# BEST of the BEST
## *from*
# *LOUISIANA II*

**Selected Recipes from Louisiana's**
# FAVORITE COOKBOOKS

*The Chalmette Battlefield and Malus-Beauregard House at the Jean Lafitte National Historical Park and Preserve. New Orleans.*

# BEST
## of the BEST
## from

*Louisiana*

# II

Selected Recipes from Louisiana's
## FAVORITE COOKBOOKS

EDITED BY
## Gwen McKee
AND
## Barbara Moseley
*Illustrated by Tupper England*

QUAIL RIDGE PRESS

## Recipe Collection © 1998 Quail Ridge Press, Inc.

Reprinted with permission and all rights reserved under the name of the cookbooks, organizations or individuals listed below.

*Big Mama's Old Black Pot Recipes* © 1987 Stoke Gabriel Enterprises; *By Special Request* © Leu Wilder; *Cajun Cuisine* © 1985 Beau Bayou Publishing Co.; *Cajun Cooking for Beginners* © 1996 Acadian House Publishing; *Cajun Men Cook* © 1994 Beaver Club of Lafayette; *Cane River's Louisiana Living* © 1994 The Service League of Natchitoches, Inc.; *Celebrations on the Bayou* © 1989 The Junior League of Monroe, Inc.; *Classic Cajun-Culture and Cooking* © 1994 Lucy Henry Zaunbrecher; *A Cook's Tour of Shreveport* © 1964 The Junior League of Shreveport, Inc.; *Cooking & Gardening with Dianne* © 1996 Dianne Cage; *The Cookin' Cajun Cooking School Cookbook* © 1997 Lisette Verlander and Susan Murphy; *Cooking New Orleans Style* © 1991 Episcopal Churchwomen of All Saints', Inc.; *Czech Out Cajun Cookin'* © 1989 Katherine Guillot & Ina Potmesil; *'Dat Little Cajun Cookbook* © 1994 Relco Publishing; *'Dat Little Louisiana Plantation Cookbook* © 1995 Relco Publishing; *'Dat Little New Orleans Creole Cookbook* © 1994 Relco Publishing; *Delicious Heritage* © 1988 Delicious Heritage, Inc.; *Dinner on the Ground: A Southern Tradition* ©1990 Stoke Gabriel Enterprises; *Evolution of Cajun & Creole Cuisine* © 1989 Chef John Folse & Company; *Extra! Extra! Read All About It!* © 1995 Corinne H. Cook; *Fessin' Up with Bon Appetit* © 1992 Sue W. Fess; *The Food of New Orleans* © 1998 Periplus Editions (HK) Ltd.; *Golliwogg Cake and Other Recipes* © 1996 The Red River Radio Network; *Gone with the Fat* © 1994 Cookbook Resources; *The Hungry Hog* © 1995 Phil D. Mayers; *Kay Ewing's Cooking School Cookbook* © 1994 Kay Ewing; *La Bonne Cuisine Lagniappe* © 1989 Episcopal Churchwomen of All Saints', Inc.; *The Little Gumbo Book* © 1986 Quail Ridge Press, Inc.; *The Little New Orleans Cookbook* © 1991 Quail Ridge Press, Inc; *Louisiana Temptations* © 1996 Louisiana Farm Bureau Federation, Inc.; *Nun Better* © 1996 St. Cecilia School; *Pass the Meatballs, Please!* © 1996 Michael Cannatella; *Plantation Celebrations - Recipes From Our Louisiana Mansions* © 1994 Chef John Folse & Company; *The Plantation Cookbook* © 1972 The Junior League of New Orleans; *River Road Recipes III: A Healthy Collection* © 1994 The Junior League of Baton Rouge, Inc.; *Roger's Cajun Cookbook* © 1987 Vernon Roger; *Roger's Lite Cajun Cookbook* © 1989 Vernon Roger; *Secrets of The Original Don's Seafood & Steakhouse* © 1996 Don's Seafood & Steakhouse of Louisiana, Inc.; *A Shower of Roses* © 1996 St. Therese Catholic Church; *Southern But Lite* © 1994 Cookbook Resources; *Tell Me More* © 1993 The Junior League of Lafayette; *Tony Chachere's Second Helping* © 1995 Tony Chachere's Creole Foods of Opelousas, Inc.; *Too Good To Be True* © 1992 Chet Beckwith; *The Top 100 Cajun Recipes of All Time* © 1995 Acadian House Publishing; *Trim & Terrific American Favorites* © 1996 Holly B. Clegg, Inc.; *A Trim & Terrific Louisiana Kitchen* © 1993 Holly Berkowitz Clegg; *Trim & Terrific One Dish Favorites* © 1997 Holly Berkowitz Clegg, Inc.; *Who's Your Mama, Are You Catholic and Can You Make a Roux?* © 1991 Marcelle Bienvenu;

### Library of Congress Cataloging-in-Publication Data

Best of the best from Louisiana II: selected recipes from Louisiana's favorite cookbooks / edited by Gwen McKee and Barbara Moseley.
p. cm.
Includes index.
ISBN 0-937552-83-6
1. Cookery, American—Louisiana style. I. McKee, Gwen.
II. Moseley, Barbara.
TX715.2.L68B47 1998
641.59763—dc21                                          98-17608
                                                              CIP

Copyright © 1998 by QUAIL RIDGE PRESS, INC.
ISBN 0-937552-83-6

First printing, June 1998 • Second, November 1998 • Third, July 2001
Fourth, March 2003

Manufactured in the United States of America
Cover and chapter opening photos courtesy of Louisiana Bureau of Tourism

**QUAIL RIDGE PRESS**
**1-800-343-1583 • Email: info@quailridge.com**
**Website: www.quailridge.com**

# CONTENTS

*Editors Gwen McKee and Barbara Moseley proudly show samplings of Louisiana's "Best."*

# PREFACE

It's been said, "Every day's a party in Louisiana—some are just more organized than others!" No doubt about it, Louisianians will surely tell you that food is what starts the party. "Come on over . . . I'm making a pot of jambalaya." "Let's bring a King Cake." "Emil's got a sack of crawfish." Where else but Louisiana? Where else does the ability to make a spicy sauce piquant or "a mean gumbo" carry such respect and admiration? Indeed, where else in the world does food receive as much love and reverence as in Louisiana?

Two words—Cajun and Creole—are almost synonymous with the word Louisiana, so famous is the state for these types of cuisine. So what is the difference? Well, as best we can determine, Cajun cooking is broadly identified as French country cooking marked by peppery seasoning. Cajun meals often come from whatever is lured out of a bayou into a black iron pot, then enhanced with "The Holy Trinity"—chopped onions, bell pepper, and celery. What results is a well-seasoned, party-starting meal of jambalaya, gumbo, sauce piquante, crawfish étouffée, and the like. Creole, in contrast, is the more sophisticated city food of New Orleans that has been influenced by many ethnic groups— French and Spanish mixed with American Indian, Caribbean, African, German, Italian, and Anglo-Saxon. In antebellum days, these people led a life of luxury as rich planters, and their seafood dishes were elaborate. Perhaps Louisiana's fertile water is the tie that binds these two incomparable cuisines together.

So many dishes were created here: Mardi Gras King Cake, Banana's Foster, Blackened Red Fish, New Orleans Barbecue Shrimp, Alligator Sauce Piquant, Pecan Pralines, Beignets and Cafe au Lait . . . "Jambalaya, Crawfish Pie, and File Gumbo". . . . yum, yum, and more yum.

But everything is not Cajun and Creole. Eating anywhere in Louisiana is a taste bud celebration! Ruston peaches, Natchitoches meat pies, so many wonderful corn and rice and recipes, plus an abundance of wild game and fish recipes from northern Louisiana ensure incredible cuisine from every corner of the state.

Amidst meandering bayous and moss-draped oaks, sugar cane fields and cypress swamps, there is an abundance of edible things that grow on bushes, in the ground, on trees, in the water, and even in the mud! (Crawfish are called mudbugs.) The settings are so impressive in Louisiana, and they all seem to relate to food. Consider the pecan trees that provide not only the sumptuous nut meats that inspire so many delectable dishes—especially a good old pecan pie and those sensational pralines—but also a shady place for a picnic. It inspires you to load up your basket with Southern Pecan Chicken, Cajun Bar-B-Que Beans, Spicy Crawfish Pasta, and Pineapple-Orange Sunshine Cake and enjoy a day in the glorious outdoors.

We so much enjoyed traveling all over the state, and were privileged to talk with the fun and food-loving people who created these recipes and published the books that contain them. Getting to know the people and sharing their heritage with you is a great pleasure for us. We hope our research will allow you to take a tour through Louisiana by way of your taste buds.

We are grateful to all the cookbook contributors who have shared a little portion of their books to make up this collection. Please find out more about each of them in the Catalog of Contributing Cookbooks section following the recipes. Our wonderful staff—especially Sheila and Annette—deserve accolades for assisting us in bringing you the essence of Louisiana in this collection of new and creative recipes as well as time-honored favorites. Our thanks to Tupper England, whose illustrations add a special touch, and to Charlie Fisher at the Louisiana Office of Tourism, who so cheerfully helped us with pictures and informative facts about the state, enabling us to add a little insight into those strange words and phrases and places that are *so Louisiana*. It is our desire to provide you with interesting reading and a lot of enjoyable eating.

*Best of the Best from Louisiana II* reaffirms that fantastic food, friendly folks, and fun, fun, fun are truly the Louisiana way of life. We hope it will bring the party to your house.

*Gwen McKee and Barbara Moseley*

# CONTRIBUTING COOKBOOKS

Allons Manger
Big Mama's Old Black Pot
A Bouquet of Recipes
By Special Request
CDA Angelic Treats
Cajun Cookin'
Cajun Cooking: From the Kitchens of South Louisiana
Cajun Cooking A Labor of Love
Cajun Cooking for Beginners
Cajun Cuisine
Cajun Men Cook
Cane River's Louisiana Living
C'est Bon, Encore
Celebrations on the Bayou
Classic Cajun—Culture and Cooking
The Cookin' Cajun Cooking School Cookbook
Cooking & Gardening with Dianne
Cooking New Orleans Style!
Cooking with Morehouse Parish Sheriff Ladies' Auxiliary
Cooking with Mr. "G" and Friends
A Cook's Tour of Shreveport
Czech-Out Cajun Cooking
'Dat Little Cajun Cookbook
'Dat Little Louisiana Plantation Cookbook
'Dat Little New Orleans Creole Cookbook
Delicious Heritage
Dinner on the Ground
The Evolution of Cajun & Creole Cuisine
Extra! Extra! Read All About It!
Family Favorites
Family Traditions
Feast of Goodness
Fessin' Up with Bon Appetit
The Food of New Orleans
From Mama to Me
Golliwogg Cake

# CONTRIBUTING COOKBOOKS

Gone with the Fat
Heart of the Home
The Hungry Hog
In The Pink
Just For Kids
Kay Ewing's Cooking School Cookbook
Kooking with the Krewe
L' Heritage Du Bayou LaFourche
La Bonne Cuisine Lagniappe
The Little Gumbo Book
The Little New Orleans Cookbook
Louisiana Temptations
Northeast Louisiana Telephone Co, Inc.'s
Fiftieth Anniversary Cookbook
Nun Better
Pass the Meatballs, Please!
Pigging Out with the Cotton Patch Cooks
Plantation Celebration
The Plantation Cookbook
Recipes From Bayou Pierre Country
River Road Recipes III
Roger's Cajun Cookbook
Roger's Lite Cajun Cookbook
Secrets of The Original Don's Seafood & Steakhouse
Shared Treasures
A Shower of Roses
Sisters' Secrets
Southern But Lite
St. Philomena School 125th Anniversary
Tell Me More
Tony Chachere's Second Helping
Too Good To Be True
The Top 100 Cajun Recipes
Trim & Terrific American Favorites
A Trim & Terrific Louisiana Kitchen
Trim & Terrific One-Dish Favorites
Who's Your Mama, Are You Catholic, and Can You Make a Roux?

# Beverages
# and Appetizers

Nottoway Plantation, completed in 1859, is the largest plantation home in the South. On the Mississippi River, two miles north of White Castle.

## Coffee Mocha Punch

2 quarts brewed coffee,
  chilled
1 quart chocolate milk
1/2 gallon vanilla ice cream

1 cup heavy cream,
  whipped
1 ounce semi-sweet chocolate,
  grated

Stir coffee and chocolate milk together in a punch bowl. Spoon in vanilla ice cream. Stir slightly to combine. Place dollops of whipped cream on top and sprinkle with grated chocolate for garnish. Serves 16-20.

*Kay Ewing's Cooking School Cookbook*

## Nun Better Punch

1 (46-ounce) can unsweetened
  pineapple juice
1 (2-liter) bottle Sprite or 7-Up
1 (6-ounce) can frozen orange
  juice concentrate
1 cup water
1 fifth vodka

2 (10-ounce) bottles
  maraschino cherries
1 (20-ounce) can pineapple
  chunks
1 (6-ounce) can mandarin
  oranges

Mix all ingredients well and freeze. To serve: remove from freezer and let stand until slushy (approximately 30 minutes to 1 hour).

*Nun Better*

## Cool Eggnog

1 (1/2-gallon) carton vanilla
  ice cream
1 (2-liter) bottle lemon-lime
  carbonated beverage,
  chilled

1 tablespoon almond extract
1 1/2 cups half-and-half
1/2 cup brandy
1/2 cup white cream de cacao

Cut ice cream into pieces and place in punch bowl. Pour rest of ingredients into punch bowl and stir lightly. Pour punch into cups and sprinkle with nutmeg.

*Sisters' Secrets*

## Bloody Mary

*This is a real eye-opener when spiced up with Louisiana's own Tabasco.*

4 cups good quality,
   thick tomato juice
1 teaspoon salt
1 teaspoon black pepper
1/2 teaspoon celery salt
1 tablespoon Worcestershire sauce

8 dashes of Tabasco sauce
2 teaspoons fresh lime juice
4-5 jiggers vodka
Lime wedges to garnish

In a large pitcher, combine all ingredients and chill for at least one hour. Stir again before serving. Pour into tall glasses over chipped ice; garnish with lime. Makes 4 (8-ounce) cocktails.

*Who's Your Mama, Are You Catholic,*
*and Can You Make a Roux?*

## Muscadine Wine

4 cups sugar
1 package yeast
1 (12-ounce) can grape juice
   concentrate or 32 ounces
   muscadine juice

1 (6-ounce) can lemonade
   concentrate
Water to fill jug

Mix all ingredients well. Add enough water to fill a gallon jug 2 inches below the neck of the jug. Place a balloon on top of the jug and let stand for 21 days. Strain the wine through cheese cloth into bottles, and cork. Yield: 32 (4-ounce) servings.

Cal 128; Chol 0mg; Sat Fat 0gm; Fat 0gm; Sod 4mg; Dietary Fiber <1gm; Exchanges: not acceptable for diabetics.

*Gone with the Fat*

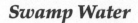

## *Swamp Water*

1 small package lime
gelatin (or sugar-
free)
1 cup hot water

1 (12-ounce) can frozen
unsweetened pineapple
juice concentrate
2 liters carbonated water

Mix lime gelatin with hot water to dissolve. Add frozen concentrate and carbonated water. Chill. Serve over ice. Yield: 10 (12-cup) servings.

Cal 38; Chol 0mg; Sat Fat <1gm; Fat <1gm; Sod 1mg; Pro <1gm; Cho 8gm; Exchanges: 1 fruit.

*Just For Kids*

## *Grape Wine*

*Delicious when used as a wine cooler.*

4 cups grape juice
concentrate

5 cups sugar
1 package yeast

Combine grape juice, sugar, and yeast. Pour into a 1-gallon small mouth jug. Fill with tap water to about ³/₄ full. Shake well to mix. Fit a punch balloon over mouth opening of jug and tape well to prevent air loss. Set aside in a warm place to ferment. Gently shake jug daily for about a week to mix ingredients. Balloon will inflate to about a basketball size. When balloon is deflated completely, the wine is done, about 3 weeks. Pour slowly into wine bottles; throw away residue. Cap or cork wine bottles and it is ready to use.

*C'est Bon, Encore*

## *Peach Brandy*

*Good after-dinner drink. Can put over your holiday cake.*

12 ripe peaches
4¹/₂ cups sugar

2 fifths bourbon

Wash peaches; do not peel. Put unpeeled fruit in 1-gallon wide-mouth jar; pour sugar over peaches. Do not stir. Pour bourbon over sugar. (You can use gin.) Cover jar tightly with plastic wrap; screw on lid to seal. Store jar in dark place for 3 months, until all sugar melts. Strain into 3 sterilized fifth bottles.

*Recipes from Bayou Pierre Country*

## Sucre Brulé
### *(Caramelized Sugar)*

1 cup sugar

1 cup water

Milk (according to taste)

Put sugar into heavy black iron pot. Cook over medium "fire;" stir constantly until sugar is deep golden. Add water carefully and stir until caramelized sugar is thoroughly diluted. Cook to consistency of thick syrup. Add, according to taste, to boiled milk. Milk should be beige color to be tasty. Sweeten with white sugar, if necessary.

The smell of this being prepared in the kitchen brings back many happy memories! Mom would fix this as coffee milk for us on cold mornings.

*Allons Manger*

## Seafood Dip

1 (4½-ounce) can shrimp

1 (6-ounce) can crabmeat

1 (8-ounce) package cream cheese, softened

¼ cup onion, minced

1 teaspoon Worcestershire sauce

4 dashes Tabasco

1 teaspoon lemon juice

4 tablespoons mayonnaise

½ teaspoon salt

⅛ teaspoon cayenne

Drain shrimp. Chop into small pieces. Combine all ingredients. Mix thoroughly. Refrigerate 12 hours to obtain maximum flavor. Makes 2½ cups.

*Dinner on the Ground*

## *Delicious Crawfish Dip*

2 bunches green onions,
 chopped
1/4 bunch parsley, chopped
1 stick oleo or butter
3 tablespoons flour
1 large can Pet milk
1 beaten egg yolk

Salt and pepper to taste
1 pound crawfish tails
 in a bag (add any
 fat from bag)
1/2 pound Mexican Velveeta
 cheese

Sauté onions and parsley in butter. Sprinkle in flour. Add Pet milk. Stir over heat until thick. Remove from heat and stir in egg yolk. Season. Add crawfish tails and cheese. Return to heat and cook over low heat for 10 minutes while stirring constantly. Serve with good crackers or chips.

*Kooking with the Krewe*

## *Light Crab Dip*

2 cans crab meat
4 ounces light Cheddar
 cheese
2 cups fat free mayonnaise

6 tablespoons fat free
 French salad dressing
2 teaspoons horseradish

Drain cans of crab. Rinse the crab meat. Mix all ingredients. Chill. Serve with fat free or low fat crackers. Yield: 18 (4-table-spoon) servings.

Cal 64; Chol 24mg; Sat Fat <1gm; Fat 1gm; Sod 580mg; Dietary Fiber 0gm; Exchanges: ½ meat, ½ bread.

*Gone with the Fat*

## *Tuna Dip*

1 (8-ounce) can spring water
 tuna fish
1 package Italian Good
 Seasons Dressing

1 (8-ounce) carton sour
 cream

Drain tuna and mash. Add dressing mix and sour cream. Mix well. Chill. Make a day ahead.

*Shared Treasures*

## Layered Nacho Dip

1 pound lean ground
  beef
1 (16-ounce) can refried
  beans
1 (1¼-ounce) package taco
  seasoning mix
1 (6-ounce) carton avocado dip
1 (8-ounce) carton sour cream

1 (4½-ounce) can chopped
  ripe olives, drained
2 large tomatoes, chopped, drained
1 onion, finely chopped
1 (4-ounce) can chopped
  green chilies, drained
3 cups shredded Monterey
  Jack cheese

Cook beef until thoroughly browned. Drain off all grease. Add beans and taco seasoning; mix well. When cooled, spread into a 9 x 13-inch glass dish. Layer all remaining ingredients (in order listed) over beef mixture; chill. Serve with Doritos or corn chips. Keeps several days.

*Sisters' Secrets*

## Black-eyed Pea Dip

1 (16-ounce) can black-eyed
  peas with jalapeño
  peppers, drained
½ cup (1 stick) margarine,
  softened
5 green onions, finely chopped

6 slices bacon, cooked and
  crumbled
1 (8-ounce) package low-fat
  processed cheese, cubed
1 teaspoon garlic powder

Mash peas in large bowl until smooth. Add margarine and blend well. Stir in green onions, bacon, cheese and garlic powder, mixing well. Pour mixture into 1-quart microwave-safe dish. Microwave at HIGH setting for 3-4 minutes or until cheese is melted. Stir well. Serve with tortilla chips or raw vegetables. Makes 1½ cups.

*Cane River's Louisiana Living*

---

The word Creole has several definitions. In Louisiana, a Creole is a white person descended from French or Spanish settlers, or a person of mixed European and African blood. It's also a style of cooking and architecture.

---

## *Hot Turnip Green Dip*

1/2 cup finely chopped onion
1/2 cup finely chopped celery
2 tablespoons butter
1 (3-ounce) can sliced
  mushrooms, drained
1 (10-ounce) package frozen
  chopped turnip greens

1/4 teaspoon grated lemon rind
1 (10³/4-ounce) can cream of
  mushroom soup
1 (6-ounce) package garlic cheese
  spread
1 teaspoon Worcestershire sauce
5 drops hot pepper sauce

Sauté the onion and celery in butter until tender. Stir in mush-rooms and set aside. Cook turnip greens and lemon rind in the bowl of a food processor, and process until smooth. In the top of a double boiler, combine sautéed vegetables, puréed turnip greens, soup, cheese, Worcestershire, and hot pepper sauce, stirring frequently until mixture is well blended and heated. Serve hot with miniature Mexican corn bread muffins. Makes 6 cups.

*Celebrations on the Bayou*

## *Christmas Cheese Ball*

*For many years I have made this cheese ball for gifts to my friends at Christmas. The red and green ingredients seem to go with the season.*

3 (8-ounce) packages cream
  cheese
1 (4-ounce) package blue
  cheese
1/2 teaspoon garlic salt
2 tablespoons chopped pimiento

2 tablespoons chopped green
  pepper
2 tablespoons chopped celery
Chopped pecans

Allow the cheese to come to room temperature. Mix all the in-gredients except pecans. Shape into a ball (or two small balls). Roll cheese ball in chopped pecans. Decorate the top of the cheese ball with strips of pimiento and green pepper to represent poin-settias.

*By Special Request*

## Home-Style Boursin

2 (8-ounce) packages cream
  cheese, softened
1/4 cup mayonnaise
2 teaspoons Dijon mustard

2 tablespoons chopped chives
2 tablespoons dill weed
1 clove garlic, minced

In a bowl, mix all ingredients together. For party spread, simply spread on favorite little party breads. For party ball, shape into a ball and roll in 1/2 cup crushed pecans. Wrap in clear wrap and refrigerate for 3 days. Serve on cheese board with favorite breads or crackers.

*Tony Chachere's Second Helping*

## Cheese Ring

1 bunch finely chopped
  green onions
Red and black pepper,
  to taste

1 pound grated cheese
1 cup mayonnaise
1 cup finely chopped nuts
1 jar red plum preserves

Combine ingredients, except preserves. Pour into greased (Pam) round bowl to form cheese ring. Place on serving dish and top with red plum preserves.

*Kooking with the Krewe*

## Shrimp Mold

1 can cream of mushroom
    soup
2 (8-ounce) package cream
    cheese
2 envelopes gelatin
1/4 cup water
2 cans shrimp, drained

1 can crab meat, drained
1 bunch green onions, chopped
1 cup chopped celery
1/2 red bell pepper, chopped
1 tablespoon lemon juice
1 cup mayonnaise
Hot sauce to taste

Heat soup. Dissolve cream cheese in soup. Dissolve gelatin in cold water. Add to soup. Add remaining ingredients. Place in mold and refrigerate. Serve with crackers.

*Sisters' Secrets*

## Shrimp Butter

1 (8-ounce) package cream
    cheese
1 stick real butter
2 tablespoons lemon juice

1 can small shrimp, drained
4 chopped green onions
1 tablespoon sugar
1/4 teaspoon seasoned salt

Soften cream cheese and butter. Place all ingredients into a bowl and mix with a mixer until smooth. Serve cold with crackers or at room temperature for sandwich spread.

*Fiftieth Anniversary Cookbook*

## Shrimp Balls

1 pound cooked shrimp
3 tablespoons cream cheese
1/2 cup celery, chopped fine
1 tablespoon grated onion
1 tablespoon green pepper,
    chopped fine
1 chopped boiled egg

1 teaspoon Worcestershire sauce
2 teaspoons horseradish
3/4 teaspoon salt
Garlic powder, black pepper
    and red pepper to taste
Chopped parsley

Grind or cut up shrimp in small pieces. Soften cream cheese. Add all other ingredients to it, except parsley. Mix well. Roll into small balls. Place chopped parsley on waxed paper and roll shrimp balls to coat with parsley. Chill until ready to serve. Makes 2-3 dozen.

*From Mama To Me*

## Sweet Potato Cheese Balls

2 cups mashed cooked
  sweet potatoes
1 (8-ounce) package light
  cream cheese, softened
1½ tablespoons minced jalapeño
1 teaspoon Worcestershire sauce
1 teaspoon Louisiana hot sauce

1 teaspoon seasoned salt
1 teaspoon Panola pepper
¼ cup minced onion
¼ cup finely chopped pecans
1 teaspoon garlic salt
1 teaspoon granulated onion

Combine the sweet potatoes and the cream cheese in a bowl and mix well. Add the jalapeño, Worcestershire sauce, hot sauce, seasoned salt, pepper sauce, onion, pecans, garlic salt, and granulated onion. Mix well and shape into balls. Place in a container. Chill, covered, for 8-10 hours. Serve with crackers. Yield: 16 servings.

*Louisiana Temptations*

## Sausage Rolls

2 cups flour
½ teaspoon salt
3 teaspoons baking powder

5 tablespoons shortening
⅔ cup milk
1 pound well seasoned sausage

Sift flour with salt and baking powder; cut in shortening until mixture resembles coarse crumbs; add milk all at once and mix. Divide dough into 2 parts; roll each out ¼-inch thick. Spread with sausage. Roll up as for jellyroll; repeat with remaining dough. Wrap in waxed paper and chill in refrigerator. When ready to serve, slice ⅓ or ¼-inch thick and bake in 400° oven for 5-10 minutes. Nice for morning parties.

*A Cook's Tour of Shreveport*

---

Those round mirrors like you see in convenience stores once hung in antebellum parlors—they were called "chaperone mirrors." And when a plantation owner died, all the clocks in the house were stopped until the next owner took over.

---

# Creamy Crab Puffs

1 cup flour
1/4 teaspoon salt
1/4 teaspoon cayenne
1 cup water

2 teaspoons margarine
4 eggs
Vegetable cooking spray

Preheat oven to 350°. Combine the flour, salt, and cayenne in a mixing bowl and set aside. Combine the water and margarine in a medium-sized saucepan and bring to a boil. Then reduce heat to low. Add the flour mixture to the water and margarine. Stir until mixture is smooth and pulls away from the sides of the pan. Remove from heat and cool for 5 minutes. Add eggs, one at a time, beating after each until the mixture is smooth. Drop the mixture one tablespoon at a time on a baking sheet that has been sprayed with vegetable spray. Bake for 20 minutes or until golden and puffy. Remove from oven and cool on a wire rack. Cut the tops off and remove some of the interior dough to form small holes. Set aside. Fill holes with Crab Filling.

**CRAB FILLING:**
1 tablespoon margarine
2 tablespoons flour
1/8 teaspoon salt
1 cup evaporated milk
1 pound lump crab meat,
   picked over for shells
   and cartilage

1/2 cup diced fresh tomato
2 tablespoons minced green
   onion
2 tablespoons minced
   parsley

Melt the margarine in a medium-sized saucepan over medium heat. Add the flour and salt. Cook for one minute, stirring constantly. Remove from heat. Add the milk and stir to mix well. Return to heat. Add the crab meat and cook for about 10 minutes, or until the mixture thickens. Add the tomato, green onion, and parsley. Cook for one minute, or until thoroughly heated. Makes 8 appetizer portions.

*Cajun Cooking for Beginners*

# Crabmeat Ravigote

*This rich crab dish is always one of our first choices as an appetizer at Antoine's Restaurant in New Orleans' French Quarter.*

1 tablespoon onion, minced
1 tablespoon tarragon vinegar
1 tablespoon green bell pepper, minced
1 tablespoon pimento, minced
1 tablespoon anchovies, minced (or anchovy paste)
1 cup mayonnaise
1 pound lump crabmeat
2 cups lettuce, washed and shredded
Whole anchovies or strips of pimento for garnish

Cook onion and vinegar together in a microwave oven for 30 seconds on high. Mix in next four ingredients; chill. Pick over crabmeat carefully to remove any pieces of shell. Gently mix crabmeat with sauce. Serve on a bed of shredded lettuce. Garnish with whole anchovies or strips of pimento. Serves 4.

*The Cookin' Cajun Cooking School Cookbook*

# Crawfish Party Mold

*This is always a hit. May be used as a centerpiece (to be eaten), or put in a different mold as a dip with fancy crackers.*

3 envelopes plain gelatin
1/2 cup hot water
1 (10-ounce) can tomato soup
3 pounds crawfish tails, chopped coarsely
1 (8-ounce) package cream cheese
1/2 cup finely chopped onion
1/2 cup finely chopped celery
1 cup mayonnaise
1 teaspoon baking soda

Dissolve gelatin in lukewarm water. Heat soup and add crawfish. Cook for 20 minutes on medium heat. Stir often to prevent sticking. Add cream cheese, onions, and celery. Cook until cheese is melted. Add gelatin and mayonnaise and stir until well blended. Remove from heat. Add baking soda and stir quickly while mixture foams. Prepare the molds by coating with extra mayonnaise or spraying with PAM. Pour the mixture directly into molds. Allow to set overnight. Garnish. Yields 6 cups.

*Classic Cajun*

# Shrimp Bayou Lafourche

*What happens when a Capri-born, European-trained chef adopts New Orleans as his home and comes into a delivery of picture-perfect local shrimp? Hopefully something like this reborn classic, named after an important bayou running along the eastern edge of Cajun Country.*

| | |
|---|---|
| 2 tablespoons extra-virgin olive oil | 1/2 teaspoon Worcestershire sauce |
| | Juice of 1 lemon |
| 4 teaspoons chopped shallots | 1 teaspoon fresh rosemary leaves |
| 2 teaspoons chopped garlic | 1/2 teaspoon salt |
| 1 teaspoon crushed red pepper | 1/4 teaspoon ground white pepper |
| 24 medium-size shrimp, peeled and deveined but with tails on | Ground red pepper |
| | 4 tablespoons unsalted butter, softened |
| 3 tablespoons brandy | 4 lemon wedges for garnish |
| 1/2 cup dry white wine | |

Heat the olive oil in a large skillet over medium-high heat and sauté the shallots, garlic, and crushed red pepper until the shallots are transparent, about 3 minutes. Then add the shrimp, and cook, turning once, just until they turn pink, about 3 minutes. Add the brandy, then remove the shrimp and keep them warm. Add all the other ingredients to the skillet, except the butter, and simmer until the sauce is reduced by a third—about 10 minutes. Whisk in the butter. Return the shrimp to the pan and cook for 3-4 minutes more, coating them well with the sauce. Garnish with lemon wedges and serve. Serves 4.

*Recipe by Andrea Apuzzo, Andrea's Restaurant*
**The Food of New Orleans**

---

New Orleans Lingo: "Where y'at?" is what they say in some neighborhoods in New Orleans instead of "How are you doing?" Those garlic braids that hang in the French Market are called prayer beads. A shotgun house is a one-room-wide house that got its name because you can shoot from the front door straight through the back door of the house without hitting anything. Voodoo is a mysterious religion involving charms and spells that came to Louisiana via the Caribbean. Gumbo YaYa is when everybody talks at once.

---

# Chester's Ultimate Pickled Shrimp

2 onions, quartered
6 bay leaves
2 ribs celery, cut into
   pieces
6 cloves garlic, halved
1 lemon, quartered
1/4 cup salt
6 dashes Tabasco

2 pounds large headless
   shrimp
1 1/2 cups salad oil
3/4 cup white vinegar
12 bay leaves
1 (3 1/2-ounce) jar capers,
   undrained
1 large purple onion,
   thinly sliced

In a large heavy pot, boil 3 quarts water with first 7 ingredients for 45 minutes. Add shrimp and cook approximately 10-12 minutes. Drain. Peel and devein shrimp. Set aside. In another saucepan, heat salad oil with vinegar. Remove from heat. Using an airtight plastic container, layer shrimp with oil/vinegar marinade, bay leaves, capers, and sliced onion. Cover and refrigerate. Turn frequently to coat shrimp. Chill at least 24 hours before serving. Keeps well in refrigerator for one week. Serve as an appetizer with party picks or as a salad with shredded lettuce, diced tomatoes, celery, and bell peppers.

*Delicious Heritage*

# Shrimp and Tasso with Five-Pepper Jelly

*Here's a new-style starter that combines the peppery flavors of Louisiana pepper sauce with the sweet-pungent taste of pepper jelly. It's a country concept that definitely made it to town.*

### FIVE-PEPPER JELLY:

6 tablespoons honey
3/4 cup white vinegar
1 each red, yellow, and green
   bell peppers, diced

1 jalapeño pepper, diced
1/4 teaspoon ground black pepper
Salt

Pour the honey and vinegar into a pot and reduce over medium heat until sticky, about 5 minutes. Add remaining ingredients and cook until peppers are soft, 3-4 minutes. Add salt to taste.

### CRYSTAL BEURRE BLANC:

1/4 teaspoon minced garlic
1/4 teaspoon chopped shallots
2 teaspoons vegetable oil
10 tablespoons hot sauce

1/4 cup heavy cream
1 1/2 pounds (6 sticks)
   unsalted butter, softened

Sauté the garlic and shallots in a pan with the vegetable oil. Add the hot sauce and reduce by 75 percent, then add the cream and reduce the liquid by half. Whip in the butter a little at a time.

### SHRIMP AND TASSO:

36 jumbo shrimp, peeled
   and deveined
1/2 pound tasso, julienned
1 cup all-purpose flour
   seasoned with salt and pepper

Vegetable oil
36 pickled okra

To finish the dish, make a 1/4-inch incision down the back of each shrimp and place a strip of tasso in each. Secure with a toothpick. Lightly dust each shrimp with seasoned flour. Heat about 2 inches of oil in a large skillet and fry the shrimp until golden. Place the cooked shrimp in a bowl with the beurre blanc and toss until well coated. Spread the pepper jelly on the bottom of a small dish and arrange the shrimp, alternating them with pickled okra. Serves 8.

*Recipe by Jamie Shannon, Commander's Palace*
***The Food of New Orleans***

# Creole Marinated Crab Claws

| | |
|---|---|
| 1/3 cup extra virgin olive oil | 1 teaspoon celery seed |
| 1/2 cup defatted chicken broth, | or flakes |
| less salt | 1/4 cup parsley flakes |
| 1/2 cup wine vinegar | 1 teaspoon light Creole |
| 1/3 cup lemon juice | seasoning |
| 2 green onions, chopped | 1 pound crab claws, rinsed |
| 2 tablespoons minced garlic | and drained |
| 1 tablespoon black pepper | Cherry tomatoes and black |
| | olives for garnish |

Mix marinade and pour over crab claws in shallow dish. Refrigerate for at least 4 hours. Drain well and serve on a platter lined with lettuce leaves. Garnish with cherry tomatoes and black olives. Yield: 6 servings.

Per Serving: Cal 101; Fat 6.6g; %Fat Cal 57; Sat Fat 0.9g; Chol 24mg; Sod 136mg.

*River Road Recipes III*

# Wine Marinated Mushrooms

| | |
|---|---|
| 20 medium-size fresh | 1/2 teaspoon celery seeds |
| mushrooms | 1/2 teaspoon mustard seeds |
| 2 small onions, thinly sliced | 1/4 teaspoon whole cloves |
| 1/3 cup vinegar | 1/4 cup vegetable oil |
| 1/3 cup water | 1 (2-ounce) jar diced pimiento, |
| 1/4 cup chablis or other | drained |
| dry white wine | 2 tablespoons chopped green |
| 3/4 teaspoon salt | onion |

Clean mushrooms with damp paper towels, set mushrooms aside. Combine sliced onions and next 7 ingredients in a 1 1/2-quart casserole. Cover with heavy-duty plastic wrap and microwave on HIGH for 5 minutes. Stir in mushrooms. Cover and microwave at HIGH for 2-3 minutes or just until mushrooms are tender. Remove mushrooms with a slotted spoon, and place in a small bowl. Strain liquid, discarding sliced onions. Add oil, pimiento, and green onions to strained liquid, pour over mushrooms, and toss gently. Cover and refrigerate at least 4 hours. Drain before serving. Yields 20 appetizer servings.

*Czech-Out Cajun Cooking*

# Stuffed Mushrooms

*Simple, but the most requested recipe.*

1 (8-ounce) package cream cheese, softened to room temperature

2 tablespoons Worcestershire sauce

1 (12-ounce) package bacon, cooked, cooled and crumbled

1 large carton mushroom caps (remove stems, wash)

Mix cream cheese with Worcestershire sauce; add crumbled bacon. Stuff with teaspoon into washed and dried mushroom caps. Place on cookie sheet and refrigerate until ready to serve. Prior to serving, broil in oven 5-7 minutes or until tops are light brown. Serve hot and provide cocktail napkins if plates are not being used.

*Family Traditions*

# Tortilla Roll-Ups

2 (8-ounce) packages cream cheese, softened

4 cloves minced garlic

1/4 cup chopped green onions

1/4 cup chopped jalapeño peppers

10-12 flour tortillas

Combine cream cheese, garlic, green onions, and jalapeños. Spread on tortillas. Roll-up jellyroll fashion. Place seam down and slice in 1-inch pieces. Serve with salsa and/or guacamole!

*Tell Me More*

## Jo Ann's Crustless Quiche

4 cups (16 ounces) grated
   Monterey Jack cheese
4 cups (16 ounces) grated sharp
   Cheddar cheese
1 (5-ounce) can evaporated
   milk

9 eggs
2 or 3 jalapeño peppers,
   chopped
1 (4-ounce) can green chilies,
   chopped

Combine Monterey Jack and Cheddar cheeses, milk, eggs, jalapeño peppers and chilies, mixing well with wooden spoon. Pour mixture into 13 x 9 x 2-inch baking dish. Bake at 350° for 40 minutes. Let stand until cool. Cut into 1-inch squares. Serves approximately 36.

*Cane River's Louisiana Living*

## Dub's Stuffed Jalapeño Peppers

3 (12-ounce) cans mild
   jalapeño peppers
   (without seeds)

1/2 pound Velveeta
   (coarsely grated)

Drain and remove stems from peppers. (All seeds must be removed from peppers.) Stuff with cheese.

3 (6-ounce) cans crabmeat
1 cup light mayonnaise
2 (7½-ounce) cartons
   Egg Beaters (vegetable
   omelette mix)
1 tablespoon onion, minced

1 tablespoon Italian
   seasoning
1 tablespoon Tony's Creole
   Seasoning
1 (15-ounce) box Italian
   bread crumbs

Combine all remaining ingredients and mix thoroughly. Pat mixture into small patties 1/4 inch thick. Patties must be large enough to wrap around stuffed pepper. Mixture should seal off entire surface of pepper. Deep fry 4-5 minutes in hot oil or until browned. Makes 21.

**Note:** Add more mayonnaise if there is difficulty with mixture adhering to peppers.

*Dinner on the Ground*

## *Sausage Bread*

1 pound hot sausage, crumbled
1 pound mild sausage, crumbled
1 pound hickory-smoked sausage, chopped
3 bunches green onions, chopped
1 (4-ounce) can mushrooms
4 cups shredded Cheddar cheese
4 cups shredded mozzarella cheese

2 cups grated Parmesan cheese
1 (4-ounce) can chopped black olives
1 (7-ounce) jar pitted green olives, chopped
Chopped jalapeños (optional)
1 (3-loaf) package frozen bread dough, thawed
¼ cup melted butter

Brown the sausages together in a large saucepan, stirring frequently and adding the green onions and mushrooms before the sausage is cooked through. Drain and set aside. Combine the Cheddar, mozzarella, and Parmesan cheeses in a large bowl. Add the olives, jalapeños, and sausage mixture to the cheese mixture; mix well and set aside. Flatten one loaf of the bread dough to the size of a dinner plate on a floured surface. Place ⅓ of the sausage and cheese mixture in the middle of the bread. Bring up the sides to enclose the filling; pinch the seams to seal. Follow the same procedure for the remaining 2 loaves. Place 2 of the loaves seam-side-down in a lightly greased 9 x 13-inch baking pan and place the remaining loaf in a smaller pan. Brush with melted butter. Bake at 350° for 30 minutes or until golden brown. Yield: 36 servings.

**Variations:** For an appetizer or party food, spread the sausage and cheese mixture in crescent rolls. For a pizza loaf, spread pizza sauce on the bread before adding the sausage and cheese mixture.

*Louisiana Temptations*

 Baton Rouge—a name which refers to the red stick that once marked the boundary between two Indian tribes.

## Apache Cheese Bread

*Use this cheese dip to start your Fiesta.*

1 (9-inch) Apache* loaf of
   bread
16 ounces sharp Cheddar
   cheese, grated
1 (8-ounce) package cream
   cheese, softened

1 (8-ounce) carton sour cream
1/2 cup minced green onions
1 teaspoon Worcestershire sauce
2 (41/2-ounce) cans green chilies,
   chopped
1 cup chopped ham

Cut the top off the bread (*any hard round loaf of bread may be used), reserving top, and scoop out the inside. Combine remaining ingredients and mix well. This will be a very stiff mixture. Fill the bread with the cheese mixture, replace the top, and place on a cookie sheet. Bake in a 350° oven for 1 hour and 10 minutes. Serve with tortilla chips or tear and dip with the bread.

*Celebrating on the Bayou*

## Sausage Spinach Bread

*This is one of those versitile recipes that can be used on many occasions. Serve it as an appetizer or as a bread.*

2 loaves frozen French
   bread dough
1 (10-ounce) package frozen
   chopped spinach
1 pound hot pork sausage

2 tablespoons chopped onion
1 egg
10 ounces grated mozzarella
   cheese
1/2 cup grated Parmesan cheese

Allow dough to thaw. Cook spinach according to package directions. Drain well. Brown sausage and drain off fat. Add onion and cook until onions are soft. Beat egg. Add about half of it to the drained spinach and reserve the rest to brush over the top of the bread. Working with one loaf of bread at a time, roll the bread out into a rectangle, about 9 x 13 inches. Spread half of the spinach, sausage, and mozzarella cheese over the dough. Sprinkle with half of the Parmesan cheese. Roll up, jellyroll-style, sealing all edges tightly so the filling remains inside. Pierce tops of bread loaves with fork a few times. Brush with beaten egg. Bake at 375° for 20 minutes or until brown. Serve hot. Repeat steps with second loaf. Makes 2 loaves.

*Extra! Extra! Read All About It!*

## Janet's Party Sandwiches

1 bunch broccoli flowerets,
  chopped fine
1/2 cup stuffed olive,
  chopped fine
1/4 cup chopped green onion

1/2 cup mayonnaise
4 hard-boiled eggs, chopped
  fine
Salt and pepper to taste
Garlic powder, if desired

Combine all ingredients. Spread on wheat bread. Trim crusts. Cut in 3 or 4 pieces.

*In The Pink*

## Cheese Crunchies

8 ounces sharp grated
  cheese
2 sticks margarine, softened
2 cups flour

1/2 teaspoon salt
1/4 teaspoon black pepper
1 teaspoon cayenne pepper
2 cups Rice Krispies

Combine cheese and margarine in large bowl. Mix thoroughly. Sift together flour, salt, and peppers and add to cheese and margarine. Mix well. Add Rice Krispies and mix lightly. Roll into marble-size balls and press lightly just to flatten to about the size of a 50 cent piece. Bake at 350° for about 20 minutes. Do not brown. Yield: 100-150.

*LaBonne Cuisine Lagniappe*

## Cheese Cookies

2 sticks (1/2 pound) butter
  or margarine
16 ounces Cheddar cheese
  (New York Sharp), grated

2 cups flour
1 teaspoon salt
1 teaspoon cayenne pepper
1 1/2 cups chopped pecans

Cream butter and cheese together. Add flour, salt, and pepper, then blend in pecans. It will be a very stiff dough. With wax paper make small, long rolls of the dough and refrigerate overnight. Slice thin and bake on ungreased cookie sheet in 275°-oven for 45-50 minutes. Cool on a rack. Dough will keep several days in refrigerator or a couple of months in the freezer. Serves 50 for cocktails or with coffee or tea.

*Golliwogg Cake*

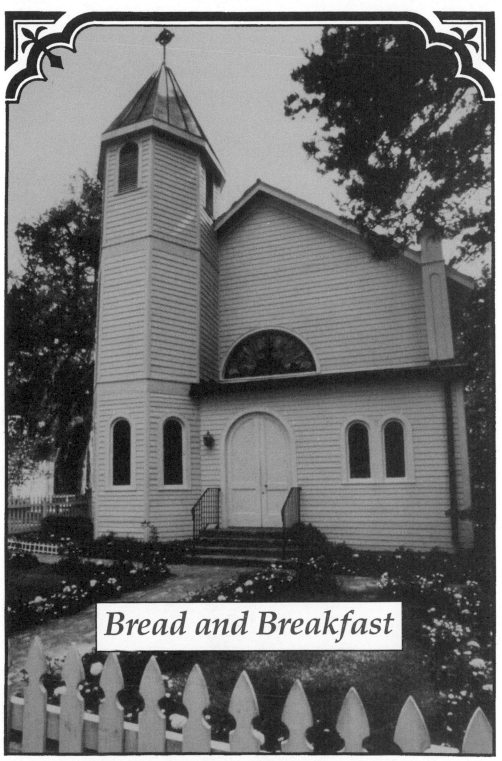

# *Bread and Breakfast*

The oldest building in St. Tammany Parish, the Christ Episcopal Church
in Covington was consecrated in 1846.

## Sweet Potato Pumpkin Bread

*Both sweet potatoes and pumpkins are indigenous to South Louisiana and are most often cooked in desserts or sweetened casseroles. Here, the two are combined with a simple bread mix to create a quick and easy bread recipe that is sure to please.*

| | |
|---|---|
| 3/4 cup cooked cubed sweet potatoes | 2 tablespoons nutmeg |
| 3/4 cup cooked cubed pumpkin | 3 1/2 cups all-purpose flour |
| 3 cups sugar | 1 teaspoon salt |
| 4 eggs | 2 teaspoons baking soda |
| 1/2 cup oil | 1/2 cup water |
| 2 tablespoons cinnamon | 3/4 cup raisins |
| | 1 cup pecans |
| | Pecan halves for garnish |

Preheat oven to 350°. Parboil sweet potatoes and pumpkin cubes until tender. Remove, mash and set aside. In a large bowl, mix sugar and eggs until creamy. Add oil, sweet potatoes, and pumpkin. Mix on high speed until creamy; reduce to low and add dry ingredients alternately with water. Beat until well blended. Stir in raisins and pecans and pour into a large greased cake pan. Bake for one hour or until top is golden brown. Garnish with pecan halves. For an added touch, glaze with Louisiana cane syrup. Serves 6.

**Note:** You may wish to use 8-ounce cans of sweet potatoes and pumpkin, rather than fresh.

*Plantation Celebration*

## Sweet Potato Bread

3 cups sugar
1 cup cooking oil
4 eggs
3½ cups sifted flour
2 teaspoons soda
½ teaspoon salt

1 teaspoon cinnamon
1 teaspoon nutmeg
⅔ cup water
2 cups cooked, mashed
  sweet potatoes
1 cup chopped pecans

Combine sugar and oil; beat well. Add eggs and beat. Combine dry ingredients and add to egg mixture alternately with water. Stir in sweet potatoes and chopped pecans. Pour batter into 3 greased loaf pans. Bake at 350° for one hour. Yield 3 loaves.

*L' Heritage Du Bayou Lafourche*

## Brown Breakfast Bread

1 cup all-purpose flour
2 tablespoons sugar
½ teaspoon salt
1 teaspoon baking soda
2 cups finely ground
  graham cracker crumbs

1 cup sour milk*
1 cup dark syrup or
  molasses
½ cup raisins
½ cup pecans, chopped
  fine

Preheat oven to 350°. Mix flour, sugar, salt, and baking soda. Add graham cracker crumbs, sour milk, and dark syrup. Add raisins and nuts. Bake one hour in 9 x 5-inch loaf pan prepared with vegetable cooking spray. Cool on rack. Slice into 12 slices, using serrated knife. Freezes well. Yield: 12 slices.

**Note:** *Sour milk = 1 cup skim milk plus 1 tablespoon vinegar or lemon juice.

Cal 245; Chol 0mg; Sat Fat <1gm; Fat 5gm; Sod 185mg; Pro 4gm; Cho 46gm.

*Just For Kids*

---

Festivals in Louisiana include ones for strawberries, rice, pecans, sweet potatoes, sugar cane, peaches, crawfish, frogs, goats, etc. And parties gather for cochon de laits, crawfish boils, Mardi Gras parades, LSU football games, fais do does . . . and for absolutely no reason at all.

# Butterscotch Banana Bread

*When plain banana bread doesn't seem exciting enough, this variation is just the ticket.*

1³/₄ cups all-purpose flour
2 teaspoons baking powder
¹/₂ teaspoon baking soda
¹/₂ teaspoon ground
   cinnamon
¹/₂ teaspoon ground nutmeg
1 cup mashed bananas
   (2 large bananas)

³/₄ cup sugar
1 large egg
2 large egg whites
¹/₄ cup canola oil
¹/₄ cup skim milk
¹/₂ cup butterscotch chips

Preheat the oven to 350°. Coat a 9 x 5 x 3-inch loaf pan with nonstick cooking spray. Combine the flour, baking powder, baking soda, cinnamon, and nutmeg in a bowl; set aside. In a mixing bowl, combine the mashed bananas, sugar, egg, egg whites, and oil, blending well. Add the flour mixture alternately with the milk to the banana mixture. Stir in the butterscotch chips. Pour into the prepared loaf pan. Bake for 50 minutes to 1 hour or until a toothpick inserted in the center comes out clean. Cool in pan. Makes 16 slices.

Cal 167; Fat 5.5g; Cal for Fat 29.9%; Sat Fat 1.7g; Sod 119mg; Chol 13mg.

*Trim & Terrific American Favorites*

## *Mignonne's Spinach Bread*

1 (10-ounce) package frozen
  spinach, thawed and
  chopped
1 (10-ounce) package French
  rolls or twin loaves
  French bread
1/4 cup margarine, softened
1 medium onion, chopped

1/4 cup margarine, melted
1 (16-ounce) roll jalapeño
  cheese
1 teaspoon Worcestershire
1/8 teaspoon pepper
2 cups (8 ounces) shredded
  mozzarella cheese

Drain spinach and squeeze dry with paper towel; set aside. Cut rolls in half lengthwise; spread with 1/4 cup softened margarine. Sauté onion in 1/4 cup melted margarine. Add cheese roll, stirring until cheese melts. Remove from heat; add spinach, Worcestershire sauce, and pepper, stirring well. Spread spinach mixture on bread, sprinkle with mozzarella cheese. Bake at 350° for 8 minutes or until cheese melts. Serve immediately. Yields 12 servings.

*Heart of the Home*

## *Beer Bread*

*This quick bread is too good for words, and you can eat it without guilt!*

3 cups self-rising flour
1/3 cup sugar
1 (12-ounce) can light beer

2 tablespoons light
  margarine, melted
  (room temperature)

Combine all ingredients, mixing until just moistened. Pour batter into a 9 x 5 x 3-inch loaf pan coated with nonstick cooking spray and dusted with flour. Bake at 350° for 50 minutes. Serve warm. Yield: 16 slices.

Cal 111; Chol 0mg; Fat 0.9g; Cal from Fat 7.6%.

*A Trim & Terrific Louisiana Kitchen*

## Mexican Cornbread

1 cup yellow cornmeal
1/2 teaspoon salt
1/2 teaspoon soda
1/3 cup melted shortening
1 (8-ounce) carton sour cream
1 (8-ounce) can cream-style
  corn

2 eggs, beaten
1 cup shredded Cheddar
  cheese
1 (4-ounce) can chopped green
  chilies, drained

Combine above ingredients and pour into heated, greased 8- or 9-inch heavy skillet. Bake at 375° for 35-40 minutes or until golden brown. Yields about 6-8 servings.

*A Bouquet of Recipes*

## Broccoli Cornbread

1 stick butter
1 (10-ounce) box chopped
  broccoli, thawed
1 onion, chopped
4 eggs (or egg beaters)

2 cups lite Cheddar cheese,
  grated
1 (8 1/2-ounce) package jiffy
  corn muffin mix

Melt butter in microwave in a 9 x 9-inch pan. Combine broccoli, onion, eggs, cheese, and muffin mix, and mix well. Pour over butter. Bake at 400° for 30 minutes. Cool 10 minutes before cutting. (The extra butter that comes to the top, after pouring batter, will be absorbed in baking).

*A Shower of Roses*

## *Cajun Crawfish Corn Bread*

2 cups cornmeal
1 teaspoon salt
1 teaspoon baking powder
6 eggs
2 medium onions, chopped

¹/₂ cup jalapeño peppers
16 ounces Cheddar cheese
²/₃ cup oil
2 cans cream corn
2 pounds crawfish tails

In bowl combine cornmeal, salt, and baking powder. In medium bowl beat eggs, chopped onions, and jalapeño peppers. Grate cheese and add beaten eggs, onions, peppers, cheese, oil, corn, and crawfish tails. Combine this mixture with cornmeal; mix well. Pour into greased 12 x 4-inch baking dish. Bake at 375° for 55 minutes or until golden brown.

*Family Favorites*

## *Hushpuppies*

1¹/₂ cups cornmeal
1 cup flour
3 eggs
1 onion, grated
2¹/₂ cups hot milk
1 cup chopped corn
2 teaspoons baking powder

1 red pepper, chopped
2 tablespoons chopped jalapeño
  pepper
1¹/₂ cups grated Cheddar
  cheese
2 tablespoons butter, melted

Combine cornmeal and flour in mixing bowl. Beat eggs and add to cornmeal mixture. Add onion, milk, corn, baking powder, red pepper, and jalapeño pepper. Stir. Add Cheddar cheese and melted butter. Blend well. Drop by the spoonful into hot oil. Fry until golden brown. Drain on paper towels.

*Roger's Cajun Cookbook*

 A 5,000-egg omelet? Absolutely. Abbeville has a festival around the occasion.

# Ursula's Cornbread Dressing

*This cornbread dressing has graced our table for as long as I can remember. Ursula Beaugh was my neighbor, and this recipe is a family heritage recipe. I cannot imagine a holiday meal without this dressing. However, I do not use it just at holiday time. The dressing enhances Sunday dinner, whether it's baked chicken or a roast. Seasoned ground meat is added to the cooked cornbread.*

## CORNBREAD:

2¹/₂ cups cornmeal
³/₄ cup flour
1¹/₂ teaspoons salt
3 tablespoons baking powder

1 tablespoon sugar
3 tablespoons oil
3 eggs
3 cups milk

Mix all ingredients together. Pour into greased (11-inch) heavy skillet and bake at 425° for 30-35 minutes.

## MEAT MIXTURE: (URSULA'S)

2 pounds lean ground
  beef
2 onions, chopped
1 bell pepper, chopped
3 cloves garlic, chopped
1 cup chopped celery
Salt, black pepper and
  cayenne pepper

1 (14¹/₂-ounce) can beef
  broth
2 (10³/₄-ounce) cans cream of
  mushroom soup
1 teaspoon Kitchen Bouquet
¹/₄ cup chopped fresh parsley
¹/₄ cup chopped green onions
3 eggs, lightly beaten

In large skillet, brown beef. Drain off fat. Add onions, bell pepper, garlic, and celery. Season to taste with salt, black pepper, and cayenne pepper. This should be relatively spicy because you will be mixing it with cornbread. Add beef broth and cook slowly, about 45 minutes, covered. Add cream of mushroom soup, Kitchen Bouquet, parsley, and green onions. Crumble cornbread and add it to the meat mixture. Check seasoning. Stir in the lightly beaten eggs. Spoon into large baking dish. Bake in 350° oven for 30-45 minutes or until bubbly. Serves 12-14.

*Extra! Extra! Read All About It!*

## *Cornbread Dressing*

**CORNBREAD:**

1¹/₂ cups cornmeal
³/₄ cup flour
³/₄ teaspoon salt
3 teaspoons baking powder

1 large egg
1 cup milk
2 tablespoons vegetable oil

Combine all ingredients. Bake at 400° in well greased or oiled pan for 30-40 minutes or until lightly browned. Crumble and set aside.

1 small onion chopped
2 tablespoons bell pepper, chopped
¹/₂ cup chopped celery
1 clove garlic, minced
2 tablespoons margarine

1-1¹/₂ pounds ground beef
1 teaspoon salt
¹/₄ teaspoon black pepper
¹/₄ teaspoon red pepper
1 can mushroom soup
3 cups chicken broth

Sauté onion, bell pepper, celery, and garlic in margarine. Add to cornbread. Brown beef in heavy pot; add salt and peppers and cook about 30 minutes on low heat. Mix meat, cornbread, sautéed vegetables, soup and broth together. Bake in buttered casserole dish at 350° for 45 minutes. Makes 10 servings.

*From Mama To Me*

## *Frenchies*

*Lusty crusty munchies. Better make plenty.*

1 (6-roll) package French mini-loaves
1¹/₄ sticks butter or margarine
1 teaspoon garlic powder

1 teaspoon Tabasco
1 teaspoon water
1 tablespoon parsley flakes (optional)

Slice French bread into thin rounds (a generous ¹/₄ inch). Melt margarine; add remaining ingredients. Brush both sides of bread rounds very lightly with butter mixture. Bake on 2 cookie sheets in 225° oven 40-50 minutes till dry, but not brown. Turn heat off and leave in oven 30 minutes or more (or overnight). Store in tin or cookie jar.

**Note:** If you freeze the bread first and use a knife with a serrated edge (or an electric knife), it will slice much easier and neater.

*The Little New Orleans Cookbook*

## Sausage Grits

1 pound bulk pork
  sausage
3 cups hot cooked grits
2¹/₂ cups shredded Cheddar
  cheese

3 tablespoons butter
3 eggs, beaten
1¹/₂ cups milk
Parsley, optional
Pimento strips, optional

Cook sausage until brown in heavy skillet; drain well. Spoon sausage into lightly greased 9 x 13-inch baking dish. Combine hot grits, cheese, and butter. Stir until cheese and butter are melted. Combine eggs and milk; stir into grits. Pour over sausage. Bake at 350° for one hour. Garnish with parsley and/or pimento strips, if desired. This can be made and refrigerated overnight and baked the next day.

*CDA Angelic Treats*

## Steak Creole with Cheese Grits

3 pounds lean, boneless
  top round steak
¹/₄ teaspoon pepper
¹/₄ cup all-purpose flour
1 onion, thickly sliced
2 green bell peppers,
  seeded and sliced
1 tablespoon minced garlic
2 cups canned beef broth

1 (15-ounce) can no-salt-
  added tomato sauce
1 teaspoon light brown sugar
1 tablespoon Worcestershire
  sauce
1 teaspoon dried basil
1 teaspoon dried thyme
1 teaspoon dried oregano
Cheese Grits

Trim any fat from the round steak. Season the steak with the pepper, and dredge in the flour, shaking off any excess. In a large skillet coated with nonstick cooking spray, brown the steak over medium-high heat for 5-7 minutes on each side. Remove the steak and set aside. Add the onion and pepper to the skillet and cook over moderate heat, stirring occasionally, about 5 minutes. Stir in the garlic, beef broth, tomato sauce, brown sugar, Worcestershire sauce, basil, thyme, and oregano, and bring to a boil. Return the steak to the skillet and spoon some of the sauce over it. Cover and cook over medium-low heat for 1¹/₂ - 2 hours, or until the steak is very tender, stirring occasionally. Serve with the grits. Makes 6 servings.

CONTINUED

**CHEESE GRITS:**

1 cup quick grits
3 cups water

1 cup shredded reduced-fat
Cheddar cheese

Cook the grits according to package directions, using 3 cups water and omitting any salt. After they are done, stir in the Cheddar.

Cal 487; Fat 10.4g; Cal from Fat 19.2%; Sat Fat 4.8g; Prot 61.7g; Carbo 32.9g; Sod 578g; Chol 143mg.

*Trim & Terrific One-Dish Favorites*

## Chili-Cheese Grits

6 cups water
1½ cups uncooked regular
    grits
½ cup butter or oleo
2 teaspoons seasoned salt
¼ teaspoon garlic powder

1 (16-ounce) loaf processed
    cheese spread (Cheez Whiz)
1 (4-ounce) can chopped green
    chilies
3 eggs, beaten

Bring water to a boil in a Dutch oven; add grits, cover; reduce heat and simmer 10 minutes. Add butter and next 4 ingredients, stirring until cheese melts. Stir a small amount of hot grits into the eggs; add to remaining hot grits, stirring constantly. Pour mixture into lightly greased 13 x 9 x 2-inch baking dish. Bake at 350° for 40 minutes or until mixture is set. Yields 10 servings.

*Pigging Out with the Cotton Patch Cooks*

## Cush Cush

2 cups cornmeal
1 teaspoon salt
1/2 teaspoon baking powder
1 tablespoon flour

1 1/2 cups water
1/2 cup cooking oil,
   heated well

Mix cornmeal, salt, baking powder, flour, and water thoroughly, being sure the mixture is not too dry. Place mixture into hot oil (use an iron pot, if available) and let the dough form a crust. Stir well; lower the flame to simmer. Cover and cook 15 minutes. Serve with milk as a cereal or pour pure cane syrup over top and serve with a glass of milk. Serves 4.

*C'est Bon, Encore*

## Sweet Potato Biscuits

2 1/2 cups baking mix
1/3 cup margarine
1/2 cup milk

1 cup mashed cooked
   sweet potatoes

Combine the baking mix, margarine, and milk in a bowl. Add the sweet potatoes and mix well. Drop the dough by heaping tablespoonfuls onto a floured surface and shape into biscuits. Place on a baking sheet. Bake at 275° for 15 minutes or until golden brown. Store the leftover biscuits in sealable plastic bags in the refrigerator. Yield: 6 serving.

*Louisiana Temptations*

## Sausage Cheese Biscuits

2 cups Pioneer biscuit mix
1/2 pound bulk pork sausage
1/2 pound grated Cheddar
   cheese

1/2 teaspoon red pepper
   (optional)
1 egg

Mix all ingredients. Mix well; knead lightly. Pinch off dough and form into balls to make a biscuit about 1 3/4-inch in width. Place on greased baking sheet. Bake at 325° about 25 minutes or until golden brown.

*Heart of the Home*

# Ham Brunch Rolls

1 (25-ounce) package frozen
  Parkerhouse-style rolls
1 cup finely chopped ham,
  well trimmed or 95% fat free

3 tablespoons grainy brown
  mustard
2 teaspoons prepared horseradish
1 teaspoon Worcestershire sauce

Allow the roll dough to thaw. Spread each roll into a 3-inch diameter circle. Combine the remaining ingredients to make the filling. Put one heaping teaspoon of filling in the center of the circle. Bring the edges of the dough together to encase the filling in a ball of dough. Place each roll seam-side-down in a muffin pan sprayed with vegetable oil cooking spray. Allow the rolls to rise until doubled in size. Bake for 15 minutes at 350°. Yield: 24 rolls.

Per Serving: Cal 96; Fat 2.3g; %Fat Cal 22; Sat Fat 0.8g; Chol 6mg; Sod 262mg.

*River Road Recipes III*

# Cajun Eggs

1½ teaspoons cooking oil
½ bell pepper, chopped
2 jalapeño peppers, chopped
½ cup sliced fresh
  mushrooms
½ can Ro-Tel tomatoes
3 stalks green onions, chopped

½ pound boiled crawfish
  tails, peeled
3 eggs
¼ cup Cheddar cheese
¼ cup Swiss cheese
3 dashes Tabasco sauce

In a skillet with oil, sauté bell pepper and jalapeño peppers 2 minutes. Add mushrooms, tomatoes, green onions, and crawfish. Sauté 2 minutes. Crack 3 eggs over the vegetables, leaving them whole. Top with cheeses and Tabasco. Cover the skillet and let eggs cook to desired doneness.

*Roger's Lite Cajun Coobkook*

## *Pick-Me Bread*

*Absolutely delicious. Kids love it.*

3 (10-count) cans Hungry
  Jack biscuits
1 cup sugar
3 teaspoons cinnamon

2 sticks butter
1$^1$/$_2$ cups brown sugar
1 tablespoon cinnamon
1$^1$/$_2$ cups chopped pecans

Cut biscuits into 6 pieces each. Dip in sugar and cinnamon mixture. Drop one can of biscuits into a greased bundt pan. Melt the brown sugar, butter, and 1 tablespoon cinnamon together. Pour 1/3 of mixture over the biscuits. Put in second can of biscuits, 1/3 of mixture, then third can of biscuits, then mixture. Bake at 425° until golden brown. Let set until cooler, then turn over on plate. Makes 8-10 servings.

**Cooking with Morehouse Parish Sheriff Ladies' Auxiliary**


## *Fig Coffee Cake*

2 eggs, beaten
3/4 cup sugar
1/3 cup butter, melted
1$^1$/$_2$ cups flour
1$^1$/$_2$ teaspoons baking powder

1/2 teaspoon salt
1/2 cup milk
1 teaspoon vanilla
Fig Mixture

Combine eggs, sugar, and butter; beat well. In separate bowl, combine flour, baking powder, and salt. Gradually add flour mixture to egg mixture alternately with milk. Stir in vanilla. Pour 1/2 of batter into a greased and floured 8-inch-square pan; top with 1/2 of the Fig Mixture. Pour remaining batter over fig layer, then top with remaining Fig Mixture. Bake at 350° for 40-45 minutes or until cake tests done.

**FIG MIXTURE:**

1/2 cup packed brown sugar
2 tablespoons softened butter

1/2 teaspoon ground cinnamon
10 fig bars, crumbled

Combine all ingredients; mix well.

*The Top 100 Cajun Recipes*

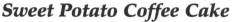

## Sweet Potato Coffee Cake

2 teaspoons cinnamon
2¼ cups flour
1½ teaspoons baking powder
1 teaspoon baking soda
½ teaspoon salt
½ cup tub margarine
½ cup brown sugar
½ cup sugar

2 egg whites plus 1 whole egg
½ cup light sour cream
⅔ cup cooked and mashed
  sweet potatoes
¾ cup nonfat yogurt
2 teaspoons vanilla
Nut topping
1 tablespoon melted tub margarine

NUT TOPPING:
⅓ cup brown sugar
2 tablespoons sugar
2 tablespoons wheat germ

1 teaspoon cinnamon
½ teaspoon nutmeg
½ cup chopped nuts

Combine first 5 ingredients. In a mixer, beat ¼ cup margarine and sugars until well blended, adding eggs one at a time. Add sour cream, sweet potatoes, yogurt and vanilla. Gradually add dry ingredients. Prepare a 10-inch tube or bundt pan with vegetable oil cooking spray and dust with flour. Combine Nut Topping ingredients. Spread ½ of batter into pan, covering with ½ of Nut Topping. Spread remaining batter over topping. Stir one tablespoon margarine into remaining Nut Topping. Sprinkle over batter. Bake at 350° for 50-60 minutes or until toothpick comes out clean. Cool 10 minutes. Yield: 16 servings.

Per Serving: Cal 247; Fat 8.9g; %Fat Cal 32; Sat Fat 1.9g; Chol 17mg; Sod 253mg.

*River Road Recipes III*

## Blueberry Coffee Cake

1 cup butter
2 cups sugar
2 eggs
1 cup sour cream
1/2 teaspoon vanilla

2 cups cake flour or 1⁵/₈
  cups all-purpose flour
1/4 teaspoon salt
1 teaspoon baking powder
1/2 - 3/4 cup blueberries (fresh,
  canned or frozen, well drained)

FILLING:
1/2 cup brown sugar
1 teaspoon cinnamon

1/2 cup chopped nuts

Cream butter and sugar, add eggs. Fold in sour cream and vanilla. Add dry ingredients and fold in blueberries. Grease and flour a bundt pan. Pour 1/3 batter in pan and spread with a knife. Sprinkle 1/2 of filling over batter. Add 1/3 more batter and spread. Sprinkle with remaining filling. Add last 1/3 of batter and swirl cake gently with a knife. Bake at 350° for 55-60 minutes. Partially cool in pan, remove and sprinkle top of cake with powdered sugar.

*Golliwogg Cake*

## Fig Preserves

6 pounds ripe figs, stems
  removed
3/4 cup soda
Water to cover figs

6 pounds sugar
16 lemon slices
8 cinnamon sticks

Using large enamel bowl or crock, soak figs in soda water for one hour. Drain and rinse well. Place figs in large shallow roasting pan and sprinkle sugar over all. Pour in 2 - 3 cups water, enough so the bottom of the pan is covered. Add lemon slices and cinnamon sticks. Bring to a vigorous boil; turn down fire so that there is always bubbling on top. Do not stir very often. Cook 1¹/₂ - 2 hours or until figs are easily pierced with a straw. Some figs will split, but whole figs are desired. Take off scum. Fill sterilized jars, being sure 2 slices of lemon and one cinnamon stick are in each. Makes 8 pints. Fig preserves are delicious on biscuits or toast. For a special treat, warm and serve over vanilla ice cream.

*The Plantation Cookbook*

## Bob's French Toast

3 eggs
4 tablespoons milk
1/4 teaspoon vanilla

2 tablespoons sugar
Powdered sugar
Sliced bread

Mix first four ingredients thoroughly in shallow bowl. Dip each side of bread in batter (do not soak). Fry in 1/4 inch hot shortening (450° in electric skillet) until brown crust forms on both sides. Butter and sprinkle with powdered sugar. Serves 4.

*A Cook's Tour of Shreveport*

## Pain Perdue
### (Lost Bread or French Toast)

1 (5-ounce) can evaporated
   milk
2 eggs, well beaten
1/2 cup sugar

1/2 teaspoon vanilla
5 slices French bread
1 cup oil or butter
Powdered sugar

Mix together evaporated milk, eggs, sugar, and vanilla; dip each slice of bread into this mixture, coating well. Drain off excess batter and fry in hot oil at 375° until brown; turn and brown other side. Drain on paper towels and sprinkle with powdered sugar. Yield: 6 servings.

*Cajun Cuisine*

## Waffles

1 cup sifted all-purpose flour
1 tablespoon sugar
1/2 teaspoon salt
1 1/2 teaspoons baking powder

1 egg, separated
1 scant cup milk
2 tablespoons melted butter

Sift dry ingredients. Beat egg yolk in milk and add to dry ingredients. Beat until batter is smooth. Add melted butter, fold in stiffly beaten egg white. Bake in hot waffle iron until golden. Serves 4.

**Variation:** 1/2 cup broken nuts, 1/4 cup crisply fried crumbled bacon, or 1/2 cup blueberries may be added before folding in egg whites.

*A Cook's Tour of Shreveport*

## Tiny Pecan Muffins

| | |
|---|---|
| 1/2 cup self-rising flour | 1 teaspoon vanilla extract |
| 1 cup light brown sugar | 1 cup chopped pecans |
| 1/2 cup melted oleo | 2 eggs, beaten |

Mix all ingredients. Bake in greased miniature muffin tins in a 350° oven for 15 minutes. Do not bake longer than 15 minutes. Makes 3 dozen. Delicious!

*Shared Treasures*

## Beignets

| | |
|---|---|
| 2 cups flour | 2/3 cup milk |
| 1/2 teaspoon salt | Oil, enough to deep fry |
| 1 teaspoon baking powder | 1/2 cup powdered sugar or |
| 2 eggs, separated | cinnamon sugar |

Sift dry ingredients into a bowl. Add egg yolks to milk; mix well and add to dry ingredients. Beat egg whites until stiff and fold into the batter. Heat oil until HOT. Drop by spoonful into deep fat. Beignets will float and pop over. Remove when light brown. Sprinkle with powdered sugar or cinnamon sugar.

**Variation:** Banana Pop-Overs: Dip 1 piece of banana into batter and drop into hot oil.

*Cajun Cookin' Memories, Photos, History, Recipes*

# Gumbos and Soups

Fat-bottomed cypress trees growing in shallow lakes and bayous are a familiar site in Louisiana, as here at Cheniere Lake Park in West Monroe.

# Microwave Roux
## (With Vegetables)

*Frozen chopped vegetables work just fine—they just sizzle a bit more and require a few more seconds cooking time. Grandmother would even be fooled by this one!*

²/₃ cup vegetable oil

²/₃ cup flour

²/₃ cup chopped onions

²/₃ cup chopped celery

²/₃ teaspoon minced garlic

²/₃ cup chopped bell pepper

²/₃ cup chopped green onions (optional)

²/₃ cup hot water

Mix oil with flour in a 4-cup glass measuring bowl. Microwave uncovered on HIGH for 6 minutes. Stir and cook another 30-60 seconds on HIGH till the color of mahogany.

Now you can add your chopped vegetables, stir well, and "sauté" them on HIGH for another 5 minutes till soft but not brown.

Now before stirring, pour oil off top. Add hot tap water, stirring till smooth. Beautiful! And it freezes for later use.

*The Little Gumbo Book*

# Seafood Gumbo

1/2 cup oil
1/2 cup all-purpose flour
2 cups onion, chopped fine
2 teaspoons green onions, chopped
1 cup celery, chopped fine
1 1/2 gallons water (boil shrimp peelings for stock water)
4 cloves garlic, minced (optional)

Salt, black and cayenne pepper, to taste
2 pounds shrimp, peeled and deveined
1/2 teaspoon parsley, chopped fine
1/2 pint shelled oysters
1 pound claw crab meat
Gumbo filé

Pour off excess oil from roux, add onions and celery. Cook until onions are wilted, then add water and garlic. Cook in heavy uncovered pot over medium heat for one hour, and season to taste with salt, black and cayenne pepper. Add shrimp and parsley to mixture; cook another 10-15 minutes. Add oysters and crab meat to the gumbo; allow to come to a boil. Serve in soup plates with cooked rice. Serves 6. Use a dash of filé in each plate, if desired.

*Secrets of The Original Don's Seafood & Steakhouse*

# Shrimp and Egg Gumbo

**ROUX:**
1 cup flour                                   2/3 cup oil

Cook flour and oil until golden brown.

1 cup celery, chopped
1 large onion, chopped
1 bell pepper, chopped

2 quarts water
1 pound fresh shrimp, peeled
6 hard-boiled eggs

When roux is golden brown, add celery, onion, and bell pepper. Cook until vegetables are limp. Add water and shrimp. Cook until shrimp are done. When cooked, add eggs. Serve over rice. Very good!

*C'est Bon, Encore*

## Mamaw's Shrimp Gumbo

*A family favorite . . . everybody loves it!*

1 stick butter or margarine
1 pound frozen cut okra
²/₃ cup vegetable oil
³/₄ cup flour
1 (12-ounce) bag frozen
  chopped onion
¹/₂ (10-ounce) bag frozen
  chopped bell pepper
3 quarts water

1 (28-ounce) can tomatoes,
  chopped
1 teaspoon chopped garlic
2 teaspoons salt
¹/₂ teaspoon ground bay leaves
¹/₂ teaspoon black pepper
1 teaspoon Tabasco
¹/₄ teaspoon crushed red pepper
3-4 pounds raw shrimp, peeled

In big, heavy pot, melt butter; add okra and cook on medium heat till not ropy anymore—about 15-20 minutes—stirring often. In another big iron pot or skillet, heat and stir oil and flour to make dark brown roux. Add vegetables which have thawed slightly (the frozen kind sizzle a bit more, but keep stirring, it works just fine.) Add a cup of hot water slowly to the roux, stirring till smooth. Now combine the two mixtures in the bigger pot.

Add tomatoes, water, garlic, and all seasonings, and bring to a boil. Add shrimp, bring back to a slight boil, lower heat and simmer about 30 minutes. Serve over fluffy rice with potato salad and buttered crackers and iced tea. Makes about 12-15 bowls.

*The Little Gumbo Book*

## Turkey Gumbo Soup

Roast turkey carcass
¹/₂ teaspoon salt, optional
1 tablespoon margarine
1 cup sliced okra, fresh
  or frozen
1 cup sliced celery
¹/₂ cup chopped onion
¹/₄ cup green pepper
1 teaspoon minced garlic

2 tablespoons flour
1 (16-ounce) can diced
  tomatoes
¹/₂ cup rice
2 tablespoons chopped parsley
¹/₄ teaspoon each: cumin, pepper
  Tabasco sauce, thyme
8 ounces cooked turkey

CONTINUED

Place turkey carcass in large pot and cover with water. Add salt. Simmer about 2 hours. Pour broth into container and chill. Skim off fat. Remove meat from bones and reserve. Sauté okra in margarine until it starts to turn brown, about 5 minutes. Add celery, onion, green pepper, and garlic. Sauté for about 2 minutes while stirring. Sprinkle with flour. Stir until blended and starting to brown. Add tomatoes. Add broth, rice, and seasonings. Simmer 30 minutes. Add meat and heat 5 minutes. Yields 8 (1$^1$/$_2$-cup) servings.

Cal 115; Chol 15mg; Sat Fat <1gm; Fat 3gm; Sod 473mg; Pro 9gm; Cho 13gm; Exchanges: 1 meat, 1 vegetable, ½ bread.

*Southern But Lite*

## Chicken Gumbo

1 cup flour
1 cup oil
1 gallon water
 Hen or fryer, cut into
   serving pieces
Salt and pepper to taste

1 cup chopped onion
¹/₂ cup chopped bell pepper
¹/₄ cup chopped celery
1 pound sausage (optional)
¹/₄ cup onion tops

Make a dark roux with flour and oil. Add water slowly and allow to boil on medium high. Add hen or fryer and season to taste. Add onion, bell pepper, and celery and continue to boil until meat is tender. If a large hen is used, boil for at least 2 hours. If a fryer is used, boil only 1 hour. If you are using sliced smoked sausage, you have to add the sausage to the pot when you add the meat. This does add a special flavor to the gumbo. Finally, add the chopped green onions and boil for 10 more minutes. Serve in gumbo bowl over rice. Serves 4-6.

*Classic Cajun*

# Father Jeff's Corn-Crab Meat Bisque

**CRAB STOCK:**

6 boiled crabs
2 onions, quartered
3 ribs celery, coarsely
   chopped

1 bell pepper, quartered
1/2 cup white wine
2 1/2 quarts water
Salt and pepper to taste

Pick boiled crabs and set aside crab meat for bisque preparation. In a heavy Dutch oven, boil shells and stock ingredients. Lower heat and simmer for 45 minutes. Remove shells and strain liquid. Set aside. Purée vegetables in blender. Set aside.

**BISQUE:**

1 stick butter
1 cup chopped yellow onion
3 tablespoons flour
1 (12-ounce) can evaporated
   milk
1/2 teaspoon tarragon
1/2 teaspoon liquid crab boil
2 quarts crab stock

2 (12-ounce) cans whole kernel
   corn, undrained
1 (8 3/4-ounce) can cream-style
   corn, undrained
Crab meat from 6 boiled crabs,
   or 1 pound lump crab meat
1/2 cup chopped parsley

Melt butter; add onion, flour, and milk. Simmer until ingredients blend smoothly and onion is transparent. Stir in tarragon, crab boil, crab stock, corn, and puréed vegetables. Cook slowly over low heat, approximately 20 minutes. Ten minutes before serving, gently fold in crab meat and parsley. Yield: 8-10 servings.

*Allons Manger*

Established in 1821, the Academy of the Sacred Heart in Grand Coteau is the second oldest institution of learning west of the Mississippi. In 1863, Union General Nathaniel Banks was briefly headquartered there. He thereafter saw to it that the nuns were taken care of and the school was kept stocked with food and other supplies. Further, he made any harm done to the nuns a crime punishable by death. In its gracious oak alley setting, the all-girls Academy has remained in continuous operation through fire, epidemics, and war. It is also the only site in the US of a miracle recognized by the Catholic Church.

## Louisiana Crab Bisque

2 cups fresh lump crab meat
  (do not use canned)
2 (10$^3$/4-ounce) cans cream
  of mushroom soup, undiluted
2 (10$^3$/4-ounce) cans cream
  of asparagus soup, undiluted
2 cups whipping cream

2$^1$/2 cups milk
1 teaspoon Worcestershire
  sauce
$^3$/4 teaspoon hot pepper sauce
$^2$/3 cup dry sherry
White pepper to taste
$^1$/4 cup chopped chives

Combine crab meat, mushroom soups and asparagus soups in blender or food processor. Blend well. Pour soup mixture into heavy saucepan. Add whipping cream, milk, Worcestershire sauce, hot pepper sauce and sherry. Heat thoroughly, stirring occasionally; do not boil. Season with white pepper. Sprinkle chives on individual servings in soup bowls or demitasse cups. Soup can be prepared one day in advance and stored in refrigerator but should not be frozen. Serves: 10-12 soup bowl portions or 20-22 demitasse portions.

*Cane River's Louisiana Living*

## Squash Bisque

*This soup is delicious cold, too!*

2 medium onions, chopped
2 tablespoons butter
1 quart chicken broth
4 cups sliced squash
$^3$/4 cup sliced carrots
2 medium potatoes, diced

1 teaspoon salt
1 teaspoon thyme
2-4 teaspoons Worcestershire
  sauce
1 (16-ounce) carton
  half-and-half

In a saucepan, sauté onions in butter. Add chicken broth, squash, carrots, potatoes, salt, and thyme, and cook only until vegetables are tender. Cool. Purée in food processor. Return to saucepan and add Worcestershire and half-and-half. Heat on low and serve. (High heat will make the soup curdle.) Makes 2 quarts.

*Celebrations on the Bayou*

# *Crawfish Bisque*

**DRESSING:**

| | |
|---|---|
| 5 pounds crawfish tails, divided | 3 tablespoons chopped parsley |
| 2 medium onions | 3 tablespoons chopped onion tops |
| 6 slices bread, toasted | 12 dozen crawfish body shells, cleaned |
| 3 cups milk | |
| 5 eggs | |

Grind 3 pounds crawfish tails and onions in coarse chopper of grinder. Soak bread in milk and press slightly to remove excess milk. Break into small pieces. Combine bread and eggs with ground mixture. Add 3 tablespoons parsley and 3 tablespoons onion tops. Season to taste and mix well. Stuff shells. Reserve remaining dressing to add to gravy. Bake stuffed shells in a shallow pan at 500° until browned. Remove from oven and set aside.

**GRAVY:**

| | |
|---|---|
| 6 tablespoons vegetable oil | 3 cups water |
| 1¼ cups flour | 1 stick butter |
| 4 onions, chopped | Salt and pepper |
| 2 cups crawfish tails (reserved from the 5 pounds) | 3 tablespoons chopped parsley |
| | 3 tablespoons chopped onion tops |

Mix oil and flour in a heavy pot to make a roux (a dark roux is preferred). Add onions, 2 cups crawfish tails, and cook 5 minutes. Add water and simmer ½ hour. Add remaining dressing, butter, baked shells, and seasonings (to taste). Simmer about 10 minutes. Add parsley and onion tops. Serve over cooked rice. Yield: 15-20 servings.

**Note:** This can be frozen when made ahead of time. Just eliminate the last 10 minutes of cooking and the parsley and onion tops. Add these when you are ready to use.

*Nun Better*

# Corn Chowder

*A crowd pleaser!*

6 slices bacon
16 ounces cream-style
  corn
1 cup milk
1 medium onion, diced

1 small green pepper, diced
3 medium potatoes, diced
Salt and white pepper,
  to taste
1/2 cup white wine

Cook bacon until crisp; drain well.  To bacon grease, add corn, milk, onion, green pepper, and potatoes.  Cook until vegetables are tender.  Add salt and pepper to taste.  Add wine.  Serve with bacon crumbled on top.  Yield: 4 servings.

*Fessin' Up with Bon Appetit*

# Corn and Crawfish Chowder

1 stick margarine
2 tablespoons flour
1 onion, chopped
1 pound crawfish
1 quart milk
2 cans cream corn
Tabasco to taste

1 (15-ounce) can whole corn
1 can cream of potato soup
1/2 teaspoon Accent
1/2 teaspoon Worcestershire sauce
1/4 cup grated provolone cheese
1/4 cup chopped shallots
Seasoned salt to taste

Blend together margarine and flour over low heat.  Add onion; sauté until wilted.  Add remaining ingredients and cook on medium heat for 40 minutes.  Serves 7 or 8.  Approximately 200 calories per serving.

*A Shower of Roses*

## *Broccoli Chowder*

1 pound fresh broccoli
1 (13³/₄-ounce) can chicken
  broth
1¹/₂ cups skim milk
1 cup evaporated skim
  milk

¹/₂ cup lean cubed ham
Salt to taste (optional)
¹/₄ teaspoon pepper
1 cup shredded lite Swiss
  cheese

Combine broccoli and ¹/₂ can chicken broth in casserole dish. Cover and cook 5 minutes in microwave. Remove broccoli and cool, cutting into small pieces. Add remaining broth to dish with milk, ham, salt, and pepper. Microwave 5 minutes or until mixture boils. Stir in broccoli and cheese and microwave 3 minutes. Yield: 4 servings.

Cal 244; Chol 38mg; Sat Fat 4gm; Fat 8gm; Sod 374mg; Pro 24gm; Cho 19gm; Exchanges 2 meat, 2 milk, 1 vegetable.

*Just For Kids*

## *Oyster Stew*

1 pint oysters with liquid
¹/₄ cup butter
1 cup milk
¹/₂ cup cream

¹/₂ teaspoon salt
¹/₄ teaspoon pepper
¹/₈ teaspoon paprika

Pour oysters and liquid into a saucepan. Bring to a brisk boil until edges of oysters begin to shrivel and curl. Add butter and stir until melted. Reduce to medium heat. Add milk and cream (curdling will occur only if milk is beginning to sour). Season with salt and pepper. Increase heat and bring to light boil. Sprinkle with paprika and serve hot. Serves 4.

**Note:** When using fresh oysters, one cup water may be used for liquid.

*Big Mama's Old Black Pot*

# *Corn Soup*

*It is hard to believe this creamy soup is not full of heavy cream. You can garnish it with chopped green onions when serving.*

1 onion, chopped
1 green bell pepper,
   seeded and chopped
1/2 teaspoon minced garlic
1 (16-ounce) bag frozen
   sweet corn
1 (8 1/2-ounce) can cream-
   style corn
1 (10-ounce) can diced
   tomatoes and green chilies

1 (14 1/2-ounce) can fat-free
   chicken broth
1 tablespoon Worcestershire
   sauce
Salt and pepper to taste
2 cups low-fat milk
1/3 cup all-purpose
   flour

In a pot coated with nonstick cooking spray, sauté the onion, green pepper, and garlic over medium-high heat until tender, about 5 minutes. Add the frozen corn, cream-style corn, diced tomatoes and green chilies, chicken broth, Worcestershire sauce, and salt and pepper. In a separate bowl, blend together the milk and flour. Gradually stir into the corn mixture. Cook for 15 minutes, until hot throughout. Makes 8 (1-cup) servings.

Cal 125; Fat .04g; Cal from Fat 2.9%; Sat Fat 0.1g; Sod 387mg; Chol 1mg.

**Trim & Terrific American Favorites**

# *Chicken and Corn Soup*

1 whole chicken fryer
2 tablespoons vegetable oil
1 cup chopped onion
1/2 cup chopped bell pepper
1/4 cup celery, minced
2 tablespoons garlic, minced
2 tablespoons parsley flakes
2 tablespoons whole sweet basil
2 teaspoons salt

1 tablespoon black pepper
1 1/4 cups diced Ro-Tel tomatos
4 cups whole kernel yellow
  corn
2 quarts chicken stock
3 tablespoons cornstarch dissolved
  in 1/4 cup water

In a 4-quart pot, boil chicken in enough water to cover until completely cooked (about 45 minutes). Chicken should be falling apart. Remove chicken to large bowl and allow to cool. Strain stock. Return to pot and boil until reduced to about 2 quarts. Reserve. Next, in a 4-quart pot, heat oil. Add onion, bell pepper, celery, garlic, parsley, and basil to hot oil and sauté until onions begin to wilt. Add salt, pepper, and Ro-Tel tomatoes and simmer on medium heat for 10 minutes. Add corn and stir well. Add reserved chicken stock and bring to boil. Reduce heat to low, cover and simmer for 30 minutes.

While mixture is simmering, pick all the meat from the boiled chicken. When mixture has simmered for 30 minutes, add all chicken to pot and stir. Add cornstarch mixture to pot and stir well. Cover and remove from heat. Serve.

*'Dat Little Cajun Cookbook*

# *Taco Soup*

1 pound ground meat
1 onion, chopped
2 cans green beans
2 cans whole kernel corn

2 cans kidney beans
2 cans Ro-Tel tomatoes
1 large can tomato juice
1 package taco seasoning

Brown the ground meat in skillet. Add the onion and sauté until clear. Add the remaining ingredients. Stir and simmer until flavors blend. This makes a large amount. Can halve recipe or freeze half. Good for potluck dinners.

*Fiftieth Anniversary Cookbook*

# Roasted Garlic Soup

1 large head (bulb) garlic
1/2 teaspoon olive oil
1/4 cup butter or margarine
1/2 onion, chopped
1/4 cup flour
2 medium baking potatoes,
　(1 pound) peeled and
　chopped

3 cups chicken broth
1 cup heavy cream
Salt and white pepper,
　to taste
Chopped parsley for
　garnish

Preheat oven to 325°. Cut a small slice off the top of the whole garlic head to expose garlic cloves. Place in a garlic roaster or small baking dish, drizzle with olive oil, cover and roast for 30 minutes. Remove cover and roast 30 minutes more. When cool enough to handle, squeeze garlic pulp from peel.

In a large saucepan, heat butter over medium heat. Add onion and sauté until tender. Add flour and cook, stirring constantly, for about 2 minutes, until lightly browned. Add roasted garlic, potatoes, and chicken broth. Bring to a boil, cover and lower heat. Cook for 15-20 minutes, stirring occasionally. Purée soup in food processor or blender until smooth. Return to saucepan and stir in cream, salt and white pepper. Heat thoroughly and taste for seasoning. Add more chicken broth if soup is too thick. Serve garnished with a little chopped parsley. Serves 6-8.

*Kay Ewing's Cookbook School Cookbook*

# Pumpkin Soup

2 tablespoons oleo
1/4 cup chopped onion
1 1/4 teaspoons curry powder
1 tablespoon flour
2 cups cooked pumpkin
  (1 can)
1 teaspoon brown sugar

1/8 teaspoon nutmeg
1 teaspoon salt
1/8 teaspoon pepper
3 1/2 cups chicken broth
  (2 cans)
2 cups cream (or milk)

Melt oleo. Sauté onion, curry powder, and flour. Combine pumpkin, sugar, nutmeg, salt, and pepper and add to oleo mixture. Add chicken broth. Bring to a simmer. Remove from heat a few minutes to blend flavors. Stir in cream and bring back to a simmer.

**Note:** You may make this the day before and add cream at time of reheating and serving.

*Shared Treasures*

# Black-eyed Pea and Sausage Soup

1 pound black-eyed peas,
  washed and soaked
  2 hours
2 tablespoons bacon drippings
2 tablespoons flour
1 large onion, chopped
6 green onions with tops,
  chopped
2 stalks celery, chopped
1/2 teaspoon garlic powder

1/2 teaspoon each: thyme and
  oregano
Salt and pepper to taste
1/4 teaspoon Tabasco sauce
2 cups chicken stock or broth
6 or more cups water
1 pound Smokey Hollow Hot
  Link Sausage, thinly sliced
1/4 - 1/2 cup sherry, optional

In a large heavy pot, make a roux of bacon drippings and flour. Add onion and cook until limp (medium heat). Add green onions and sauté about 2 minutes. Add celery and seasonings; stir, cooking about one minute. Turn heat to low; add peas, broth, water, and sausage. Stir. Bring to a boil. Cover and simmer 3-4 hours until peas are tender. Stir occasionally. Thirty minutes before serving, sherry can be added, if desired. Serve with a green salad and French bread or cornbread.

*Heart of the Home*

## Potato Soup

6-8 slices bacon
2 medium onions, chopped
6-8 Irish potatoes, cubed
Salt and pepper
2 cups water
1 can cream-style corn

Fry bacon until crisp. Remove and let cool. Pour off bacon grease, except 3 tablespoons. Add onions to bacon grease and sauté until wilted. Next, add potatoes and crumbled bacon. Season to taste. Stir as they fry, adding water when they start browning. Add corn. Cook until potatoes are tender but not overcooked. Add water as needed. Delicious with corn bread.

*Kooking with the Krewe*

## Betty's Potato Soup

*I had a group of ladies over the day I tested Betty Starnes' recipe for my column. It was such a hit that most of them stopped at the store on the way home for the ingredients, and made it for their families that evening.*

4 medium potatoes
1 medium onion, chopped
2 tablespoons margarine or
  butter
1/2 teaspoon onion salt
1/2 teaspoon seasoned salt
Cayenne pepper to taste
1 (14½-ounce) can chicken broth
1/4 teaspoon dried sweet basil
1/3 cup instant potato flakes
1 pint half-and-half
Chopped green onions
Grated Cheddar cheese
Bacon pieces

Peel and dice potatoes in very small cubes. Sauté onion in margarine until soft. Add the diced potatoes and cook until potatoes are almost tender (about 5 minutes). Season with onion salt, seasoned salt, and cayenne pepper to taste. Add the chicken broth and sweet basil. Simmer covered until potatoes are tender. Add the instant potato flakes. Stir until well blended. Add the half-and-half. Heat over low heat until hot. Do not boil. Taste for seasoning. Garnish each bowl of soup with chopped green onions, cheese and a sprinkle of bacon pieces. Serves 4-6.

*Extra! Extra! Read All About It!*

# Catahoula Courtbouillon

*As with the bouillabaisse, there are as many recipes for courtbouillon as there are Acadians and Creoles. Papa's version is a thick soup, much like a chowder, and can be made with either fresh or saltwater fish.*

²/₃ cup flour
²/₃ cup cooking oil
2 medium onions, chopped
1 sweet green pepper,
   chopped
2 stalks celery, chopped
3 cloves garlic, minced
   (optional)
1 (1-pound) can whole
   tomatoes, undrained
   and chopped

1 can Ro-Tel tomatoes
1 quart fish stock or water
1 tablespoon salt
1 teaspoon cayenne pepper
2¹/₂ pounds firm white fish,
   cut into fillets or steaks
1 bunch green onions,
   tops only, chopped
¹/₄ cup finely chopped fresh
   parsley

In a large heavy pot, make a dark brown roux with flour and oil. Add onions, green pepper, celery, and garlic; cook for 5 minutes. Add both cans of tomatoes and cook slowly over a low fire. Now, here's the secret to making a good courtbouillon—let it cook until the oil forms a thin layer, like paper, over the top of the mixture. You will have to stir occasionally, but after a half hour or so, the oil will rise to the top. Add warmed fish stock or water and seasonings, and let cook for one hour, stirring occasionally. Add the fish and cook for 15-20 minutes. Right before serving, add onion tops and parsley. Check seasonings and make any necessary adjustments. I usually put a bottle of Tabasco on the table for those who wish to make it hotter. Serve in deep bowls with rice, and of course, French bread. Serves 8.

*Who's Your Mama, Are You Catholic,*
*and Can You Make a Roux?*

# Creole Bouillabaisse

*There is no doubt in my mind that the Louisiana gumbo originated from the French bouillabaisse. The innovative Creoles, adapting to their new homeland in South Louisiana, created a new bouillabaisse by using what was available here in the bayous.*

4 (1½-pound) cleaned red
  snapper
2 pounds (31-35 count)
  head-on shrimp
2 pounds live crawfish
12 fresh cleaned crabs
1 cup olive oil
2 cups chopped onions
2 cups chopped celery
1 cup chopped red bell
  pepper
4 whole diced tomatoes

¾ cup tomato sauce
¼ cup diced garlic
4 whole bay leaves
2 medium carrots, diced
3 quarts shellfish stock
2 cups dry white wine
1 teaspoon dry thyme
1 teaspoon dry basil
1 cup sliced green onions
1 cup chopped parsley
Salt and cayenne pepper
  to taste

Pour olive oil into a two gallon stock pot. Place in layers the onions, celery, bell pepper, tomatoes, tomato sauce, garlic, bay leaves, and carrots. On top of vegetables, layer whole fish, shrimp, crawfish, and crabs. Place on medium-high heat covered, and steam approximately 3-5 minutes. Add shellfish stock, white wine, thyme, and basil. Bring to a low simmer, approximately 190°, or just below the boiling point. Top of stock should ripple, but not boil. Cook 30 minutes and remove from heat. Carefully pour off the shellfish stock, and reserve for soup. Using a spatula, remove all seafood. Peel the shrimp, crawfish, and crab. Debone all meat from the fish. Bring the stock back to a low boil and add all seafood. Reduce to a simmer and add green onions and parsley. Season to taste, using salt and cayenne pepper. Serve by placing a generous amount of the seafood in the center of a soup bowl and ladle over with hot soup. Serves 12.

*The Evolution of Cajun & Creole Cuisine*

## *Créole Turtle Soup*

4½ quarts water
1½ teaspoons salt
4 bay leaves
3 pounds fresh turtle meat, boiled (reserve broth)
½ cup shortening
½ cup flour
2½ cups chopped onions
½ cup chopped green onions
5 cloves garlic, minced
1½ cups bell pepper, finely chopped
¼ teaspoon red pepper
1 (10-ounce) can tomatoes
1 (8-ounce) can tomato sauce
1 teaspoon thyme
1 teaspoon salt or to taste
1½ teaspoons black pepper
1 teaspoon allspice
2 lemons, sliced in thin rounds
5 tablespoons Worcestershire sauce
1½ cups dry sherry wine
1½ cups celery, finely chopped
¼ cup parsley, minced
6 eggs, hard-boiled
½ ounce cognac brandy (optional)

In a large soup pot, combine water, salt, bay leaves, and turtle meat. Boil turtle meat until tender.

In a deep skillet, make a roux with shortening and flour. When roux is brown, add onions, green onions, garlic, and bell pepper; sauté until soft. Skim scum which has formed on turtle and remove bay leaves. Mix a cup of turtle meat broth with the roux. Blend in small portions in the electric blender for one minute. After blending, add turtle meat and broth. Blend tomatoes and add to turtle broth. Add tomato sauce, thyme, salt, black pepper, allspice, lemon slices, Worcestershire sauce, and sherry wine. Bring to a boil and add celery and parsley. Simmer for 45 minutes. Slice eggs in halves lengthwise. Remove yolk halves and add to soup. Chop egg whites into small pieces; add to soup. Serve hot. Serves 6-8.

**Note:** A half ounce of cognac brandy poured over each serving is delightful for your taste buds.

*Allons Manger*

## Salads

Towering pines give way to 20,000 roses at the nation's largest park dedicated to roses. The Gardens of the American Rose Center. Shreveport.

## Bridesmaids' Luncheon Chicken Salad

*One of the best chicken salads you will ever eat! Guaranteed to bring rave reviews!*

1½ cups Hellmann's
  mayonnaise
¾ cup Major Gray's Chutney
1 teaspoon curry powder
2 teaspoons grated lime peel
¼ cup fresh lime juice
½ teaspoon salt
4 cups cooked, small chunked
  white meat of chicken

2 (13¼-ounce) cans chunky
  pineapple, drained
2 cups diagonally sliced celery
1 cup thinly sliced green
  onions, tops and bottoms
½ cup toasted whole or sliced
  blanched almonds

Into a really large mixing or salad bowl, combine mayonnaise, chutney, curry, lime peel and juice, and salt. (If there are fruit chunks in the Chutney, slice them as thinly as possible.) Blend well and then gently fold in remaining ingredients. Chill for 4-6 hours. Can be prepared the night before; just be sure to toss again before serving, and be sure to go all the way to the bottom of the container to mix in all accumulated juices when tossing for the final time. Serve on crisp, chilled salad greens. Yield: 8-10 generous servings.

*Too Good to be True*

## Bon Appétit's Celebrated Chicken Salad

*At Bon Appétit, salad days never end. So it is with all who have a youthful passion for salad. Chicken salad is our all-time favorite.*

3 whole boiled chicken
  breasts, chopped
  and deboned
1 cup Hellman's mayonnaise

¾ cup celery, chopped
¾ cup green grapes, diced
½ cup dried parsley or
  fresh parsley, chopped

Mix together and serve any way your heart desires. We suggest our chicken salad in sandwiches, in tomatoes, and in avocados or on a lettuce-lined plate with fresh fruit and vegetables. Yield: 4-6 servings.

*Fessin' Up with Bon Appétit*

# "Bears" Special Salad

1 large box corkscrew colored
  noodles (rotini)
1 large broccoli with flowerets,
  cut small
2 cucumbers, seeded and cut in
  bite-size pieces
2 packages imitation crab
  meat
2 boxes fresh mushrooms,
  chopped

5 tomatoes, cubed
1 large purple onion, cut
  in rings
3 stalks celery, cut in bite-size
  pieces
3 bell peppers, cubed
3 large bottles Zesty
  Italian dressing

Boil rotini noodles until tender, and drain. In large bowl, mix noodles and all other ingredients, except salad dressing. Mix vegetables and crab meat well. Pour salad dressing over vegetables and rotini, and toss gently. Chill.

*Recipes from Bayou Pierre Country*

# Shrimp Salad

3/4 cup mayonnaise
1 teaspoon salt
2 teaspoons dry mustard
6 green onions, minced or
  diced
2 stalks celery, minced
1 teaspoon paprika

2 drops hot sauce
3 sprigs parsley, minced
2 pounds shrimp, boiled and
  peeled
Lettuce leaves
Hard-boiled eggs, halved

Combine first 8 ingredients and pour over shrimp; refrigerate for 4-6 hours. Serve on lettuce leaves and decorate with eggs.

*The Top 100 Cajun Recipes*

## Fresh Corn Salad

1/4 cup fat free sour
  cream
1/4 cup fat free
  mayonnaise
1 tablespoon prepared
  yellow mustard
1 tablespoon vinegar,
  or to taste

1 teaspoon sugar
1/4 teaspoon salt
Dash of black pepper
2 cups boiled frozen corn
  kernels
2 ounces pimientos
1/2 cup diced raw carrots
1/2 cup chopped onion

Combine sour cream, mayonnaise, mustard, vinegar, sugar, salt and pepper. Add corn, pimientos, carrots, and onion. Toss to blend. Cover and refrigerate at least one hour. It is even better to make this salad the day before. Yield: 8 (1/2-cup) servings.

Cal 58; Chol 0mg; Sat Fat 0gm; Fat 0gm; Sod 199mg; Dietary Fiber 2gm; Exchanges: ½ bread, ½ vegetable.

*Gone with the Fat*

## Beans Vinaigrette

3 (16-ounce) cans whole green
  beans
1/3 cup sugar
1/3 cup vegetable oil
1/2 cup wine vinegar
2 tablespoons soy sauce
1/4 teaspoon Tabasco sauce
2 tablespoons Worcestershire
  sauce

1 teaspoon salt
1/2 teaspoon paprika
1/2 cup chopped pimiento
3-4 green onions, chopped
1 clove garlic, pressed
1 green pepper, chopped
1 (4-ounce) can sliced
  mushrooms, drained

Drain beans. Mix sugar, oil, vinegar, soy sauce, Tabasco, Worcestershire, salt and paprika. Pour over beans. Fold in remaining ingredients and place in a large covered container. Refrigerate for at least 24 hours. Serves 8-10.

*By Special Request*

# *Spinach Salad*

**DRESSING:**

1 egg
1/2 cup sugar
1/2 cup white vinegar

3/4 teaspoon salt
11/2 teaspoons bacon fat

Beat egg. Combine egg, sugar, vinegar, salt and bacon fat in pan. Cook over low heat, stirring constantly, until mixture reaches boiling point. Cool and then chill in refrigerator until ready to serve.

**SALAD:**

1 (10-ounce) package fresh
   spinach
6 slices bacon

6 green onions
2 oranges, seedless
1/2 cup peanuts or cashews

Remove spinach stems. Clean and drain. Cook bacon. Chop green onions and bacon. Peel onions and section. Combine all ingredients and dressing. Serve.

**Note:** Red or green leaf lettuce may be substituted for spinach.

*A Bouquet of Recipes*

# *Elegant Dinner Salad*

2 cloves garlic, pressed
1/2 cup olive oil
Salt and pepper, to taste
3 ounces grated Romano cheese
1 can artichoke hearts,
   quartered
1 small can chopped
   black olives

2 stalks celery, sliced thin
2 tomatoes, sliced into
   small pieces
1 ripe avocado, mashed with
   a fork
1 can asparagus, tips only

In a large bowl, mix garlic, oil, salt, pepper, and the Romano cheese. Allow to sit for 20 minutes. Then mix in the rest of the ingredients except for the asparagus. Lay the asparagus tips over the top of the salad. Serve with wine and a special meal. Makes enough to serve two.

*Pass the Meatballs, Please!*

## *Jake's Sensation Salad*

6 ounces Romano cheese
1/3 cup crumbled bleu cheese
3/4 cup lemon juice
1/4 cup white vinegar

2 1/4 teaspoons salt
1/2 cup olive oil
1 1/2 cups Wesson oil
1 teaspoon finely chopped garlic

Grind Romano cheese in food processor until fine. Add bleu cheese and mix well. Place cheese mixture into an airtight container and keep refrigerated. Mix remainder of ingredients in a large bowl and whisk well until thoroughly blended. Pour dressing into 1-quart container. Refrigerate both containers. To serve, prepare greens, using any combination of these: Iceberg lettuce, spinach, watercress, endive, romaine, escarole. Mix greens with the oil and vinegar dressing. Toss some of the cheese mixture into the dressed greens. Serve.

*Delicious Heritage*

## *Mardi Gras Salad*

*This lively salad features the traditional Mardi Gras colors of purple for justice, green for faith, and gold for power.*

1 head lettuce
1 cup sliced purple cabbage

1 cup sliced yellow bell pepper

Wash and dry lettuce. Tear into pieces. Place in large salad bowl. Sprinkle cabbage and bell pepper on top. Pour one cup Creole Mustard Salad Dressing over salad. Toss and serve. Serves 12.

**CREOLE MUSTARD SALAD DRESSING:**
2 tablespoons Creole Mustard
2 tablespoons vinegar (cane,
    red wine, or rice)

3/4 cup oil

Blend mustard and vinegar. Slowly add oil; blend until smooth. Pour over salad.

**The Cookin' Cajun Cooking School Cookbook**

# Seven Layer Salad

1/2 head lettuce, shredded
1/2 cup green onions or
　diced red onion
1/2 cup chopped celery
1 pound frozen green peas
2 or 3 cups mayonnaise

4 tablespoons sugar
1 pound bacon, cooked crisp
　and crumbled
1/2 pound grated sharp Cheddar
　cheese

Place all vegetables in layers, placing the mayonnaise on top of vegetables; sprinkle sugar over this, then the bacon and cheese. Refrigerate overnight, covered tightly.

**Variation:** May substitute with water chestnuts, boiled egg, cauliflower, broccoli or cooked and chilled pasta.

*Cooking with Morehouse Parish Sheriff Ladies' Auxiliary*

# Marinated Broccoli and Cauliflower Salad

1 (8-ounce) bottle Italian
　salad dressing
1 cup mayonnaise
1 cup grated Parmesan cheese
2 bunches broccoli, fresh,
　raw
1 head cauliflower, fresh,
　raw

1 pound bacon, fried crisp
　and crumbled
6 hard-cooked eggs, chopped
1/4 - 1/2 cup finely chopped
　green onions
1 (8-ounce) jar pimento-stuffed
　olives, drained

Mix Italian dressing, mayonnaise, and cheese; set aside. Wash broccoli and cauliflower, bread into flowerets and place in large bowl. Add bacon, eggs, onions, and olives; toss lightly. Add dressing and toss gently to coat all ingredients. Cover tightly and marinate in refrigerator several hours before serving.

*Sisters' Secrets*

---

A Cajun fable: It is said some of the lobsters in Nova Scotia wanted to relocate with the Acadians to Louisiana, but the trip was so hard and long that they lost a lot of weight. Hence, crawfish!

---

## Pasta Salad

*A Favorite!*

| | |
|---|---|
| 1 (12-ounce) package vermicelli | 1 medium onion |
| 1 bunch celery | 1 small bell pepper, optional |
| 1 large can pimentos | 2-3 cups Kraft Miracle Whip |
| 4 jalapeño peppers, or to taste | Salt and pepper to taste |

Cook vermicelli according to directions. Drain and cool. Finely chop celery, pimentos and peppers. Grate onion. Add cooled vermicelli; mix and add salad dressing, salt and pepper. Keep in refrigerator, covered, for 24 hours. It is good when kept 4 or 5 days. Popular before pasta was so popular!

*Cooking & Gardening with Dianne*

## Paella Salad

*This attractive salad of many colors and textures will convince even the heartiest eaters that a salad can make a satisfying meal.*

| | |
|---|---|
| 2 (5-ounce) packages saffron yellow rice | 1 (14-ounce) can quartered artichoke hearts, drained |
| 1/4 cup balsamic vinegar | 3/4 cup chopped green bell pepper |
| 1/4 cup lemon juice | |
| 1 tablespoon olive oil | 1 cup frozen green peas, thawed |
| 1 teaspoon dried basil | 1 cup chopped tomato |
| 1/8 teaspoon pepper | 1 (2-ounce) jar diced pimientos, drained |
| Dash of cayenne pepper | |
| 1 pound medium shrimp, peeled and cooked | 1/2 cup chopped red onion |
| | 2 ounces chopped prosciutto |

Prepare the rice according to package directions, omitting any oil and salt. Set aside. In a small bowl, mix together the vinegar, lemon juice, oil, basil, pepper, and cayenne; set aside. In a large bowl, combine the cooked rice with the shrimp, artichoke hearts, green pepper, peas, tomato, pimientos, red onion, and prosciutto, mixing well. Pour the dressing over the rice mixture, tossing to coat. Cover and refrigerate at least 2 hours before serving. Makes 6 servings.

Cal 325; Fat 3.9g; Cal from Fat 10.8%; Sat Fat 0.7g; Prot 24.3g; Carbo 48.8g; Sod 1,277g; Chol 152mg.

*Trim & Terrific One-Dish Favorites*

## *Fletcher Miller's Potato Salad*

*Absolutely wonderful! Garlic and vinegar combination is secret to this recipe. Do not eliminate or cut down on garlic. Mix vinegar, etc., exactly as directed.*

5 pounds medium-sized "new potatoes," cooked, cooled, and sliced
3 large ribs celery, chopped
1 bell pepper, diced
10 or more sprigs parsley, snipped
1 medium white onion (not green onion), chopped
6 large cloves garlic, minced
2 teaspoons salt
1 teaspoon cracked black pepper
1 teaspoon cracked red pepper
2 heaping teaspoons dry mustard
1/4 teaspoon sugar
3/4 cup apple cider vinegar
1 1/3 heaping cups Hellmann's mayonnaise

Mix first 9 ingredients above in large mixing bowl. Be gentle so as not to tear up the potatoes any more than necessary. Mix a small amount of vinegar with the mustard to make a paste. Let stand 10 minutes by the clock. Add sugar to paste and mix. Let stand 5 minutes. Add remaining vinegar and mix well. Pour over potato mixture and combine well, still trying not to break up potatoes any more than necessary. Add mayonnaise and mix some more. Check seasonings. Add more salt, pepper, and red pepper, if necessary. Yield: 8-12 generous servings.

*Too Good to be True*

77

# Orange Almond Salad

*A great combination of flavors with a sweet and tangy dressing.*

³/₄ cup sugar
1 teaspoon dry mustard
1 teaspoon salt
¹/₃ cup cider vinegar
1 cup vegetable oil
Leaf lettuce

1 (11-ounce) can mandarin
   oranges, chilled and drained
¹/₂ cup chopped green onion
¹/₂ cup slivered almonds,
   toasted

Combine sugar, mustard, salt, and vinegar in a food processor. With machine running, add oil through feed tube until combined. Chill.

To serve, prepare individual plates of lettuce, oranges, green onion, and almonds. Spoon dressing over salads. Serves 6.

*Kay Ewing's Cooking School Cookbook*

# Blueberry Salad

2 (3-ounce) packages
   grape gelatin
2 cups boiling water
1 (20-ounce) can crushed
   pineapple
1 (21-ounce) can blueberry
   pie filling

1 (8-ounce) package cream
   cheese, softened
¹/₂ cup sugar
1 cup sour cream
¹/₂ cup chopped pecans
1 teaspoon vanilla extract

Dissolve the gelatin in the boiling water in a bowl. Stir in the undrained pineapple and pie filling. Spoon into a 9 x 13-inch dish. Chill for one hour or until set. Beat the cream cheese and sugar in a mixer bowl until fluffy. Add the sour cream, pecans, and vanilla. Spread over the congealed layer. Chill until serving time. Yield: 8 servings.

*Louisiana Temptations*

### Apricot Pineapple Salad

1 large can apricots, drained
    and chopped
1 large can crushed pineapple,
    drained
2 small packages orange Jell-O

2 cups boiling water
1 cup combined apricot and
    pineapple juice
3/4 cup miniature marshmallows

Drain and chill fruit, reserving all juice. Dissolve Jell-O in boiling water. Add 1 cup juice, reserving rest for topping. Chill until mixture has congealed slightly. Fold in fruit and marshmallows. Pour into 9 x 11-inch shallow dish. Chill until firm and spread with topping.

TOPPING:
1/2 cup sugar
3 tablespoons flour
1 egg, slightly beaten
1 cup pineapple and apricot
    juice mixed

2 tablespoons butter
1 cup whipped cream or Cool
    Whip
3/4 cup grated cheese

Combine sugar and flour; blend in egg, then gradually stir in juice. Cook over low heat until thickened, stirring constantly. Remove from heat, stir in butter. Cool. Fold in whipped cream and spread over gelatin mixture. Sprinkle with grated cheese. Cut in squares and serve on lettuce.

*A Bouquet of Recipes*

### Horseradish Salad

1 (3-ounce) package lemon
    Jell-O
1 (3-ounce) package lime
    Jell-O
2 cups boiling water
1 cup mayonnaise

3 tablespoons prepared
    horseradish
1 (15 1/2-ounce) can crushed
    pineapple, undrained
1 (2-ounce) jar diced
    pimento, undrained

Dissolve Jell-O in boiling water. Combine Jell-O mixture, mayonnaise, and horseradish in blender until smooth. Stir in pineapple and pimento. Lightly oil or spray Pam in 11 3/4 x 7-inch pan, or use mold. Chill until firm.

*Shared Treasures*

## Broccoli-Grape Salad

4 cups chopped broccoli
   florets
Ice water
1/2 cup thinly sliced purple
   onion, cut in half-moon
   slivers

1/2 cup green grape halves
1 cup diagonally sliced
   water chestnuts
12 slices bacon, cooked and
   crumbled

DRESSING:
1 cup mayonnaise
2 tablespoons cider vinegar

1/4 - 1/3 cup sugar

Prepare salad 12-24 hours in advance of serving. Crisp broccoli in ice water. Drain well. Combine broccoli, onion, grapes, water chestnuts and bacon. Prepare dressing by combining mayonnaise, vinegar and sugar, blending well. Pour dressing over vegetable mixture, tossing to coat. Serves 8.

*Cane River's Louisiana Living*

## Cornbread Salad

1 (10-inch) skillet of
   cornbread, baked,
   cooled and crumbled
1 cup chopped celery
1 cup chopped pecans

2 ripe tomatoes, chopped
1 cup chopped bell peppers
2 bunches of chopped
   green onions
1 pint mayonnaise

Toss all together and refrigerate overnight.

*Family Traditions*

# *Vegetables*

The Olivier raised cottage by the Gabriel Oak at the Longfellow-Evangeline
Commemorative State Park. St. Martinville.

## *Orange Garlic Roasted Potatoes*

2 teaspoons extra virgin
  olive oil
1 teaspoon grated orange peel
1/2 teaspoon dried sage

1/4 teaspoon ground pepper
1/4 teaspoon garlic powder
3 medium red potatoes,
  cut into wedges

Preheat oven to 425°. Mix the first 5 ingredients, add potatoes and toss. Transfer to a baking sheet. Bake until crisp and crown, turning once, about 40 minutes. Yield: 4 servings.

Per Serving: Cal 114; Fat 2.4g; %Fat Cal 18; Sat Fat 0.3g; Chol 0mg; Sod 7mg.

*River Road Recipes III*

## *Stuffed Baked Potato with Crab*

6 medium baking potatoes
1/2 cup butter, softened
1/2 cup light cream
1 teaspoon salt
1/8 teaspoon white pepper
3 1/2 teaspoons onion, grated

1 cup sharp Cheddar cheese,
  grated
1/2 pound fresh lump crab meat
  (or artificial crab meat)
1/4 cup fresh mushrooms
1/2 teaspoon paprika

Scrub potatoes and bake for 30 minutes. Pierce potatoes with fork and turn over. Bake another 20-30 minutes or until done. Remove from oven and cool briefly. Cut each potato in half lengthwise. Scoop potato from the skin into a medium-size mixing bowl. Add butter, cream, salt, pepper, and onion. Whip with electric mixer until smooth. Fold in cheese, crab meat, and mushrooms that have been sautéed with a little grated onion in 1/4 cup of oil. Fill each potato half with mixture, mounding slightly. Sprinkle with paprika. Bake in 450° oven for 15 minutes. Yield: 6 servings.

*Fessin' Up with Bon Appétit*

## Christmas-Jalapeño Potatoes

4 medium red potatoes
1 small bell pepper
1 small can pimento
Salt and pepper to taste
1/2 stick butter

1 tablespoon flour
1 cup milk
1/2 roll garlic cheese
1/2 roll jalapeño cheese

Boil potatoes in jackets in salted water until tender. When cool, peel and slice; layer in casserole. Add green pepper, pimento, salt and pepper.

In saucepan melt butter; add flour and stir until well blended. Gradually add milk, stirring constantly. Add cheeses that have been sliced or cubed. Cook until melted. Pour over potatoes. Bake at 350° for 45 minutes to 1 hour. Serves 6-8.

*Cooking with Morehouse Parish Sheriff Ladies' Auxiliary*

## Onioned Potatoes

4 medium baking potatoes
1/4 cup soft butter or oleo

1/4 envelope (3 tablespoons)
   onion soup mix

Scrub potatoes (do not pare). Cut each lengthwise in 1/4-inch slices. Blend butter or oleo and onion soup mix; spread on one side of each potato slice. Reassemble potatoes; wrap each in foil, sealing securely. Bake on grill top over coals for one hour, or until done, turning once. Makes 4 servings.

*Pigging Out with the Cotton Patch Cooks*

## Left Over Potato Puffs

2 cups creamed potatoes
   (leftovers)
2 eggs

Chopped green onions
Red pepper to taste
1 cup flour

Mix all ingredients together and shape in small flat balls and fry in deep oil. Very good.

*Czech-Out Cajun Cooking*

# Oven French Fries

Butter flavor cooking
  spray
2 tablespoons oil
2 tablespoons powdered
  butter substitute

Pepper to taste
4 medium potatoes, peeled
  and sliced into thin strips

Prepare sheet pan with vegetable cooking spray. Mix oil, butter substitute, and pepper together. Place sliced potatoes in bowl and add oil mixture, coating potatoes well. Spread on sheet pan, being careful not to overlap potatoes. Bake at 350° for 30-45 minutes, depending on thickness of potatoes. Occasionally turn potatoes while cooking to brown evenly. Yield: 8 servings.

Cal 103; Chol 0mg; Sat Fat 2gm; Fat 3gm; Sod 179mg; Pro 2gm; Cho 17gm; Exchanges: 1 bread.

*Just For Kids*

# Sweet Potato Casserole

3 (16-ounce) cans sweet
  potatoes, mashed
1/3 cup sugar

1 stick margarine, melted
2 eggs, well beaten
1 tablespoon vanilla

Mix all ingredients well and pour into a 9 x 13-inch pan.

3/4 cup brown sugar
1/3 cup milk
1/3 cup flour

3/4 stick margarine, melted
1 cup very coarsely chopped
  pecans

Mix these ingredients and slowly pour on top of the sweet potato mixture; spread evenly without disturbing the sweet potato mixture. Bake at 350° for one hour or until the topping is set as a pecan pie would be. Makes approximately 12 servings.

*Cajun Cookin' Memories, Photos, History, Recipes*

---

Chretien Point Plantation just north of Lafayette features the stairway that was reproduced for Tara in *Gone With the Wind*. Legend has it that a thieving pirate was shot on his way up that staircase, and that his ghost climbs it still.

---

# Sauced Sweet Potatoes

3 pounds sweet potatoes
1/4 cup butter or margarine
1/4 cup heavy cream
1/4 cup sugar
1 teaspoon vanilla

1/2 cup butter
1/4 cup flour
3/4 cup light brown sugar
1/2 cup water
1/2 cup miniature marshmallows

Place sweet potatoes in a large pot, cover with water and bring to a boil over high heat. Cook until tender, drain and rinse with cold water. Peel and place potatoes in a large mixing bowl. Add butter, cream, sugar, and vanilla. Mash together until smooth and spoon into a medium-size greased baking dish.

Preheat oven to 350°. In a small saucepan over medium heat, melt butter. Stir in flour and cook for 2 minutes. Add brown sugar and combine. Stir in water and marshmallows and cook, stirring constantly, until marshmallows melt and sauce thickens. Pour sauce over sweet potatoes, cover with foil and bake for 15-20 minutes until hot. Serves 8-10.

*Kay Ewing's Cooking School Cookbook*

# Patate Douce Bourre
### (Stuffed Sweet Potato)

6 medium sweet potatoes
1/4 cup softened butter
1/4 cup sugar
1 egg
1 teaspoon grated orange rind

1/2 teaspoon allspice
1/4 teaspoon salt
1/4 teaspoon ground nutmeg
1/2 cup miniature marshmallows
1/2 cup chopped pecans

Bake sweet potatoes at 300° until syrup comes out and potatoes are soft. Slice skin away from top of each sweet potato. Carefully scoop out pulp. Leave shells intact. Mash pulp. Stir in the next 7 ingredients. Stuff mixture evenly into shells. Top with marshmallows and pecans. Place in an oven-proof dish and bake at 350° until marshmallows are a golden brown. Yield: 6 servings.

*CDA Angelic Treats*

## Cajun Bar-B-Que Beans

1 pound ground meat
1 medium onion, chopped
1 medium bell pepper,
  chopped
1 (31-ounce) can pork and
  beans
6 tablespoons catsup
4 tablespoons Worcestershire
  sauce
¼ cup packed dark brown sugar
½ cup barbecue sauce
Dash of Tabasco sauce

Brown the meat in a large skillet. Pour off the grease. Stir in the onion and bell pepper and sauté slightly. Transfer the ground meat, onion, and bell pepper into a 2-quart casserole. Add remaining ingredients. Mix well. Bake at 350° for 45 minutes.

*Cooking New Orleans Style!*

## Husband Pleasin' Baked Beans

1 pound ground beef
2 medium onions, chopped
½ stick margarine
3 (15-ounce) cans Ranch
  Style beans
2 (16-ounce) cans pork and beans
¼ cup prepared mustard
¼ cup maple syrup
½ cup brown sugar
1 cup catsup

Brown beef and onions in margarine and combine with remaining ingredients. (This can be refrigerated overnight or popped in the oven.) Bake at 300° for 1½ hours. Serves 12 generously.

**Variation:** For a delicious one-dish meal, increase beef to 2 pounds. Great for a barbecue dinner.

*Cooking with Mr. "G" and Friends*

On Mardi Gras Day in 1699, Pierre le Moyne, Sieur d'Iberville, founded a military outpost named Point Mardi Gras at the mouth of the Mississippi River. The state of Louisiana has been celebrating Mardi Gras ever since. The statewide party begins on January 6th, the Twelfth Night Feast of the Epiphany, and ends on "Fat Tuesday" (Mardi Gras Day), 46 days before Easter.

# Lundi Red Beans and Rice

*When it's Monday in New Orleans, it's time for red beans and rice. So good, and good for you . . .*

| | |
|---|---|
| 1 pound dry red beans | 2 cloves garlic, minced |
| 8 cups water | 2 bay leaves |
| 1 meaty ham bone or | Few shakes Tabasco sauce |
|   ham hocks | Salt and pepper to taste |
| 2 onions, chopped | |

Place all in a big heavy pot. When it come to a boil, lower heat and let it simmer, stirring occasionally, for at least 3 hours, but longer is fine. When they are soft enough, mash some of the beans against the side of the pot—makes for a wonderfully creamy sauce to serve over hot fluffy rice. Serves 6-8.

**Note:** Soaking the beans overnight cuts the cooking time in half. The seasoning meat varies: My Aunt Tiel wouldn't dream of making red beans without pickled pork, MaMère insisted on ham hocks, and my daddy liked hot sausage in his. But the real New Orleans secret is the ham bone marrow. Crack the bone to release that wonderful full-bodied flavor and creamy texture. A tradition that is still alive and well today, red beans and rice has always been cooked on Monday with the bone leftover from Sunday's ham. Before washing machines, that fit in quite well with the all-day chore of Monday washing. (Lundi is French for Monday; Mardi is Tuesday—bet you knew that.)

*The Little New Orleans Cookbook*

## Green Bean Bundles

2 cans whole green beans        1½ pounds bacon, cut in half

Drain green beans. Put 5-7 beans on ½ slice of bacon, roll and secure each bundle with a toothpick. Repeat bundles until all bacon is used. Arrange on broiling pan and broil bundles until bacon is cooked.

**SAUCE:**

2½ tablespoons butter        1 teaspoon paprika
2½ tablespoons vinegar       1 teaspoon fresh parsley
1½ teaspoons salt            1 teaspoon onion juice

Combine all ingredients. Cook over low heat until boiling. Pour over the cooked bean bundles and serve. Beans and sauce may be done ahead of time and refrigerated. Reheat at serving time. Yield: 8-10 servings.

*Nun Better*

## Green Beans and Stewed Potatoes

3 slices bacon                4 small fresh potatoes,
3 cups fresh green beans,       scraped
  snapped                     3 tablespoons margarine,
4 cups water                   melted
1 teaspoon salt              2 tablespoons flour
½ teaspoon pepper

Brown bacon in large saucepan. Add green beans, water, salt, pepper, and potatoes. Cover and simmer 40-50 minutes or until potatoes are tender. (Gently stir at 10 minute intervals to prevent sticking. Additional water may be added, if needed.) After potatoes are cooked, remove ½ cup hot liquid from beans and potatoes. Combine with margarine and flour to make creamy paste. Stir paste into beans and potatoes while still cooking. Simmer 10 minutes or long enough to thicken liquid. Serves 4.

*Dinner on the Ground*

## Stuffed Squash

3 yellow squash
2½ cups water
2 teaspoons salt
1 tablespoon bacon drippings
1 garlic clove, crushed

½ pound ground beef
½ cup rice, uncooked
½ teaspoon pepper
2 cups stewed tomatoes

Cut squash lengthwise. Scrape out seeds. Add 2 cups water and one teaspoon salt into a heavy pot with tight-fitting lid. Bring to boil. Add squash with sliced-side down and cook over medium heat for 5 minutes or until tender. Remove squash and let drain. Heat bacon drippings in a heavy skillet. Add garlic and ground beef. Cook until browned (approximately 10 minutes). Add rice, one teaspoon salt, pepper, tomatoes, and ½ cup water. Cover and cook over low heat for approximately 20 minutes, or until liquid is absorbed. Fill squash halves with mixture and arrange in bottom of baking pan.

SAUCE:
2 tablespoons butter
2 tablespoons flour
½ teaspoon dry mustard
¼ teaspoon salt

¼ teaspoon red pepper
1 cup milk
¼ cup cheese

Melt butter in a saucepan. Stir in flour, mustard, salt, pepper, and milk. Bring to a boil, stirring until thickened. Reduce heat and add cheese. Cook slowly until cheese is melted and mixture is smooth. Pour ½ of cheese sauce over squash. Bake 15-20 minutes. Add remainder of sauce before serving. Serves 6.

*Big Mama's Old Black Pot*

## Squash Dressing

8 yellow squash, chopped
1 onion, chopped
1 bell pepper, chopped
2 tablespoons butter
1 package Mexican cornbread

1 can cream of mushroom
  soup
1/2 pound Velveeta cheese
1 small jar pimento

Sauté vegetables in butter. Cook cornbread, cool, crumble, mix with vegetables. Add soup, cheese, pimento; heat till blended. Pour into casserole and bake in 350° oven for 20-30 minutes until bubbly.

*Family Traditions*

## Sesame Zucchini

2 medium zucchini
1 tablespoon Asian
  sesame oil*
1 1/2 teaspoons sesame seeds,
  lightly toasted

1 teaspoon soy sauce
1 tablespoon lemon juice
Salt and pepper

Halve the zucchini lengthwise and cut into 1/2-inch pieces. Steam over simmering water, covered, until just tender—about 5 minutes. Toss the zucchini with sesame oil, seeds, soy sauce, lemon juice, and salt and pepper to taste. Makes 2 servings.

**Note:** *Sesame oil is available in grocery store's Oriental section.

*Golliwogg Cake*

## Stuffed Mirliton

5 mirlitons
1/4 stick butter substitute
1 cup chopped onions
1/2 pound peeled shrimp,
 chopped
1 cup white crab meat
1 cup sliced smoked turkey,
 breasts, chopped
3 tablespoons chopped
 green onions

1 tablespoon chopped parsley
1/2 teaspoon salt
1/4 teaspoon red pepper
1/4 teaspoon black pepper
1/4 teaspoon thyme
1 teaspoon Worcestershire sauce
1/2 teaspoon Louisiana Hot Sauce
Italian breadcrumbs
Parmesan cheese

Halve mirlitons lengthwise. Remove seeds from center. Boil mirlitons until tender. Scoop mirliton meat out, leaving about 1/4 inch of meat on peeling walls. Reserve mirliton pulp.

Heat butter substitute in black skillet. Add onions, shrimp, crab meat and turkey. Simmer 2-3 minutes. Add mirliton pulp, green onions, parsley, dry seasonings, Worcestershire sauce and hot sauce. Simmer 2 minutes. Add enough breadcrumbs to make firm mixture (1/2 to 1 cup).

Stuff equal amounts of mixture into mirliton halves. Sprinkle with Parmesan cheese and bake in 350° oven for 15 minutes.

*Roger's Cajun Cookbook*

## Skillet Mirlitons

6-8 mirlitons
Nonstick cooking spray
1/3 cup milk

Salt and pepper to taste
1/2 cup grated Cheddar cheese
 (more, if desired)

Scrub mirlitons. Boil with skins on, about 30 minutes. Cool, peel and mash. Drain as much liquid as possible. In sprayed skillet, place mirlitons, milk, and seasonings. Cook on low heat 10-15 minutes, or until milk is almost gone. Cover with cheese and let melt. Serve in skillet or remove carefully to serving dish.

*Cajun Men Cook*

## Cabbage Rolls

1 head cabbage
2 tablespoons chopped onion
1¼ cups cooked rice
2 eggs
½ teaspoon salt
½ teaspoon pepper

1 pound ground pork
  sausage
3 pounds ham hocks
1¼ cups tomato sauce
1 cup water

Wash head of cabbage and drop into boiling water for 5 minutes. Remove from water and allow to drain. Add onion, rice, eggs, salt and pepper to sausage. Roll the meat mixture in cabbage leaves and secure with a toothpick. Place the ham hocks in the bottom of a cast iron pot with enough water to cover the bottom. Place cabbage rolls over ham hocks. Make a mixture of tomato sauce and one cup water. Pour over cabbage rolls. Cover and cook over medium-low heat approximately one hour. Serves 4-6.

*Big Mama's Old Black Pot*

## Hot and Spicy Cabbage

2 ounces center-cut
  smoked ham
½ cup chopped onions
½ cup chopped bell pepper
Olive-oil-flavored cooking
  spray

1 (10-ounce) can chopped
  Ro-Tel tomatoes
½ teaspoon sugar
4 cups cabbage, sliced
⅛ teaspoon white and black
  pepper

Stir-fry ham, onions, and bell pepper in cooking spray. Add Ro-Tel tomatoes and sugar; simmer 2-3 minutes. Add cabbage and peppers. Simmer 15 minutes. Yield: 8 servings.

Cal 30; Chol 4mg; Sat Fat 3gm; Fat <2gm; Sod 244mg; Pro 2gm; Cho 5gm; Exchanges 1 vegetable.

*Southern But Lite*

---

 The Louisiana Bald Cypress can grow to 80 feet in height and 40 feet in circumference.

---

# Tony's Cabbage Casserole

1 medium head cabbage
4 tablespoons margarine
1 pound lean ground meat
1 medium onion, chopped
2 cloves garlic, minced
Tony's Creole Seasoning

1 (10¾-ounce) can cream of
  mushroom soup
¼ cup chopped green onions
1 cup steamed rice
¼ cup bread crumbs

Cut cabbage in small chunks and in a medium pot, boil in salted water until tender, but still green. Drain and reserve the liquid. Melt margarine in a deep skillet and fry ground meat with onion and garlic until brown. Add Tony's Creole Seasoning. In a large bowl, mix cabbage with meat, adding mushroom soup, green onions, and rice.

Pour mixture into greased, flat baking dish. Top with bread crumbs. If you think the casserole is too dry, add some of the water from the boiled cabbage. Bake at 300° for 20-30 minutes. Yields 6 servings.

*Tony Chachere's Second Helping*

# Cousin Patty's Carrot Soufflé

*Extra good and colorful.*

³/₁ cup sugar
3 tablespoons flour
¼ teaspoon salt
¼ teaspoon black pepper
1 teaspoon baking powder
1 stick (¼ pound) butter,
  softened

1 teaspoon vanilla
2 tablespoons rum (optional)
1 (16-ounce) can carrots,
  drained
3 eggs

Preheat oven to 350°. Whisk together sugar, flour, salt, pepper, and baking powder. Combine all ingredients in blender and blend thoroughly. Pour into casserole and bake for 45 minutes. Serve hot. Serves 4-6 hungry hogs!

*The Hungry Hog*

## Beignets De Carottes
### (Carrot Fritters)

8 boiled, mashed carrots   ½ tablespoon flour
1 egg                      1 inch cooking oil in skillet
½ cup sugar (or artificial sweetener)

Combine carrots, egg, sugar, and flour; mix well. Drop by spoonful into hot cooking oil to deep fry to desired brown color.

*Allons Manger*

## Corn Maque Choux

*This is one of the choice corn dishes in southwest Louisiana. Handed down from the Indians, the flavor is outstanding.*

4 tablespoons bacon fat      1 teaspoon cayenne pepper
  or butter                  ½ teaspoon garlic powder
8 cups fresh of the cob      1 bay leaf
  sweet corn, or frozen      1 teaspoon black pepper
1 cup fresh or canned whole  1 cup chicken stock or
  tomatoes                     chicken bouillon
2 cups onion, chopped fine   1 cup milk
1 cup bell pepper, chopped   1 teaspoon sugar
  fine                       1 teaspoon basil

Melt bacon fat or butter in 6-quart iron pot. Add one cup corn and parch to a medium brown (do not burn), about 10 minutes. Strain and set aside. Reserve one cup. Add to the drippings, all vegetables except corn. Cook on high heat for 10 minutes. Stir frequently to keep from sticking or burning. Add corn and all other ingredients except chicken stock, milk, sugar, and basil. Set aside cup of browned corn. Stir well and cook at high heat, covered, for 5 minutes. Uncover, scrape corn crust from bottom of pot and cook for 5 minutes, continuing to stir crust from bottom to prevent burning. Remove bay leaf, add browned corn and continue to cook on high heat for about 10 minutes. Continue to scrape and mix crust formed at the bottom of the pot. Now add chicken stock, milk and sugar. Cover, and simmer on low heat for 15 minutes. If corn is a little dry, add more milk, add basil. Adjust seasoning as needed and simmer for 5 more minutes. Stir occasionally. Serves 10.

*Cajun Men Cook*

## Corn Creole

1 large onion, chopped
1 small green pepper,
  chopped
3 tablespoons bacon drippings
  or oil
1 pound ground beef
1 (20-ounce) can cream-style
  corn

1 egg
Milk (¹/₃ cup)
¹/₂ cup cornmeal
2 teaspoons salt
Pepper to taste
¹/₂ cup bread crumbs
2 tablespoons butter

Sauté the onion and pepper in drippings until wilted. Add the meat and brown well. Add the corn and cook for one minute. Beat the egg and milk; add to meat mixture with cornmeal and seasoning. Pour into a 1-quart baking dish. Top with bread crumbs and dot with butter. Bake at 350° for 45 minutes. Yield: 4-6 servings.

*CDA Angelic Treats*

## Eggplant Casserole

2 medium eggplants
3 tablespoons bacon drippings
1¹/₂ pounds ground beef
3 tablespoons onion, chopped
3 tablespoons green pepper,
  chopped

3 small hot peppers, chopped
1 teaspoon garlic, chopped
1¹/₂ teaspoons salt
¹/₄ teaspoon pepper
1¹/₂ cups rice, cooked
2 teaspoons lemon juice

Peel and chop eggplants. Heat fat in skillet. Add eggplant, ground beef, onion, peppers, garlic, salt and pepper. Cook on medium heat, stirring constantly, for 10 minutes or until eggplant begins to tender. Stir in rice. Put into greased baking dish. Bake at 375° for 30 minutes. Remove from oven and sprinkle with lemon juice. Serves 5-7

*Big Mama's Old Black Pot*

## Stuffed Eggplant

4 medium eggplants
1 cup onions, chopped fine
½ cup celery, chopped fine
¼ pound oleo
12 stale saltine crackers
2 eggs

2 pounds boiled shrimp, peeled
  and deveined
1 pound white crab meat
Parsley and green onions
Italian bread crumbs

Cut each eggplant into 2 equal parts; remove middle and chop. Add onions, celery, and oleo; smother until done. Crush crackers and put in bowl with eggs. Mix well with chopped boiled shrimp, smothered eggplant, crab meat, parsley and green onions. Season to taste. Boil shells of the eggplant for 10 minutes or until tender and then stuff them with mixture. Top each eggplant with Italian bread crumbs. Bake 20-25 minutes at 350°. Serves 8.

*Secrets of The Original Don's Seafood & Steakhouse*

## Eggplant and Tomato Casserole

1 medium eggplant
2 tomatoes, peeled and
  coarsely chopped
1 onion, coarsely chopped
1 green pepper, coarsely
  chopped

2 cloves garlic, minced
4 tablespoons butter or
  margarine
Salt and pepper to taste
½ - ¾ cup grated Cheddar
  cheese

Peel eggplant and cut into chunks. Place in a saucepan and cover with water. Boil until eggplant is tender (about 15 minutes). Drain. Sauté onion, pepper, and garlic in butter until tender. Stir in tomatoes and cook for another 2 minutes. Combine vegetables, salt and pepper. Pour into a greased casserole and top with grated cheese. Bake at 350° for 30-35 minutes. Serves 4-6.

*By Special Request*

## Oyster Spinach Madeline

2 (10-ounce) packages frozen
  chopped spinach
4 tablespoons butter
2 tablespoons flour
2 tablespoons onions, chopped
1/2 cup evaporated milk
1/2 cup vegetable liquor
1/2 teaspoon black pepper
3/4 teaspoon celery salt
3/4 teaspoon garlic salt
Salt to taste
1 (6-ounce) roll jalapeño cheese
1 teaspoon Worcestershire sauce
Red pepper to taste
1 dozen oysters

Cook spinach according to directions on package. Drain and reserve liquid. Melt butter in saucepan over low heat. Add flour, stirring until blended and smooth, but not brown. Add onions and cook until soft. Add liquid slowly, stirring constantly to avoid lumps. Cook until smooth and thick; continue stirring. Add seasonings and cheese which has been cut into small pieces. Stir until melted. Combine with cooked spinach and oysters. Bake in 350° oven for 15 minutes. Serves 8.

*Allons Manger*

## Spinach-Artichoke Casserole

1 stick butter
1/2 cup finely chopped onion
2 (10-ounce) packages frozen
  chopped spinach, thawed
  and drained well
2 (14-ounce) cans artichoke
  hearts, drained and chopped
1 1/2 pints sour cream
10 shakes hot pepper sauce
1 tablespoon lemon juice
1 teaspoon Worcestershire sauce
1/4 teaspoon garlic powder
Salt and black pepper
1/2 cup Italian bread crumbs
1/2 cup freshly grated Parmesan
  cheese

In a large skillet, melt butter, add onion, and sauté until wilted. Add spinach and artichoke hearts and mix well. Simmer 3-4 minutes. Remove from heat. Add sour cream, hot pepper sauce, lemon juice, Worcestershire, and garlic powder. Season with salt and pepper, bread crumbs and Parmesan cheese. Bake uncovered in 350° oven for 20-30 minutes or until hot. Makes 10 servings.

*Celebrations on the Bayou*

## *Mustard or Turnip Greens*

2 or 3 bunches mustard greens
  or turnip tops
½ pound salt pork, bacon
  or sausage

Salt and pepper to taste
1 large onion, chopped
2 large turnip bottoms,
  peeled and cubed

Stem and pick the greens; wash several times. Put greens in large pot (the water on the leaves from washing is sufficient, do not add any). Add meat, seasoning, onion, and turnip bottoms. Cook slowly until meat and greens are tender. Serve with corn bread. To be eaten with the pot likker.

*Czech-Out Cajun Cooking*

Pine and Oak Alley was the site of a famous 1870 wedding. The father of the bride imported a spider from China to spin huge webs in the trees, then the webs were sprinkled with gold and silver dust for the procession. The remnants of the two-mile alley (near St. Martinville) can be seen today.

## Stuffed Green Peppers

2 large green peppers
1/2 pound lean ground beef
1/4 cup uncooked instant rice
1 (8-ounce) can tomato sauce, divided
2 tablespoons chopped onion

1 egg, beaten
1/2 teaspoon salt
1 tablespoon Parmesan cheese
1/2 teaspoon Worcestershire sauce
Dash of pepper

Cut peppers in half lengthwise, and remove seeds. Combine ground meat, rice, 1/4 cup tomato sauce and remaining ingredients. Stuff peppers with mix and place in a greased baking dish. Spoon remaining tomato sauce over stuffed peppers and then sprinkle with additional Parmesan cheese. Cover and bake at 350° for 50 60 minutes. Yields 4 servings.

*By Special Request*

## Vegetable Casserole

1 onion, chopped
1/2 stick butter
Water chestnuts, sliced and chopped slightly

1 cup Hellmann's mayonnaise
1 cup grated cheese
2 cans Veg-All, drained
1/2 cup crushed potato chips

Sauté chopped onion in butter. Mix all ingredients except potato chips, and pour in casserole. Top with potato chips last 10 minutes of baking time. Bake 30 minutes at 350°.

*A Bouquet of Recipes*

## Swiss Vegetable Medley

1 bag frozen broccoli, carrots and cauliflower
1 can cream of mushroom soup

1 cup shredded Swiss cheese
1/3 cup sour cream
1/4 teaspoon black pepper
1 can French friend onions

Combine vegetables, soup, 1/2 cup cheese, sour cream, pepper, and 1/2 can onions. Pour into 1-quart casserole. Bake covered at 350° for 30 minutes. Top with remaining cheese and onions. Bake uncovered for 5 more minutes.

*Cooking with Mr. "G" and Friends*

¼ pound salt pork, cut up
1 tablespoon shortening
1 large onion, chopped
1 small bell pepper, chopped
1 cup sliced okra, fresh or frozen

1 (8-ounce) can tomato sauce
1 (16-ounce) can corn,
   whole or cream-style
1 (16-ounce) can lima beans
1 tablespoon sugar

Bring salt pork to a boil in water and scald; drain and fry well in shortening. Add onion and fry lightly; add bell pepper, okra, and tomato sauce; cook at medium heat for about 15 minutes. Add corn, lima beans, and sugar; cook ½ hour on low heat. If mixture becomes too thick, add water as needed.

*Cajun Cooking*

1 tablespoon cornstarch
3 tablespoons vinegar
3 tablespoons sugar or
   sugar substitute

1 teaspoon salt
½ cup beet juice
1 can beets

Combine all ingredients except beets in a medium saucepan. Heat until thickened. Cool. Add beets. Serve warm or cold.

*L' Heritage Du Bayou Lafourche*

1½ pounds mushrooms, sliced
4 cloves garlic, chopped
3 tablespoons whole basil
1 tablespoon ground thyme
½ cup fresh parsley, chopped

4 tablespoons olive oil
½ cup port wine
½ cup heavy cream
Salt and pepper

In a large bowl, thoroughly mix mushrooms, garlic, basil, thyme, and parsley. Cover bowl with plastic wrap and refrigerate for 2 hours. Using a skillet large enough to hold the mushroom mixture, heat the olive oil over a medium-high heat. Add the mushroom mixture and cook for 6 minutes, stirring constantly. Add wine, lower heat to medium-low and cook for 4 more minutes. Add cream and continue to cook for 5-7 minutes. Remember to stir constantly to prevent sticking and keep the sauce smooth.

*Pass the Meatballs, Please!*

# Pasta, Rice, and Jambalaya

*Avery Island is the home of Tabasco sauce, abundant wildlife, and a jungle garden and bird sanctuary. It's "Bird City" is home to thousands of Snowy Egrets.*

## Spinach Stuffed Manicotti

1 pound ground meat
1 onion, chopped
1 teaspoon chopped garlic
1/2 bell pepper, chopped
14 ounces chopped spinach
1/4 cup cottage cheese

2 eggs, well beaten
14 cooked manicotti shells
1 jar spaghetti sauce
1/2 cup grated Parmesan cheese
1 cup shredded mozzarella cheese

Cook ground meat, onion, garlic, and bell pepper seasoned to taste. Drain well and set aside to cool. Cook and drain spinach, cool; add cottage cheese and eggs; mix well. Add to meat mixture. Stuff shells with mixture and place in oiled 13 x 9-inch pan. Pour spaghetti sauce over manicotti shells. Sprinkle with Parmesan cheese, then sprinkle the mozzarella cheese. Preheat oven to 350° and bake for 30 minutes.

*Sisters' Secrets*

## Chicken Primavera

1 (12-ounce) package
    linguine
1 1/2 pounds skinless, bone-
    less chicken pieces
1/4 cup olive oil
3 cloves garlic, minced
1/2 pound mushrooms, sliced
1 onion, chopped

1 red bell pepper, chopped
1/2 teaspoon dried oregano
1/2 teaspoon dried basil
1/2 teaspoon dried thyme
Salt and pepper to taste
1 cup frozen peas
1/4 cup grated Parmesan
    cheese

Cook linguine according to directions on package; drain. In large frying pan, cook chicken pieces in olive oil and garlic until lightly brown and done. Watch carefully, tossing to keep from sticking. Add mushrooms, onion, red pepper, and seasonings, sautéing until tender. Add peas, tossing until heated. When pasta is ready, add to vegetable mixture, combining well. Add Parmesan cheese and serve. Yield: 6-8 servings.

Cal 365; Chol 51mg; Fat 9.7g; Cal from Fat 23.8%.

*A Trim & Terrific Louisiana Kitchen*

*Make this ahead of time and freeze, especially for vacation. Once it has thawed, follow baking instructions—tastes like it was just made!!*

3 pounds chicken
1 cup chicken stock
9 lasagna noodles
1 tablespoon oil
1 large can whole tomatoes
3 large sliced carrots
1 large onion, sliced
3 zucchini, sliced
3 yellow squash, sliced
  (optional)
2¹/₂ tablespoons margarine

1 medium onion, chopped
1 small bell pepper, chopped
2 stalks celery, chopped
3 tablespoons flour
1¹/₂ teaspoons dried basil
1¹/₂ teaspoons Italian seasoning
1¹/₂ cups 2% milk
1 cup frozen peas
Salt and pepper to taste
³/₄ pound grated mozzarella
  cheese

Season chicken and boil until cooked. Remove bones and chop meat into bite-size pieces. Reserve one cup of chicken stock. Cook lasagna noodles according to package directions, adding one tablespoon oil and salt to water. Drain and rinse with cold water. Lay flat on baking sheet and cover.

Drain and slice tomatoes, discarding excess juices. Steam carrots, onion, zucchini and squash, if used. Melt margarine; add onion, bell pepper, and celery, and cook until clear. Season vegetables while they are sautéing. Add flour and stir over low heat one minute. Stir in dried herbs. Slowly add milk and stock. Boil one minute; add steamed vegetables, diced chicken and frozen peas. Mix well and cook 5 minutes more. Adjust seasonings to taste.

Spoon enough sauce from chicken mixture to cover bottom of 9 x 13-inch glass dish. Layer 3 noodles and pour ¹/₂ of chicken mixture over noodles. Top with sliced tomatoes and sprinkle ¹/₃ of mozzarella over all. Top with 3 more noodles. Spread remainder of chicken mixture and top with ¹/₃ of mozzarella over all. Top with final 3 noodles and sprinkle remainder of cheese. Cover with foil and bake at 375° until bubbly, about 40 minutes. Uncover and bake additional 5 minutes or until top is golden. Let stand 5-10 minutes before serving.

*Tell Me More*

### Creole Shrimp Spaghetti

4 tablespoons chopped onion
1/2 cup sliced celery
2 tablespoons butter, melted
1/4 cup flour
1 teaspoon salt
1/4 teaspoon pepper

4 cups cooked tomatoes
1 cup sliced mushrooms
  (fresh, if possible)
1 teaspoon sugar
1 pound cooked shrimp
8 ounces spaghetti

Cook onion and celery in butter until tender. Stir in flour, salt and pepper. Add juice from tomatoes (2 cups) and stir until smooth. Crush tomatoes and add to sauce along with mushrooms and sugar. Simmer over low heat for 40 minutes. Add cooked shrimp. Serve over cooked spaghetti. Best if prepared ahead of time. May be frozen. Cook 1/2 hour to reheat. Add water if necessary.

*A Cook's Tour of Shreveport*

### Shrimp and Spaghetti

6-8 dozen raw unpeeled
  shrimp
2 sticks butter
1 cup chopped onion
2/3 cup coarsely chopped
  celery
1 green pepper, cut in strips
1/4 cup dry white wine

1/4 cup water
2 bay leaves
1 teaspoon thyme
Salt, pepper and Tabasco,
  to taste
1 pound spaghetti
1/2 cup chopped parsley
Romano cheese

Peel and devein shrimp. Melt 1 1/2 sticks butter and sauté onion. Add celery and green pepper and cook just until crunchy (about 2 minutes). Add shrimp; cook until pink (about 5 minutes). Remove shrimp and vegetables with slotted spoon. Add wine and water and boil 5 minutes. Reduce heat, add bay leaves, thyme, salt, pepper, and Tabasco and simmer 20 minutes. Stir in 1/2 stick butter, shrimp, and vegetables. Serve this over cooked spaghetti with parsley and Romano cheese.

*In The Pink*

# Spicy Crawfish Pasta

*Great dish served with garlic bread and salad.*

| | |
|---|---|
| 1 package rotini (spiral) pasta | 1 (1-pound) package crawfish tails |
| 1 stick butter or margarine | 1 pint half-and-half |
| 1 bunch green onions, chopped | 6-8 ounces jalapeño-Jack cheese |
| 1 medium yellow onion, chopped | Salt, black and red pepper, to taste |
| 1 teaspoon minced garlic | Parmesan cheese (optional) |

Prepare pasta according to package. Drain and set aside to cool. In a large nonstick skillet, melt butter. Add onions and garlic; sauté approximately 3 minutes. Add crawfish and sauté another 3 minutes. Reduce heat to medium and add half-and-half. Reduce heat to low and add slices of jalapeño-Jack cheese to the sauce. Stir sauce frequently until the cheese is thoroughly melted (sauce will be slightly lumpy). Season to taste, but go lightly with pepper; the jalapeños in the cheese make the sauce very spicy.

In a large casserole dish, combine drained, cooked pasta and crawfish sauce. Sprinkle with Parmesan cheese and serve while hot. (Can be prepared ahead and reheated in oven at 350°.) Serves 4-5 adults.

*Fiftieth Anniversary Cookbook*

## Hot Pepper Rice

3 cups cooked long-grain
  rice
1 cup sour cream
1 (4-ounce) can chopped
  green chilies, drained

1 medium fresh jalapeño pepper,
  seeded and diced
1 (8-ounce) package Monterey Jack
  cheese, shredded and divided
1/2 cup (2 ounces) shredded
  Cheddar cheese

Combine rice, sour cream, green chilies, and jalapeño pepper. Layer half of rice mixture in a lightly greased 11 x 7 x 2-inch baking dish; top with half of the Monterey Jack cheese. Repeat procedure and sprinkle with Cheddar cheese. Bake at 350° for 15 minutes or until cheese melts and casserole is heated through. You may omit the jalapeño pepper if you desire a milder dish. Yield: 6-8 servings.

*Cooking with Mr. "G" and Friends*

## Nakatosh Rice Casserole

1 cup uncooked converted rice
2 bunches green onions,
  chopped
1 large green bell pepper,
  chopped
1-2 tablespoons vegetable oil
1/2 cup margarine
2 (4-ounce) cans sliced
  mushrooms, drained

2 (3-ounce) jars diced pimiento,
  drained
1 tablespoon soy sauce
1 tablespoon Worcestershire
  sauce
Salt to taste
1/4 teaspoon black pepper
1 1/2 teaspoons Italian seasoning
1 teaspoon dry parsley flakes

Prepare rice according to package directions. Sauté green onions and bell pepper in oil and margarine until softened. Combine sautéed vegetables, rice, mushrooms, pimiento, soy sauce, Worcestershire sauce, salt, black pepper, Italian seasoning and parsley, mixing well. Spread mixture in 2-quart casserole. Bake at 350° until hot and bubbly. Unbaked casserole can be stored in refrigerator for up to 2 days. Serves 8.

*Cane River's Louisiana Living*

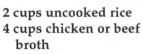
2 cups uncooked rice
4 cups chicken or beef
  broth
1 stick butter

$^{1}/_{2}$ cup chopped green onions
1 clove garlic, minced
1 pound mushrooms, sliced

Cook rice in broth. While rice is cooking, in a skillet sauté green onions and garlic until tender. Add mushrooms and continue to cook until mushrooms are tender. Add mushroom mixture to warm rice and mix well. Cover and let stand 10-15 minutes to let flavor develop before serving.

*Nun Better*

$^{1}/_{2}$ cup oil
$^{1}/_{2}$ cup flour
1 pound ground beef
1 pound ground pork
$^{1}/_{2}$ pound ground pork
  liver
1 bell pepper, chopped
3 onions, chopped

4 stalks celery, chopped
1$^{1}/_{2}$ cups water
Salt, black pepper, and cayenne
  pepper to taste
1 bunch green onion tops,
  chopped
$^{1}/_{2}$ cup minced parsley
3 cups cooked rice

Make a light brown roux with oil and flour. Sauté beef, pork, and liver in another pot until light brown; add bell pepper, onions, and celery, and continue cooking until onions are transparent. Add roux and water to meat mixture and simmer 30-45 minutes. Add salt, black pepper, cayenne pepper, green onion tops, and parsley, and mix well. When ready to serve, add cooked rice, and mix well. Yield: 6-8 servings.

*Cajun Cuisine*

 Konriko in New Iberia is America's oldest rice mill.

## Dirty Rice Dressing

1/2 pound chicken gizzards
1/2 pound chicken livers
1 tablespoon oil
1/2 pound ground pork
2 teaspoons cayenne pepper
2 teaspoons salt
1 1/2 teaspoons black pepper
1 teaspoon paprika
1 teaspoon dry mustard

2 medium onions, chopped
2 ribs celery, chopped
2 cloves garlic, minced
1 bell pepper, chopped
3 cups stock
1 1/2 cups uncooked rice
2 stalks green onions, chopped
2 sprigs parsley, chopped

Place gizzards and livers in 3 cups boiling water. Boil until tender (about 20 minutes). Remove and save water as stock. Separate and chop livers and gizzards.

Add one tablespoon of oil to skillet and brown ground pork and gizzards, about 6 minutes. Add seasonings, onions, celery, garlic, and bell pepper. Stir thoroughly. Add the stock, and simmer for 5 minutes. Add the rice, chicken livers, green onions, and parsley. Stir and simmer 5 minutes. Cover and reduce to lowest heat level. Cook until rice is fluffy (about 10 minutes).

*Roger's Cajun Cookbook*

## Jambalaya Casserole

1 pound pork sausage
1 large onion, chopped
1 bell pepper, chopped
1 (4-ounce) can mushrooms
1 pound ground beef
1 (14 1/2-ounce) can tomatoes
1 can tomato soup
1 (1-pound 15-ounce) can
  pork and beans

1 (15-ounce) can red beans
1 teaspoon salt
1 tablespoon Worcestershire sauce
Garlic powder
Black pepper to taste
Red pepper to taste
1 1/2 cups grated cheese

Brown sausage. Add onion, bell pepper, and mushrooms. Cook until onions are transparent. Add beef and cook until no pink shows. Add all other ingredients except cheese. Bake at 350° for one hour, uncovered. Add cheese and bake 15 more minutes.

*Cooking with Morehouse Parish Sheriff Ladies' Auxiliary*

## Quick and Delicious Jambalaya

1 pound ground beef,
  browned
1½ pounds peeled shrimp
1½ cups raw rice, washed
1 (10½-ounce) can cream
  of chicken soup

1 (10½-ounce) can onion
  soup
½ cup chopped bell pepper
1 stalk celery, chopped
Salt and pepper to taste
Tabasco sauce to taste

Mix all ingredients in a large bowl. Place mixture in a 2-quart casserole. Bake covered in a 350° oven for 1½ hours or until done. Serves 6.

*Cooking with Mr. "G" and Friends*

---

The sweet scent of magnolia blossoms fills the air at Houmas House Plantation and Gardens in Darrow. *Hush, Hush, Sweet Charlotte,* starring Bette Davis was filmed there. The drawing below is of its garconnierre (where the boys stayed when they came to visit).

---

## *Pork Chop Jambalaya*

*This is a very simple way to fix jambalaya.*

2 pounds pork chops
Salt and pepper
1/4 inch oil in bottom
   of pot
1 cup chopped onions
3/4 cup chopped bell pepper

1/4 cup chopped celery
1 cup water
4 cups cooked rice
1 1/2 cups chopped green
   onion tops

Brown pork chops that have been seasoned to taste. Remove chops from pot. Sauté onions, bell pepper, and celery in oil that chops were browned in. Remove all oil from the pot that you can and add a small amount of water to form a gravy. Put chops back into the pot. Cook on medium heat for about 20 minutes. Add cooked rice and onion tops and stir well. Cover and simmer for 10 minutes. Serves 4.

*Classic Cajun*

*Jambalaya has become the best known rice dish in America. The origin of this dish cannot be disputed. When the early Spanish settlers came to New Orleans in the early 1700s, they brought the recipe for their famous paella. Since the ingredientswere not to be found in South Louisiana, their recipe was quickly adapted to the products at hand. Oysters and crawfish replaced clams and mussels in the recipe. Andouille took the place of ham, and the new dish emerged from the paella pans of the Spanish. Since the main ingredient was rice, the dish was named "Jambon a la yaya." Yaya is the African word for rice. Today, the dish is made with many variations and with whatever is available. The most popular combination, however, is pork, chicken and andouille.*

1/4 cup shortening or bacon
   drippings
2 pounds cubed pork
1 pound sliced andouille
2 cups chopped onions
2 cups chopped celery
1 cup chopped bell pepper
1/4 cup diced garlic

7 cups beef or chicken stock
2 cups sliced mushrooms
1 cup sliced green onions
1/4 cup chopped parsley
Salt and cayenne pepper,
   to taste
Dash of hot sauce
4 cups long grain rice

In a 2-gallon Dutch oven, heat Crisco or bacon drippings over medium-high heat. Sauté cubed pork until dark brown on all sides and some pieces are sticking to bottom of pot, approximately 30 minutes. This is very important, as the brown color of jambalaya is derived from the color of the meat. Add andouille and stir-fry an additional 10-15 minutes. Tilt pot to one side and ladle out all oil, except for one large cooking spoon. Add onions, celery, bell pepper, and garlic. Continue cooking until all vegetables are well caramelized, however, be very careful, as vegetables will tend to scorch since the pot is so hot. Add beef stock, bring to a rolling boil and reduce heat to simmer. Cook all ingredients in stock approximately 15 minutes for flavors to develop. Add mushrooms, green onions, and parsley. Season to taste using salt, cayenne pepper, and hot sauce. I suggest that you slightly over-season since the rice tends to require a little extra seasoning. Add rice, reduce heat to very low, and allow to cook 30-45 minutes, stirring at 15 minutes intervals. Serves 6.

***The Evolution of Cajun & Creole Cuisine***

## J. C.'s Creole Jambalaya

*I know you'll enjoy this one!*

2 chicken bouillon cubes
1 cup hot water
1 cup chopped onion
1/4 cup chopped bell pepper
1/4 chopped celery
1 teaspoon chopped garlic
1/4 cup vegetable oil
1 cup chopped ham
1 1/4 cups short grain rice

1 pound chopped shrimp meat
1/3 cup tomatoes, peeled and
   chopped
1 teaspoon salt
1/4 teaspoon black pepper
1 teaspoon Tabasco sauce
1 tablespoon Tabasco jalapeño
   sauce
2 tablespoons chopped parsley

Dissolve bouillon cubes in hot water. Over medium fire sauté onion, bell pepper, celery, and garlic in oil until wilted. Add ham and rice and stir-fry for 5 minutes. Add shrimp, tomatoes, bouillon water, salt, black pepper, and Tabasco sauces and bring to a boil. Lower heat, cover and cook for 30 minutes. Stir in parsley. Serve hot. Serves 4-6 hungry hogs!

*The Hungry Hog*

## Shrimp-Chicken Jambalaya

2 medium onions, chopped
2 cloves garlic, minced
2 ribs celery, chopped
1 large green pepper,
   chopped
2/3 cup uncooked regular
   rice
2 cups chicken broth

8 ounces chicken breast,
   cooked and cubed
1 (16-ounce) can stewed
   tomatoes
8 ounces shrimp deveined
   and rinsed
1/2 teaspoon hot sauce
1/4 teaspoon pepper

Coat a large skillet with cooking spray; place over medium heat until hot. Add onions, garlic, celery, and green pepper; sauté until tender. Add remaining ingredients. Bring to a boil, cover, reduce heat, and simmer 25 minutes or until rice is done, stirring occasionally. Yields 4 servings.

Cal 311; Chol 129mg; Sat Fat 1gm; Fat 3gm; Sod 650mg; Pro 36gm; Cho 35gm; Exchanges 4 meat, 1 bread, 3 vegetable.

*Southern But Lite*

# Louisiana Chicken Jambalaya

2 cups white onions,
  chopped
1 cup chopped celery
3 cloves garlic
1 tablespoon tomato paste
1 pound skinned chicken
  breast, cut in
  bite-size pieces
1 pound Healthy Choice
  ground beef

$1/2$ teaspoon salt
$1/2$ teaspoon pepper
Dash of red pepper
1 cup cold water
5 green onion tops,
  chopped
$1/2$ teaspoon parsley, chopped
3 cups cooked rice

Heat large Dutch oven that has been sprayed with vegetable cooking spray. Add onions, celery, garlic, and tomato paste. Cook over medium heat uncovered until white onions are wilted. Add meats, salt, pepper, and red pepper. Stir well until the meat starts to brown. Add one cup of cold water and continue to cook an additional 40 minutes on low heat. Stir occasionally. Add green onion tops and parsley. Simmer over low heat uncovered for an additional 15 minutes. Remove from heat. Add cooked rice and mix thoroughly. Serve with French bread and salad. Yield: 8 servings.

Cal 248; Chol 72mg; Sat Fat 1gm; Fat 4gm; Sod 332mg; Dietary Fiber 1gm;
Exchanges: 3 meat, 1 bread, 1 vegetable.

*Gone with the Fat*

## Black-Eyed Pea Jambalaya

1 pound ground beef
1 tablespoon vegetable oil
1/2 pound cubed ham
1 cup chopped onion
1/2 cup chopped bell pepper
1 (15 1/2-ounce) can black-
  eyed peas
1 (15 1/2-ounce) can black-
  peas with jalapeños

1/2 tablespoon Worcestershire
  sauce
1/4 teaspoon salt
1/8 teaspoon black pepper
4 cups cooked rice
2 tablespoons chopped green
  onion
2 tablespoons chopped parsley

In a large Dutch oven, brown the beef in the vegetable oil over medium heat, cooking for about 10 minutes, stirring often. Add the ham and cook for 3 minutes. Add the onion and bell pepper and cook for 6-8 minutes, stirring often, until vegetables are soft. Add the black-eyed peas, Worcestershire sauce, salt, pepper and rice and reduce heat to medium-low. Cook for 5 minutes, or until rice is warmed through. Add the green onion and parsley and serve immediately. Makes 8 servings.

*Cajun Cooking for Beginners*

# Seafood

Shrimp boats line the banks of a South Louisiana bayou.

1/2 cup crabmeat
1/4 cup Italian bread crumbs
1 ripe tomato, chopped
1 tablespoon whipping cream
Salt, red and black pepper
  to taste
1 tablespoon teriyaki sauce

1 tablespoon chopped green
  onions
1/2 tablespoon chopped parsley
1/2 teaspoon grated lime zest
1 (2-pound) red snapper,
  cleaned, head and tail on

**SEASON MIX:**
1/4 teaspoon salt
1/8 teaspoon white pepper

1/4 teaspoon garlic powder

Combine first 9 ingredients and set aside. Pour teriyaki saue over cleaned fish (outside and inside cavity). Season with Season Mix. Open cavity; add crab mixture. Make 2 vertical 1/4-inch slits on top and bottom of fish.

Place fish on grill. Add wet hickory chips to coals. Grill 25-30 minutes, until fish is flaky. Top with 2 lime slices and serve with salad.

*Roger's Lite Cajun Cookbook*

1 pound catfish fillets
1/4 cup skim milk
1/2 cup fine dry bread crumbs
1/4 cup yellow corn meal
1 tablespoon toasted sesame
  seed

1 tablespoon Mrs. Dash
1/4 teaspoon dry mustard
1/8 teaspoon garlic powder
Dash pepper
Parsley

Thaw fish if frozen. Measure thickness of fish. Pour milk into a shallow dish. Combine crumbs, corn meal, sesame seed, Mrs. Dash, mustard, garlic powder, and pepper. Dip fish into milk; coat with crumb mixture. Spray a 13 x 9 x 2-inch baking pan with nonstick coating. Place fish in pan. Sprinkle with parsley. Bake in 450° oven until golden and fish flakes easily. Allow 4-6 minutes per 2-inch thickness. Yield: 4 servings.

Cal 216; Chol 4mg; Sat Fat 1gm; Fat 4gm; Sod 114mg; Pro 22gm; Cho 23gm; Exchanges 4 meat, 1 bread.

*Southern But Lite*

# Blackened Red Fish

*When done right, this is a delicacy. This procedure is rather simple to do, but should be done outdoors and not inside because of the smoke it generates. You will need a good consistent burner and a large frypan— preferably a cast iron black skillet of at least 12 inches or more in size. In preparing the pan for blackening, the pan is pre-heated with nothing in it for 10 minutes or more until it is very very hot. Just any pan will not do very well. You will also need a baking dish or container to hold seasoned fillets; a dish containing melted butter (no salt, or light salt); and, a dish or container to place blackened fillets when done.*

### Red fish fillets

The fillets are seasoned with a good blackened fish seasoning. I prefer K. Pauls. There are several others. Red fish fillets can be seasoned ahead of time and kept refrigerated until ready to cook. After pan is very hot, dip seasoned fillets one at a time in the melted butter and coat both sides and then place in the frying pan. A 12- or 13-inch pan will hold 2 or 3 fillets at one time. Be sure to turn the fillets quickly to avoid over burning or blackening on the first side. Be attentive and turn as needed. About 2 minutes per side does the job, and the fish will begin to flake when probed with a fork. Place the blackened fillets in a dish and put in a 200° oven until all fillets are ready to be served.

*Cajun Cooking: A Labor of Love*

# Basin Fish Fry Á La Skerrett

2 teaspoons salt
1 teaspoon lemon pepper
1/2 teaspoon cayenne pepper
10 bass fillets

2 cups cracker meal
Vegetable oil for frying
1 large onion, diced
   for frying

Mix seasonings together in a small bowl; be sure fillets are moist but not wet; season both sides of the fillet, rubbing into the meat gently. Put cracker meal into a brown paper bag along with fillets. Shake to coat fillets with meal. Put enough oil in a cast iron frying pan to depth approximately half the average thickness of the fillets. Heat oil until 360° or until a fleshy onion piece will curl up as it floats on the surface of the oil. Add fillets and fry on one side until golden brown. When fillets are turned over to fry the other side, add the onions over the fish. When fish is done, remove with onions and place on a platter covered with brown paper bag. Adjust seasoning, if needed, and serve immediately. Makes 4 servings.

*Cajun Men Cook*

## Tartar Sauce

1 cup mayonnaise
2 tablespoons dill pickle
  relish
1 small onion, grated

1 tablespoon horseradish
Salt and hot pepper sauce,
  to taste

Combine all ingredients; let stand at least 30 minutes before serving. Serve with fried seafood.

*Cajun Cuisine*

# Onion Baked Catfish

6 catfish fillets, each
  about 6 ounces
1/2 teaspoon Creole seasoning
1 cup (8-ounces) sour
  cream

1 cup mayonnaise
1 (1-ounce) package ranch-style
  dry salad dressing mix
1 (2.8-ounce) can French fried
  onion rings

Preheat the oven to 350°. Put the fillets in a shallow bowl and sprinkle them evenly with the Creole seasoning. Set aside. In a small bowl, combine the sour cream, mayonnaise, and salad dressing mix. Blend well. Pour the mixture into a shallow bowl. Process the onion rings in a blender or food processor until finely crushed. Put these in another shallow bowl. Dip the fillets first in the sour cream mixture, then in the crushed onion rings and coat evenly. Put the fish in an ungreased shallow baking pan. Bake uncovered until fish flakes easily when tested with a fork, about 20 minutes. Makes 6 servings.

*Cajun Cooking for Beginners*

# Tommy's Terrific Trout

*This is one terrific recipe! The fillets are cooked in a garlic-butter Worcestershire mixture. Do not overcook the fillets. If your fillets are thin, adjust cooking time. The fish, a crisp green salad and hot French bread are all you need for a perfect meal.*

6 trout fillets
6 tablespoons butter or
  margarine
2 cloves garlic, minced
1 1/2 tablespoons Worcestershire

Salt, black pepper and
  cayenne pepper to taste
1/2 cup Italian bread crumbs
1 lemon, sliced for garnish
1/3 cup white wine

Season fish with salt and pepper. Melt butter in (9 x 13-inch) baking dish. Add garlic and Worcestershire sauce to butter. Coat both sides of fish with the butter mixture and place fillets in dish. Bake in 400° oven for 20 minutes, depending on size of your fillets. Pull out oven rack and sprinkle crumbs over fish. Garnish with lemon slices. Add wine to pan juices. Turn oven to broiler heat. Return fish to oven. Broil until surface is brown and crispy. Serve piping hot. Serves 3-6, depending on size of fillets.

*Extra! Extra! Read All About It!*

8-12 trout fillets (allow
   1/3 pound per person)
Milk to cover (flavored
   with 1 teaspoon salt
   and 6 drops Tabasco)
3/4 cup flour
2 sticks butter

1/2 teaspoon Tabasco
1/2 cup finely chopped
   green onions
1/2 cup finely chopped
   green pepper
2/3 cup dry white wine

Soak fillets one hour in flavored milk to cover. Dry fish well and salt generously on both sides. Dredge in flour and shake off excess. Put one stick of butter and Tabasco in baking dish (not aluminum) large enough to hold fillets without crowding. Place pan on middle shelf in broiler and let butter start to bubble. Remove from oven and sprinkle green onions and green pepper in bottom of pan, laying fillets on top. Use remaining butter to dot tops, and return to broiler. Cook 15-20 minutes (depending on size of fillets), basting twice. When fish are done and browned on top, remove them with a spatula to a heated serving platter, and keep warm. Add wine to pan juices and place pan over a medium flame on top of range. Allow sauce to bubble rapidly, stirring constantly for 3-4 minutes. Spoon some sauce over trout and serve the rest in a heated sauceboat.

*The Plantation Cookbook*

## Broiled Stuffed Flounder

1 medium onion, minced
8 tablespoons butter, divided
2 stalks celery, chopped fine
1 cup shrimp, cleaned and
  peeled
1 small can mushrooms
1/2 pound crab meat
1 small bay leaf
1 tablespoon Worcestershire

1/2 cup cream
Bread crumbs
Salt and pepper
3 ounces white wine plus
  1/2 ounce for basting
2 (2 - 2 1/2-pound) flounders
2 tablespoons oil
Juice of 1/2 lemon

Sauté the finely chopped onion in 6 tablespoons butter until soft; add celery and sauté 2 or 3 minutes longer. Add shrimp and mushrooms (with their liquid) and sauté until the shrimp are pink; then add crab meat, bay leaf, Worcestershire, cream, and enough bread crumbs to hold the dressing together. Season to taste. Add the wine and stuff the fish. Close the slits with the aid of small skewers and lace up.

Heat 2 tablespoons oil along with 2 tablespoons butter in broiler pan and place the fish in the pan. Broil the fish slowly under a low flame, basting with the butter/oil mixture as the fish begins to brown. Add a little more wine to the broiler pan to increase basting liquid and keep the fish moist. It is not necessary to turn the fish. Keep the flame low and when the top of the fish is golden brown or slightly darker, the fish will be cooked through. Spoon the remaining sauce from the pan over the fish. Sprinkle with lemon juice. Serves 4.

*St. Philomena School 125th Anniversary*

Louisiana is a fisherman's paradise. Lakes, rivers, streams, bayous, and the Gulf of Mexico are all abounding with fish that seem anxious to jump onto your hook! The Atchafalaya Basin is a magnificent 800,000-plus-acre natural swampland, and Toledo Bend Reservoir is a 186,000-acre bass fishing paradise. One cannot go very far in Louisiana without coming upon a great place to fish.

## Trout Meuniére

*Many recipes call for clarified butter, as does this one. To clarify butter, melt it over low heat. Do not brown. Strain melted butter through very fine cheesecloth.*

| | |
|---|---|
| **4 trout fillets** | **Capers** |
| **1/2 cup milk** | **Worcestershire sauce** |
| **Salt and pepper** | **Lemon slices** |
| **Flour to coat** | **Parsley, minced** |
| **1 1/2 sticks clarified butter, divided** | |

Soak fish in milk. Drain and pat dry. Season with salt and pepper. Coat with flour. Melt 1/4 cup butter in a heavy skillet. When hot, brown fillets on both sides. Remove to warm platter. Pour butter out of skillet. Place remaining butter in skillet. When hot, add capers and Worcestershire sauce. Brown. Pour mixture over fish fillets. Garnish with lemon slices and parsley. Serves 4. *Created by Lee Barnes.*

**The Cookin' Cajun Cooking School Cookbook**

## Baked Trout with Lemon Sauce

| | |
|---|---|
| **2 pounds trout fillets** | **1 tablespoon chopped parsley** |
| **Salt and pepper, to taste** | **Paprika** |
| **4 green onions, chopped** | |

Place fillets on baking sheet lined with foil. Sprinkle with salt and pepper, green onions, and parsley. Then sprinkle with paprika. Cover with Lemon Sauce. Bake at 375° for 20-25 minutes. Baste with Lemon Sauce during cooking. Serves 6.

**LEMON SAUCE:**

| | |
|---|---|
| **1/4 cup light margarine, melted** | **2 tablespoons lemon juice** |
| | **2 cloves garlic, minced** |

Combine all ingredients and pour over prepared fish.

**L' Heritage du Bayou Lafourche**

## *Shrimp and Catfish Fricassee*

*A fricassee or stew is usually a mixture of whatever is at hand. I've discovered many combinations in Louisiana fricassees from seafoods and meats to vegetables and game. In the city of Chalmette, below New Orleans, the hunters and trappers combine blue channel catfish with river shrimp to create an incomparable fricassee.*

| | |
|---|---|
| 1 pound peeled river or gulf shrimp | 4 bay leaves |
| 3 pounds cubed catfish | Pinch of thyme |
| 1 cup oil | Pinch of basil |
| 1 cup flour | 3 quarts fish stock |
| 1 cup chopped onions | 1 cup chopped parsley |
| 1 cup chopped celery | 1 cup sliced green onions |
| 1 cup chopped bell pepper | 6 eggs |
| 2 tablespoons diced garlic | Salt and cracked pepper to taste |
| 1 tablespoon diced cayenne peppers | Hot sauce, to taste |

In a 2-gallon heavy bottom stock pot, heat oil over medium-high heat. Sprinkle in flour and using a wire whisk, stir constantly until dark brown roux is achieved. Should black specks appear, discard and begin again. Add onions, celery, bell pepper, and garlic. Sauté 3-5 minutes or until vegetables are wilted. Add cayenne peppers, bay leaves, thyme, and basil, blending well into roux mixture. Add approximately 2 cups of the cubed fish and stir into roux. Slowly add fish stock, one ladle at a time, until a rich stew consistency is achieved. Remember, the remaining fish are 90% water and will thin the stew considerably when added. You may wish to keep the stew just a little thicker until the remaining fish are incorporated. Reserve the remaining stock for later use. Bring to a rolling boil, reduce to simmer and cook approximately 30 minutes. Add the remaining fish, shrimp, green onions, and parsley. Stir into the stew mixture and continue to cook until fish is tender, approximately 10-15 minutes. Crack the eggs into the simmering stew and allow to poach for 10 minutes. Season to taste using salt, pepper, and hot sauce. Serve over steamed rice or pasta. Serves 6-8.

*Plantation Celebrations*

## Creole Catfish

1 stick butter
3 tablespoons flour
1 can tomato sauce
1 can tomatoes
1 can Ro-Tel tomatoes
1 tablespoon Worcestershire
1 clove garlic, minced
1 large onion, chopped
1 small bell pepper, chopped
3 stalks celery, chopped
1/2 pound mushrooms, sliced
2-3 pounds catfish filets or
   5-6 pounds whole catfish
1/4 cup chopped parsley
1/4 cup green onions
Salt and pepper to taste

Make sauce combining all ingredients except fish, green onions and parsley; let cook for about one hour. Add fish and cook for 15-25 minutes. Add parsley and green onions. Mix well. Season to taste. Serve over rice.

*From Mama To Me*

## Grilled Shrimp with Pineapple Rice

12 large shrimp, peeled
   and deveined)
1/2 bell pepper, cut in
   1-inch squares
1 onion, sliced
2 tablespoons teriyaki sauce
2/3 cup cooked rice
2 tablespoons crushed pineapple,
   drained
1 tablespoon chopped parsley
Basting Sauce

Combine shrimp, green pepper, onion, and teriyaki sauce in bowl. Cover and marinate one hour in refrigerator.

BASTING SAUCE:
1/4 stick margarine
4 dashes Worcestershire sauce
1 tablespoon honey
1 teaspoon lemon juice
1/2 teaspoon garlic powder

In saucepan melt margarine, add Worcestershire sauce, honey, lemon juice, and garlic powder. Simmer one minute. Alternate shrimp, bell pepper, and onion slices on 2 skewers. Place on grill and charbroil till shrimp are done, about 8-10 minutes. Wet mesquite chips can be added to coals to give a nice smoked flavor.

Combine rice, pineapple and parsley. Place one skewer on each side of rice mixture.

*Roger's Cajun Cookbook*

## *Fried Shrimp*

1 cup all-purpose flour
1/2 teaspoon sugar
1/2 teaspoon salt
1 cup ice water (leave 1 or 2
  cubes in)

1 slightly beaten egg
2 tablespoons oil
2 pounds fresh, frozen shrimp,
  unpeeled

Combine ingredients, except shrimp; stir until smooth, then set in refrigerator or freezer to chill. Peel shells from shrimp, leaving tail intact; "butterfly" shrimp by cutting lengthwise to tail. Dry shrimp, dip into batter, fry in deep hot fat (350° - 400°) till floating and golden brown, 3-5 minutes. Serve immediately.

**Note:** Also good for frying soft- and hard-shelled crabs, eggplants, onions, etc.

*Cajun Cooking*

## *Seafood Cocktail Sauce*

2/3 cup catsup
3 tablespoons chili sauce
2 tablespoons horseradish

3 tablespoons fresh lemon
  juice
Hot pepper sauce, to taste

Mix all ingredients well; refrigerate until ready to serve. This is served with any fried or boiled seafood.

**Note:** Minced onion may be added.

*Cajun Cuisine*

## Stuffed Shrimp

1 cup oil
1 cup chopped onion
1 cup chopped bell pepper
1 cup chopped celery
1 pound crab meat
Salt and pepper, to taste
Bread crumbs

1 pound large shrimp, peeled
  (leave on tips of tails
  and last segment of shell)
2 eggs
1 cup evaporated milk
Corn flour
Oil for frying

Sauté in oil the onion, bell pepper, and celery until tender. Add crab meat, seasonings, a small amount of water and bread crumbs to make a stiff dressing.

"Butterfly" shrimp by making a vertical cut in the back; stuff center with mixture, squeezing shrimp in hand to form a croquette. Freeze shrimp.

Mix eggs and evaporated milk; dip frozen shrimp into egg/milk mixture, then into corn flour. Fry while frozen in deep oil until brown.

**Note:** Crabs and flounder can be stuffed with same dressing.

*The Top 100 Cajun Recipes*

## Shrimp and Artichoke Casserole

1 (14-ounce) can artichoke
  hearts (drained)
1$^1$/$_2$ pounds shrimp, boiled
1 clove garlic, chopped
1 small onion, chopped
$^1$/$_4$ pound mushrooms, sliced
3 tablespoons butter or
  margarine
1 can cream of mushroom
  soup

$^1$/$_2$ cup mayonnaise
1 tablespoon Worcestershire
  sauce
2 tablespoons sherry (optional)
$^1$/$_2$ cup grated Parmesan
  cheese
Salt, pepper and paprika,
  to taste
1 (10-ounce) package frozen
  chopped spinach

Place artichokes in buttered 2-quart casserole. Add shrimp. Sauté garlic, onion, and mushrooms in butter. Add undiluted soup, mayonnaise, Worcestershire sauce, sherry, cheese, salt and pepper. Add spinach which has been thawed and well drained. Pour mixture over shrimp. Sprinkle with cheese and paprika. Bake 20 minutes at 375° or until bubbly.

*L' Heritage Du Bayou Lafouche*

## Shrimp with Eggplant Casserole

1 large eggplant
16 ounces raw shrimp
1 cup chopped onion
1 cup chopped bell pepper
1 cup chopped celery
1 clove garlic, minced

10 ounces Campbell's Healthy Request cream of mushroom soup
1/2 teaspoon black pepper
4 ounces light Cheddar cheese
1/2 cup dry seasoned bread crumbs

Puncture eggplant several times and cook on HIGH in microwave for 3 minutes. Set aside to cool. When cool, pull skin off and chop. Sauté shrimp, onion, bell pepper, celery, and garlic in cooking spray until the shrimp turn pink. Add soup, pepper, and cheese; heat and set aside. Mix with 1/4 cup seasoned bread crumbs and chopped eggplant. Top with remaining bread crumbs and spray with cooking spray. Bake at 350° for 25 minutes. Yield: 8 servings.

Cal 162; Chol 94mg; Sat Fat 1gm; Fat 4gm; Sod 562mg; Dietary Fiber 1gm; Exchanges: 2 meat, ½ bread, 1 vegetable, ½ fat.

*Gone with the Fat*

## Baked Shrimp, New Orleans Style

2 pounds large shrimp, unpeeled and with heads on
1/2 pound (2 sticks) margarine, melted
4 cloves garlic, chopped
1/2 teaspoon Italian seasoning

2 tablespoons paprika
2 teaspoons coarse ground black pepper
1/8 teaspoon cayenne pepper
1/2 teaspoon salt
2 tablespoons fresh lemon juice

Preheat oven to 450°. Put the shrimp in a large baking pan and spread evenly. Combine the remaining ingredients in a small saucepan and mix well. Pour mixture over the shrimp and bake for about 10-12 minutes, stirring a few times during the cooking time. (Shrimp is done when the shell separates from the shrimp at the tail section.) Serve with lots of hot French bread to "sop up" the butter and juices. Makes 4-6 servings.

*Cajun Cooking for Beginners*

# *Barbecue Shrimp*

*Serve Barbecue Shrimp with French bread to dip in the sauce. This wonderful shrimp dish is worth messing up your hands to eat. I also like to serve Barbecue Shrimp with pasta. I made this dish on the NBC Weekend Today Show and received 3,000 letters in the mail requesting the recipe. I guess Barbecue Shrimp is everyone's favorite!*

| | |
|---|---|
| 4 tablespoons olive oil | 1 teaspoon dried oregano |
| 1/2 cup fat-free Italian dressing | 1 tablespoon dried rosemary |
| 1 tablespoon minced garlic | 1 teaspoon dried thyme |
| 1 teaspoon hot pepper sauce | 1 lemon |
| 1/3 cup Worcestershire sauce | 2 pounds headless large shrimp, unpeeled |
| 4 bay leaves | 1/3 cup white wine (optional) |
| 1 tablespoon paprika | |

In a large, heavy skillet, place the olive oil, Italian dressing, garlic, hot sauce, Worcestershire sauce, bay leaves, paprika, oregano, rosemary, and thyme and cook over medium heat until the sauce begins to boil. Squeeze the lemon into the sauce and then place both halves in the sauce. Add the shrimp and cook approximately 10-15 minutes. Add the wine, if using, and cook another 10 minutes, or until the shrimp are done. Serve the shrimp with the sauce, from which the bay leaves have been removed and discarded. Makes 4-6 servings.

Cal 160; Fat 5.2g; Cal from Fat 29.3%; Sat Fat 1g; Sod 510mg; Chol 168mg.

*Trim & Terrific American Favorites*

## Cajun Peppered Shrimp & Grits

*A delightful combination of flavors straight from the South! Try serving this impressive dish for brunch.*

**GRITS:**

6 cups water
2 teaspoons salt
1½ cups Quick grits
2 tablespoons butter

1 roll garlic cheese
1 cup grated Cheddar cheese
1 teaspoon Worcestershire

Preheat oven to 350°. Grease a large saucepan with cooking spray, add water and bring to a boil over high heat. Stir in salt and grits. Lower heat and cook, stirring occasionally, until water is absorbed and grits thicken. Add butter, cheeses, and Worcestershire. Cook until cheese melts. Pour in a greased casserole dish and bake for about 20 minutes to set.

**SHRIMP:**

½ cup butter or margarine
¼ cup olive oil
3 pounds medium shrimp, peeled
1 clove garlic, minced
1 cup chopped green onion
1 cup sliced mushrooms
½ cup chopped parsley

½ teaspoon salt
1 teaspoon pepper
¼ teaspoon cayenne pepper
½ teaspoon paprika
¼ teaspoon basil, thyme and oregano
1 tablespoon lemon juice

In a large saucepan, melt butter and oil over medium heat. Add shrimp and sauté just until pink. Stir in all other ingredients and seasonings. Simmer about 10 minutes. Mixture will be very saucy.

Serve a scoop of grits surrounded with shrimp and sauce. Serve with hot French bread for dipping. Serves 8.

*Kay Ewing's Cooking School Cookbook*

---

Bayou Lafourche is know locally as the Longest "Street" in the World. It connects communities that developed along its shores: Thibodaux, Raceland, Lockport, Larose, Cut Off, Galliano, Golden Meadow, Leeville, and Port Fourchon. It ends at Grand Isle, the only inhabited barrier island in Louisiana.

## *Shrimp Janus*

| | |
|---|---|
| 1 medium onion | 1 teaspoon dried parsley flakes |
| 1 small bell pepper | 2 teaspoons lemon pepper |
| 1 small red bell pepper | 1 teaspoon Tony Chachere's |
| 4 stalks celery | seasoning |
| 1/2 cup white wine | 1 cup water |
| 1 package Knorr white | 1 pound medium peeled |
| sauce mix | shrimp |
| 2 cups milk | 1/4 cup chili sauce |
| 1/2 cup half-and-half | Angel hair pasta |

Chop onion, bell peppers, and celery. Sauté in 1/2 cup white wine. Mix white sauce following package directions, except that you use only 2 cups of milk and 1/2 cup half-and-half. Combine vegetable mixture with sauce, adding parsley flakes, lemon pepper, Tony Chachere's seasoning, and 1 cup of water. Simmer on medium heat for 20-30 minutes, stirring constantly with wire whisk. Add shrimp and chili sauce. Cook on low heat for 20 minutes. Cook pasta per directions. Serve shrimp sauce over pasta.

**Note:** Sauce may be frozen or prepared ahead of time.

*Kooking with the Krewe*

# Shrimp and Gravy

| | |
|---|---|
| 1 pound shrimp | 4 tablespoons green onions, |
| 1/2 onion, chopped | chopped |
| 3 cloves garlic, minced | Salt and pepper to taste |
| 1 cup bread crumbs | 3 tablespoons flour |
| 2 tablespoons Worcestershire | 2 eggs |

Grind shrimp, onion, and garlic. Add remaining ingredients and mix thoroughly. Shape into small balls and roll in flour.

**GRAVY:**

| | |
|---|---|
| 3 tablespoons flour | 3 cups water |
| 4 tablespoons oil | 1 cup tomato sauce |
| 1/2 onion, chopped | 1/2 teaspoon sugar |
| 1 green pepper, chopped | Salt and pepper |

Make a roux with flour and oil. Sauté onion and green pepper in roux. Add water and stir until mixture is smooth. Combine remaining ingredients and stir until well blended. Add shrimp balls and simmer 2 hours. Makes 12-15 balls.

**Note:** Additional water may be added, if needed.

*Big Mama's Old Black Pot*

# Shrimp Fried Rice

| | |
|---|---|
| 2 cups chopped cooked shrimp | 1 teaspoon salt |
| 1/4 cup oil | Black pepper |
| 2 eggs, lightly beaten | 4 cups boiled rice |
| 1 (4-ounce) can mushrooms, | 2 tablespoons soy sauce |
| drained | 1/2 cup scallions, chopped |

Fry shrimp in oil in deep frying pan for one minute, stirring constantly. Add eggs, mushrooms, salt and pepper and fry over medium heat for 5 minutes, stirring constantly. Add rice and soy sauce and fry for 5 minutes, stirring frequently. Mix with chopped scallions.

*Pigging Out with the Cotton Patch Cooks*

# Cheesy Shrimp-Rice Casserole

*Prepare this incredibly quick shrimp and rice dish with the hint of cheese and salsa once and your family will request it again and again.*

1 onion, chopped
1 teaspoon minced garlic
1/2 cup chopped red or green
  bell pepper
1 1/2 pounds medium shrimp,
  peeled
1 (8-ounce) can mushroom
  stems and pieces
1 1/2 cups shredded reduced-
  fat Cheddar cheese

1/3 cup salsa
1 tablespoon Worcestershire
  sauce
1/2 cup evaporated skimmed
  milk
1 bunch green onions
  (scallions), sliced
2 tablespoons canned diced
  green chilies, drained
3 cups cooked rice

In a large skillet coated with nonstick cooking spray, sauté the onion, garlic, pepper, shrimp, and mushrooms over medium-high heat for about 5-7 minutes. Add the Cheddar, salsa, Worcestershire sauce, evaporated milk, green onions, and green chilies. Stir in the rice and cook until the cheese is melted and well combined, about 10 minutes. Makes 6 servings.

Cal 323; Fat 7.4g; Cal from Fat 20.6%; Sat Fat 4.4g; Prot 29.4g; Carbo 32.4g; Sod 674g; Chol 182mg.

*Trim & Terrific One-Dish Favorites*

# Shrimp Creole

1/4 cup flour
1/4 cup oil
1 cup chopped onions
1/4 cup chopped celery
1 (8-ounce) can tomato
  sauce
2 teaspoons salt

1/2 teaspoon black pepper
1/4 teaspoon red pepper
2 pounds shrimp
3 tablespoons green onions,
  chopped
1/4 - 1/2 cup sherry wine
3 tablespoons parsley

Make a golden roux with flour and oil. Add onions and celery; cook until clear, about 10 minutes. Add tomato sauce and seasonings; cook 10 minutes more. Add raw shrimp and green onions. Cook 10 minutes, then add sherry wine and parsley; cook 10 minutes more. If too thick, add 1 tomato sauce can of water after adding sherry and consistency is checked. Serve over rice.

*From Mama To Me*

# *Shrimp Creole*

1/4 cup flour
1/4 cup bacon grease
2 cups chopped onions
1/2 cup chopped green onions
2 cloves garlic, minced
1 cup chopped green pepper
1 cup chopped celery, with
  leaves
1 teaspoon thyme
2 bay leaves
3 teaspoons salt
1/2 teaspoon pepper
6 ounces tomato paste

1 (16-ounce) can tomatoes,
  coarsely chopped, and liquid
8 ounces tomato sauce
1 cup stock (made from boiling
  shrimp heads and shells),
  or 1 cup water
4 pounds peeled, deveined,
  raw shrimp
1 teaspoon Tabasco
1/2 cup chopped parsley
1 tablespoon lemon juice
2 cups cooked rice

In a 4-quart Dutch oven, make a dark brown roux of flour and bacon grease. Add onions, green onions, garlic, green pepper, celery, thyme, bay leaves, salt, and pepper, and sauté, uncovered, over medium fire until onions are transparent and soft, about 30 minutes. Add tomato paste, and sauté 3 minutes. Add tomatoes, tomato sauce, stock (or water). Simmer very slowly, partially covered, for one hour, stirring occasionally. Add shrimp and cook until shrimp are just done, about 5 minutes. Add Tabasco, parsley, and lemon juice. Stir, cover, and remove from heat. Serve over rice.

This dish is best when allowed to stand several hours or overnight. Let cool and refrigerate. It also freezes well. Remove from refrigerator one hour before serving. Heat quickly, without boiling, and serve immediately.

*The Plantation Cookbook*

## Creole Crawfish Casserole

2 large onions, chopped
3 stalks celery, chopped
1 green bell pepper, chopped
1/2 cup margarine
1 pound cooked crawfish tails, peeled
1 egg
1 tablespoon minced parsley
3 cups cooked rice

1 (10³/4-ounce) can cream of mushroom soup, undiluted
1½ cups (6 ounces) grated mozzarella cheese, Cheddar cheese, or pasteurized process cheese spread
Cajun seasoning salt or salt and black pepper to taste
Bread crumbs

Sauté onions, celery, and bell pepper in margarine in large saucepan until vegetables are softened. Add crawfish and cook for several minutes. Stir in egg, parsley, and rice, mixing well. Add soup and cheese. Season with seasoning salt or salt and black pepper. Spread crawfish mixture in 2-quart casserole and sprinkle with breadcrumbs. Bake at 375° for 25 minutes. Serves 6.

*Cane River's Louisiana Living*

## Crawfish Étouffée

1/4 pound butter
1 cup onion, chopped
1/2 cup bell pepper, chopped
1/4 cup celery, finely chopped
2 tablespoons garlic, minced
2 tablespoons parsley flakes, dried

1 teaspoon salt
1 teaspoon Cajun seasoning
1 tablespoon all-purpose flour
1 cup crawfish, chicken stock or water
1 pound peeled crawfish tails

In a large skillet, melt butter on high heat. As soon as butter is almost melted, add onion, bell pepper, celery, garlic, parsley, salt, and Cajun seasoning. Stir well and simmer, lowering the heat slightly, until onions begin to wilt. Add flour and stir in well. Continue to stir until flour begins to stick to the bottom of the skillet. Slowly add stock a little at a time and stir until all is added and blended. Simmer for 2 minutes or until a bubble is reached. Add crawfish tails and stir well. Bring back to a bubble, reduce heat to low, and simmer, covered, for 10-15 minutes. Serve over rice.

*'Dat Little Louisiana Plantation Cookbook*

# Crawfish Étouffée

| | |
|---|---|
| 1 bunch green onions, chopped | 1 can Ro-Tel tomatoes |
| 1 bell pepper, chopped | 1 can tomato sauce |
| 4 tablespoons butter | 1 can cream of mushroom soup |
| | 1 pound crawfish tails |

Sauté green onions and bell pepper in butter until wilted. Add Ro-Tel tomatoes, tomato sauce, and mushroom soup. Over low heat, bring to a boil; add crawfish and let cook until thick. Serve over rice.

*In The Pink*

# Crawfish Fettuccine

*A delicious first course.*

| | |
|---|---|
| 3 sticks butter | 1 tablespoon chopped parsley |
| 3 onions, chopped | 1/2 cup flour |
| 2 green bell peppers, chopped | 1 pint half-and-half |
| 3 stalks celery, chopped | 1 pound Kraft Jalapeño Cheese, |
| 3 pounds crawfish tails | cubed |
| 3 cloves garlic, minced | 12 ounces fettuccine |

In a saucepan, melt butter and sauté onions, bell peppers, and celery until tender. Add crawfish and simmer 10 minutes, stirring occasionally. Add garlic, parsley, flour, and half-and-half and mix well. Simmer on low heat for 30 minutes, stirring occasionally. Add cheese and stir until melted. Meanwhile, cook noodles, drain, and cool. Combine noodles and sauce. Pour into a greased 6-quart casserole or 2 greased 3-quart casseroles. Bake uncovered in a 300° oven for 20 minutes or until heated thoroughly. Freezes well. Makes 12 servings.

*Celebrations on the Bayou*

# *Crawfish Pie*

²/₃ cup defatted chicken broth, less salt, divided
3 tablespoons diet margarine
1 large onion, chopped
¹/₂ green pepper, chopped
¹/₂ cup sliced celery
2 tablespoons all-purpose flour
1 pound crawfish tails, lightly rinsed and drained

6 ounces shredded low-fat mozzarella cheese (1¹/₂ cups)
¹/₂ cup plain bread crumbs
¹/₃ cup sliced green onions
¹/₄ teaspoon salt
Pepper to taste
1 egg white
2 light pie crusts

In large skillet, heat ¹/₃ cup of broth and margarine. Sauté onion, bell pepper, and celery. Add flour; mix well. Add remaining ¹/₃ cup broth and stir until well blended (this is a very thick mixture). Add crawfish tails and stir over medium heat about 5 minutes. Add cheese, bread crumbs, green onions, and salt and pepper. Mix well and remove from heat. Prepare pie crust. Place ¹/₂ crust mixture into a deep 9-inch pie plate. Place the remaining crust drapped in plastic in the refrigerator. Pour the crawfish mixture into the unbaked prepared pie shell. Roll out the remaining crust between wax paper. Peel off one sheet of wax paper, place shell over pie and remove the wax paper. Pinch edges together, trimming pie shell as needed. Cut several slits in pie shell and brush with beaten egg white. Bake at 350° for 35 minutes. Yield: 6 servings.

Per Serving: Cal 338; Fat 15.4g; %Fat Cal 41; Sat Fat 3.8g; Chol 90mg; Sod 353mg.

*River Road Recipes III*

## Crawfish Remoulade

2 teaspoons horseradish
  mustard
1/2 cup tarragon vinegar
2 tablespoons catsup
1/2 teaspoon paprika
1 clove garlic, minced
1 teaspoon cayenne pepper

1 cup salad oil
1/2 cup chopped green onions
1/2 cup chopped celery
2 teaspoons mustard
1/2 teaspoon salt
3 pounds cooked crawfish

Combine all ingredients except crawfish in blender. Pour over crawfish and marinate overnight. Serve chilled.

*Roger's Cajun Cookbook*

## Crawfish Cardinale

3 green onions, bulb only,
  minced
6 tablespoons butter
2 tablespoons flour
1 cup light cream
1/4 cup tomato ketchup
3/4 teaspoon salt
1/4 teaspoon white pepper

1/2 teaspoon Tabasco
2 teaspoons lemon juice
1 ounce brandy
1 pound boiled, peeled crawfish
  tails*
8 thin lemon slices
Paprika

In a skillet sauté onions in 4 tablespoons butter about 5 minutes. In a saucepan, melt 2 tablespoons butter. Blend in flour; add cream and ketchup, stirring constantly until sauce thickens. Add salt, pepper, Tabasco, and lemon juice. Flame brandy and slowly stir into sauce. Combine contents of both pans; add crawfish tails and stir. Divide the mixture into 8 ramekins and bake in 350° oven, until warm, approximately 12-15 minutes. Garnish with lemon slices and paprika.

**Note:** *1 pound cooked, peeled shrimp may be substituted for crawfish tails.

*The Plantation Cookbook*

## Tony's Crawfish Supreme

*One of Mr. Tony's favorites.*

| | |
|---|---|
| 1 pound crawfish tails | 1/2 onion, minced |
| Tony's Creole Seasoning | 1 (3-ounce) can sliced |
| 4 tablespoons margarine | mushrooms |
| 3 tablespoons all-purpose flour | 1 (10-ounce) package frozen |
| 2 cups milk | chopped spinach |
| 4 egg yolks, slightly beaten | 1/4 cup grated Parmesan cheese |
| 2 tablespoons chopped parsley | Cooking spray |

In a Dutch oven, season crawfish tails with Tony's Creole Seasoning and sauté in 2 tablespoons margarine for 5 minutes. Remove crawfish and set aside. Add remainder of margarine and flour. Stir until smooth. Gradually add milk and cook until thick, stirring constantly. Carefully add egg yolks and cook to boiling point, but do not boil. Remove from heat; adjust seasoning, if necessary. Stir in parsley, onion, and mushrooms.

In another pot, cook spinach as directed on package. Drain. Place spinach in the bottom of a 1½-quart casserole coated with cooking spray. Add crawfish and pour sauce over crawfish. Sprinkle Parmesan cheese on top of casserole. Bake at 375° for 10 minutes. Yields 4 servings.

*Tony Chachere's Second Helping*

## Crawfish Dog

| | |
|---|---|
| 3 tablespoons shortening | 1/2 cup crawfish fat |
| 3 tablespoons flour | 1/4 cup water |
| 1 medium onion, chopped | 1 teaspoon red pepper |
| 1/2 pound crawfish tails, peeled and ground | 2 teaspoons salt |

Make roux with shortening and flour; cook until light brown. Add onion; cook until done. Add crawfish and fat, water, and seasoning. Cook 20 minutes and serve on open-face hot dog bun.

*Cajun Cooking*

# Crawfish Pistolettes

1 onion, chopped
1 bell pepper, chopped
2 ribs celery, chopped
1 clove garlic, chopped
1 stick butter
2 pounds crawfish tails
1 can mushroom pieces, drained

Tony Chachere's Creole Seasoning, to taste
1 can cream of mushroom soup
3 tablespoons chopped parsley
30 pistolettes (like French mini-rolls)

Sauté vegetables in butter. Add crawfish, mushrooms, and seasoning. Cook for 15 minutes. Add mushroom soup and parsley. Simmer 5 minutes on low heat. Let cool. Cut off tip of pistolette. Remove some of the bread from the inside and replace with crawfish mixture. Replace bread tip. Spread melted butter and garlic powder on top of pistolette. Bake at 450° for 8 minutes.

**Variation:** Add 1/2 pound melted Velveeta cheese.

*St. Philomena School 125th Anniversary*

## *Broiled Softshell Crab*

*The hard shell crab will molt its shell at different times during the year. During this period, this delicacy can be brought to the table. Whether broiled, deep fried or pan sautéed, softshell crab is a masterpiece in Cajun cooking.*

| | |
|---|---|
| 12 softshell crabs | 2 cups flour |
| Eggwash (1 egg, ½ cup | 1 pound melted butter |
|   milk, ½ cup water, | Salt and cayenne pepper, |
|   beaten) |   to taste |

Preheat broiler to 500° or oven to 450°. Have your seafood supplier clean the softshell crabs in advance or clean them yourself in the following manner. Lift the pointed end of the top shell away from the main body. Scrape off the lungs or white spongy substance located at each end of the crab. Using a sharp paring knife or scissors, cut away the eyes and mouth portion located in the center-front of the crab. You may also wish to remove the "apron" or small loose shell which comes to a point in the middle of the undershell. Once completed, wash the crab thoroughly in cold water. Dredge crabs in eggwash and then in flour, shaking off all excess. On a large baking sheet with a 1 inch lip, place crabs shell-side-up. Drizzle each crab with melted butter. Crabs should be drenched. Season to taste using salt and pepper. Place crabs under broiler and allow to cook 10-12 minutes. Turn crabs to opposite side and cook an additional 10-12 minutes, basting occasionally. They may be served with lemon and parsley butter or with tartar sauce. This dish may also be eaten po-boy style. Serves 6.

*The Evolution of Cajun & Creole Cuisine*

Zydeco (Zah-dee-ko) is the most contemporary expression of Black Creole music. The music is said to have originated from many sources, but the influence of the blues and soul music is most significant in its development. Zydeco is translated to mean "snap bean," and can be played on accordians, metal washboards, thimbles, spoons, bottle openers.

# Aunt Weenie's Stuffed Crabs

*You must try these!*

4 slices toast
2/3 cup evaporated milk
1/2 cup chopped onion
1/2 cup chopped celery
1/4 cup chopped bell
   pepper
2 tablespoons olive oil
1/2 block butter

1 pound crab meat
1 large egg
1 teaspoon lemon juice
1 1/2 teaspoons salt
1/2 teaspoon black pepper
1 teaspoon Tabasco sauce
8 cleaned crab shells
Bread crumbs

Preheat oven to 375°. Soak toast in evaporated milk. Simmer vegetables in olive oil and butter over medium flame until tender. Add crab meat and continue to cook for a couple of minutes. Lower flame and add soaked bread (which has been squeezed to remove excess milk), egg, lemon juice, salt, pepper, and Tabasco, stirring thoroughly until mixed. Cook over low heat for an additional 5 minutes and continue to stir to prevent sticking. Fill crab shells with hot mixture. Sprinkle with bread crumbs, dot with butter, and bake for 10-15 minutes until brown. Serve hot. Serves 4 hungry hogs!

*The Hungry Hog*

# *Crab Chops*

*At Cypremort Point we ate crab chops on paper plates as we sat on the pier. Every person had his own garnish. My sister doused hers with ketchup. I daintily spread mine with tartar sauce. My brother sandwiched his between two chunks of French bread with mustard. We all agreed they went well with shoestring potatoes. Ah, the good old days.*

3 green onions, minced
3 tablespoons butter or
   margarine
2 tablespoons flour
1 cup milk
1 pound crab meat
20 saltine crackers,
   crumbled
1 egg, beaten

1/2 teaspoon salt
1/4 teaspoon cayenne pepper
2 dashes Tabasco sauce
Cracker meal or bread crumbs
   for dredging
Butter and vegetable oil for
   frying
Boiled crab claws for garnish
   (optional)

Sauté onions in butter or margarine. Alternate adding flour and milk, stirring constantly to make a medium-thick white sauce. Remove from heat and add crab meat, cracker crumbs, egg, salt, cayenne pepper, and Tabasco. Gently mix together and set aside to cool thoroughly. Shape into 6 patties and dredge in cracker meal or bread crumbs. Put about 1/2 inch of equal parts vegetable oil and butter in a skillet and fry patties on both sides until they are golden brown. Serves 6.

*Who's You Mama, Are You Catholic,*
*and Can You Make a Roux?*

## Pan-Fried Eggplant with Crab Meat

1 large eggplant, peeled
1 egg, beaten
1/2 cup milk
2 cups seasoned white flour
1 cup vegetable oil
1 stick butter or margarine

1/4 cup chopped green onions
1 pound lump crab meat
1 tablespoon lemon juice
Salt and pepper to taste
Meuniere Sauce
Hollandaise Sauce

Slice eggplant into 1/4-inch thick round medallions. Combine egg and milk. Dip eggplant in egg mixture and lightly coat with flour. Heat vegetable oil in heavy saucepan over medium-high heat. Sauté eggplant medallions until brown on first side. Turn over and cook approximately 2 more minutes or until tender. Remove from pan and keep warm. Place another sauté pan on medium-high heat. Add butter and sauté green onions for 30 seconds. Add lump crab meat, lemon juice, salt and pepper to taste. Sauté for 3 minutes. Place equal amounts of Meuniere Sauce on warm plates. Place one sautéed eggplant slice on sauce, top with lump crab meat and a teaspoon of Hollandaise Sauce. Yield: 6 servings. *Recipe by Chef John D. Folse, Lafitte's Landing*

**MEUNIERE SAUCE:**

1/2 cup butter
1 tablespoon chopped parsley
1 tablespoon chopped green
   onion
2 tablespoons lemon juice

1/2 teaspoon salt
1/2 teaspoon pepper
Dash Tabasco
Dash Worcestershire sauce

Mix ingredients in order. Simmer briefly over low heat. Serve over fish or seafood. Yield: 1/2 cup.

**BLENDER HOLLANDAISE SAUCE:**

2 egg yolks
2 tablespoons fresh lemon
   juice

1/2 cup butter, melted
Salt and pepper to taste

Place egg yolks and lemon juice into blender. Whirl at top speed until light yellow in color and frothy. Open small disk on top of blender cover. Gradually pour in hot butter and continue beating at top speed. Blend until thick and creamy and butter is absorbed. Season with salt and pepper. Yield: 1 cup.

*Delicious Heritage*

## Crabmeat à la Landry

1 cup onions, chopped fine
1/3 cup celery, chopped fine
1/4 pound oleo or butter
Pinch sage
Pinch thyme
Pinch nutmeg
Pinch oregano
Pinch marjoram

1 teaspoon salt
1/2 teaspoon cayenne
1 tablespoon flour
1 can evaporated milk
1 cup cornflakes
1 pound white crabmeat
1 cup Ritz crackers, crumbled

Sauté onions and celery in oleo or butter until onions are wilted. Add sage, thyme, nutmeg, oregano, marjoram, salt, cayenne, and flour. Add milk, stirring constantly. Toast the cornflakes and crumble; then mix with the crabmeat. Mix well. Combine crabmeat with the spices and put into ramekins or casseroles. Sprinkle with crumbled Ritz crackers. Add a pat of butter and bake for 20-25 minutes at 375°. Serves 6.

*Secrets of The Original Don's Seafood & Steakhouse*

## Cajun Crab Casserole

1 stick margarine
1 1/2 cups chopped onion
1/4 cup chopped green pepper
1/4 cup chopped red pepper
2 cloves garlic, minced
1/2 cup chopped celery
1 (10-ounce) can tomatoes
   with green chilies
1/4 cup chopped pimientos

2 slices bread
1 (10 1/4-ounce) can cream of
   mushroom soup
1 teaspoon Worcestershire sauce
1 teaspoon hot pepper sauce
3 cups crabmeat
3 cups cooked rice
1/4 cup snipped parsley
1/4 cup chopped green onion tops

Sauté onion, green pepper, red pepper, garlic, and celery in the melted margarine in a saucepan. Add tomatoes and pimientos. Soak the bread in water; squeeze. Add the bread, soup, Worcestershire sauce, hot pepper sauce, and crabmeat. Blend well. Add cooked rice, parsley, and onion tops. Spoon into greased 2 1/2-quart casserole; cover with buttered bread crumbs if you desire. Bake 20 minutes at 400°. Yields 6 servings.

*C'est Bon, Encore*

## *Crabmeat au Gratin*

½ stick margarine plus
   1 tablespoon
2 tablespoons flour
1 cup milk
½ onion, minced
2 stalks celery, chopped
3 tablespoons bell pepper, chopped

1 clove garlic, minced
1 pound crabmeat
Onion tops and parsley
1 cup Velveeta hot cheese
1 cup bread crumbs

Melt 1 stick margarine; add flour; add milk; make white sauce. Melt 1 tablespoon margarine in saucepan; add onions, celery, bell pepper, and garlic. Sauté. Add crabmeat, onion tops, parsley, Velveeta cheese. Add ½ cup bread crumbs. Season to taste and top with remaining bread crumbs. Bake at 350° for 30 minutes.

*From Mama To Me*

## *Seafood Quiche*

4 green onions, chopped
½ cup fresh mushrooms
2 tablespoons butter
½ pound crab meat
½ pound shrimp
4 eggs, beaten

¾ cup cream
1¼ cups milk
½ cup white wine
Salt and pepper to taste
½ pound Swiss or mozzarella
   cheese

Sauté onions and mushrooms in butter. Place crab and shrimp in bottom of baked 9-inch pie shell. Mix eggs, cream, milk, wine, salt and pepper. Fill the shell and top with cheese. Bake at 375° for 30-40 minutes or until a knife inserted in center of pie comes out dry. Cool 10 minutes before cutting. Yield: 6 servings.

*Fessin' Up with Bon Appétit*

# Barbecued Oysters

*This New Creole dish, finished outdoors on a grill, intriguingly blends several familiar local presentations with a Mediterranean element not usually encountered. Like so many of Chef Mike Fennelly's best creations, this dish shows a powerful Asian influence as well.*

2 tablespoons tomato paste
2 garlic cloves, minced
2 shallots, minced
2 teaspoons minced red onion
2 teaspoons minced fresh
  cilantro
1/2 teaspoon toasted Szechuan
  peppercorns
2 teaspoons mild chile, minced
2 1/2 tablespoons white vinegar
1/3 cup finely packed brown
  sugar

1/3 cup sesame oil
4 teaspoons freshly grated
  ginger root
1/2 teaspoon ground red pepper
Juice of 1 1/2 lemons
1/2 cup teriyaki sauce
1/3 cup soy sauce
3 dashes hot pepper sauce
1/2 pound pancetta (Italian bacon),
  thinly sliced
2 dozen oysters in the shell

Blend all ingredients, except the pancetta and oysters, until smooth. Place the pancetta on a cookie sheet and roast in a 350° oven for just 2-3 minutes, until lightly browned. Pat dry with a paper towel and cut into 1/4-inch squares. Prepare a hot fire in a grill.

Shuck the oysters and discard the top half of the shell. Rinse to remove shell particles. Place the oyster on the half shell over hot coals and pour some of the sauce over each oyster. Sprinkle with the pancetta. Grill for 5-7 minutes, or until bubbly. Serves 8.                    *Recipe by Mike Fennelly, Mike's on the Avenue*
                                        **The Food of New Orleans**

---

The Acadians were French-speaking refugees from Nova Scotia (Acadia) who came to south Louisiana in 1763. Their name was soon shortened to "Cajuns." Farmers by tradition, they settled along the dense swamps and bayous, and by the Gulf where they harvested shrimp, crabs, crawfish and oysters. They built boats out of cypress trees—pirogues— and trapped for furs. Cajuns are fun-loving people who shrug off their cares in song and dance.

# *Oyster Lover's Pie*

*A slice of Oyster Pie makes a nice hot appetizer or a delicious main dish. Commercially prepared crusts can be used. I generally make my pie crust. If using for appetizers, I make them in regular-size muffin tins and serve individual pies.*

| | |
|---|---|
| 1 stick butter | 1/3 cup chopped fresh parsley |
| 3/4 cup flour | 1/2 cup chopped green onions |
| 1 1/2 pints oysters, drained and reserve liquid | Salt, black pepper and cayenne pepper to taste |
| 1 clove garlic, chopped | 1 (9-inch) unbaked pie crust |
| 1/3 cup chopped celery | |

Melt butter in skillet. Add flour to butter and stir constantly until mixture is golden brown, about the color of a paper sack. Add the drained oysters, garlic, celery, parsley, and green onions. Season to taste. Cook only about 5 minutes or until edges of oysters curl. Remove from heat and stir in about 1/3 cup of the oyster liquid. If mixture is too thick, add a little more of the oyster liquid. As the pie bakes, the oysters will thin the filling. Check for seasoning. This needs to be spicy. Pour into unbaked pie crust. Bake in 350° oven for 30-40 minutes or until crust is golden brown. Serves 4-6.

*Extra! Extra! Read All About It!*

## New Orleans Patties

2 tablespoons bacon fat or
  oleo
1 pod garlic, minced
2 stalks celery, chopped
3 green onions and tops,
  chopped fine
2 tablespoons flour

3 dozen oysters
2 tablespoons oyster liquid
Dash of Accent
Dash of cayenne pepper
Salt and pepper to taste
2 tablespoons parsley, chopped
Patty shells

Melt fat in pan. Add garlic, celery, and onions; cook until soft. Blend in flour, oysters, oyster liquid, Accent, cayenne, salt and pepper. Cook on low heat, stirring constantly until oysters make more liquid. Simmer for 20 minutes. Add uncooked parsley and cool. Fill prepared patty shells and bake in 300° oven until heated, about 15 minutes.

This recipe fills 5-6 large patty shells. It is also delicious served in bite-sized shells as an appetizer.

*A Cook's Tour of Shreveport*

# Poultry and Game

Masked, costumed horsemen ride the Cajun countryside each Mardi Gras, stopping at rural farmhouses to ask in French for a chicken for the community gumbo. Mamou, Church Point, and other Cajun towns.

# Parmesan Chicken Bake

| | |
|---|---|
| ¹/₂ cup dry bread crumbs | ¹/₈ teaspoon thyme |
| 2 tablespoons grated | ¹/₈ teaspoon lemon pepper |
| Parmesan cheese | 6 (4-ounce) chicken breasts, |
| 1 tablespoon parsley flakes | skinned |
| 1 teaspoon salt | 3 tablespoons margarine |

Preheat oven to 350°. Combine bread crumbs, cheese, and seasonings in shallow dish. Dip chicken in crumb mixture. Coat both sides. Melt margarine in baking dish in oven. Add chicken, turning to coat both sides with margarine. Bake uncovered for one hour. Yield: 3 servings.

Cal 221; Chol 75mg; Sat Fat 1gm; Fat 9gm; Sod 523; Pro 30gm; Cho 5gm; Exchanges: 4 meat, 1 fat.

***Southern But Lite***

## *Chicken Cannatella*

2 tablespoons granulated
  garlic
1/2 cup olive oil
1 bunch green onions,
  tops only, chopped
6 chicken breasts, boneless
  and skinless, cut into
  bite-size pieces
3 sticks butter, (do not use
  margarine)
2 large onions, chopped
1 large red or gold bell
  pepper, chopped

2 stalks celery, chopped
2 cans golden mushroom
  soup
1 cup chicken stock
1 pound Velveeta, cubed
8 ounces Swiss cheese, cubed
4 ounces cream cheese, softened
  at room temperature
1/2 teaspoon cayenne pepper
1 tablespoon black pepper
Salt to taste
1/2 cup parsley, chopped
1/2 cup Italian bread crumbs

First, prepare the marinade by mixing the garlic, olive oil, and green onions together. Stir in the chicken and refrigerate for 2 hours. Do not discard the liquid! You will use the marinade liquid in the final steps.

In a heavy pot, melt and butter and add onions, bell pepper, celery. Sauté until vegetables are tender. Add mushroom soup and chicken stock and cook for 5 minutes on a medium-low heat. Then add all cheeses and cook for 5 minutes on a low heat, stirring constantly, until they melt. Add red pepper, black pepper, salt, parsley, and bread crumbs and cook for 5 more minutes. Be sure to stir constantly at this point to prevent scorching. Turn off the fire and remove from heat.

Next, heat a large skillet to a medium-high heat. Add the chicken and all the marinade ingredients and liquid. Cook for 20 minutes. Pour all the ingredients from the skillet into the pot and mix. Serve over rice or angel hair pasta. Serves 6. Enjoy!!

*Pass the Meatballs, Please!*

The Acadian Cultural Center in Lafayette tells the story of the Acadians who settled the prairies, bayous, and marshes of southern Louisiana. Acadian Village and Vermilionville are replicas of early Cajun communities.

# Charcoal Grilled Chicken

*Simple and delicious.*

**2-2¹/₂ pounds ready-to-cook broiler/fryer, halved, quartered
or disjointed**

**BARBECUE SAUCE:**

| | |
|---|---|
| ¹/₂ cup melted butter | 1 minced clove garlic |
| ¹/₂ cup cooking oil | 1 teaspoon oregano |
| ¹/₃ cup lemon juice | ¹/₂ teaspoon salt |
| ¹/₂ cup soy sauce | ¹/₂ teaspoon pepper |

Mix.  Let chicken refrigerate in barbecue sauce one hour.  Place
on grill over hot coals and cook until tender, about 30 or 45 minutes, turning with tongs and brushing occasionally with sauce.

**Note:**  For a barbecue sauce shortcut, add 2 packages of herb-
seasoned or garlic salad dressing mix to ¹/₂ cup of melted butter
and ¹/₂ cup cooking oil.

*Pigging Out with the Cotton Patch Cooks*


# Grilled Chicken

| | |
|---|---|
| 1 chicken (fryer) | ¹/₂ teaspoon garlic salt |
| ¹/₄ cup butter | ¹/₂ teaspoon onion powder |
| 1 cup Worcestershire sauce | ¹/₂ teaspoon celery salt |
| 3 tablespoons lemon juice | ¹/₄ teaspoon pepper |

Cut chicken in half.  Place on hot grill and sear.  Turn and sear
other side.  Melt butter in pan.  Add all ingredients and stir until
mixture boils.  Baste chicken halves and turn.  Continue basting
and turning every 5-10 minutes until cooked.  Grill approximately
40 minutes.  Serves 4.

*Big Mama's Old Black Pot*

# Atchafalaya Shish Kabobs

**MARINADE:**

| | |
|---|---|
| 1 onion, chopped | 1 teaspoon thyme |
| 1/2 bell pepper, chopped | 1 bay leaf |
| 1 rib celery, chopped | 1 teaspoon allspice |
| 1 tablespoon butter substitute | 1 teaspoon white pepper |
| 1 cup vinegar | 3/4 tablespoon low sodiun |
| 1/4 cup sherry | soy sauce |
| 3 sprigs parsley, chopped | 3 dashes Tabasco sauce |

Sauté onion, bell pepper, and celery in one tablespoon butter substitute. Add vinegar, sherry, parsley, thyme, bay leaf, allspice, pepper, soy sauce, and Tabasco sauce.

| | |
|---|---|
| 4 boneless, skinless chicken breasts | 1 bell pepper, quartered |
| | Cherry tomatoes |
| 1 onion, quartered | Fresh mushrooms |

Cut chicken breasts into chunks and add to cooled marinade. Marinate overnight. Place chicken breasts on skewers with bell pepper, cherry tomatoes and fresh mushrooms. Place over hot coals. Baste kabobs 3-4 times with basting sauce. Add wet hickory chips to coals and cook chicken until no longer pink.

**BASTING SAUCE:**

| | |
|---|---|
| 1 cup water | 1 teaspoon lemon juice |
| 2 tablespoons melted butter substitute | 3/4 tablespoon low sodium soy sauce |

Mix all ingredients. Baste shish kabobs.

*Roger's Lite Cajun Cookbook*

153

## *Coq Au Vin*
### *(Chicken in Wine Sauce)*

½ cup butter
6 chicken breasts, boneless
  and skinless
½ cup green onion, finely
  chopped
1 teaspoon whole thyme
1 teaspoon whole basil
1 bay leaf

1 teaspoon black pepper
2 cups quality white wine
2 tablespoons butter
¼ cup onion, finely chopped
2 tablespoons all-purpose flour
1 cup fresh mushrooms,
  quartered

Preheat oven to 350°. In a large skillet, melt ½ cup butter; add chicken breasts. Cook on high heat to brown both sides of the chicken. After turning chicken once, add green onion, thyme, basil, bay leaf, and pepper. Remove chicken and sauté green onion for one minute. Place chicken into a large oven pan. Add wine to butter mixture and sauté until combined, then pour over the chicken. Cover with foil, place in oven, and bake for 50 minutes.

Meanwhile, in the same skillet, melt remaining butter, add onion, and sauté for 5 minutes. Add flour and whisk until flour is almost a paper bag color. Remove from heat and continue to whisk until pan cools slightly. Mixture should have darkened some more. Reserve.

When chicken is done, remove from oven. Remove chicken and reserve. Place pan on burner on high heat. As soon as mixture begins to bubble, slowly add the flour mixture, whisking as you add, until all is added. Continue to whisk until mixture thickens. Return chicken to pan, and add mushrooms. Reduce heat, and sauté for 2 minutes. Remove from heat, cover and let stand for 3 minutes. Serve.

*'Dat Little New Orleans Creole Cookbook*

# *Italian Chicken*

*This is way too easy to be so good!  The Italian herbs give that finishing touch.*

1½ cups water
1 cup rice
1 (10-ounce) can diced
   tomatoes and green
   chilies, drained
½ cup chopped onion
½ cup shredded part-skim
   mozzarella cheese
2 teaspoons dried basil,
   divided

2 teaspoons dried oregano,
   divided
1 teaspoon minced garlic
1½ pounds skinless, boneless
   chicken breasts, cut into
   strips
¼ cup grated Parmesan
   cheese

Preheat the oven to 375°.  In a 2- to 3-quart oblong baking dish coated with nonstick cooking spray, combine the water, rice, tomatoes and chilies, onion, mozzarella, 1 teaspoon of the basil, 1 teaspoon of the oregano, and the garlic, stirring well.  Top the rice mixture with the chicken strips and sprinkle with the remaining basil and oregano and the Parmesan.  Bake, covered, for 45 minutes.  Uncover and continue baking 15 minutes longer, or until the chicken is tender and the rice is cooked.  Makes 4 servings.

Cal 469; Fat 8.7g; Cal from Fat 16.7%; Sat Fat 3.8g; Prot 48.3g; Carbo 46.2g; Sod 539g; Chol 116mg.

*Trim & Terrific One-Dish Favorites*

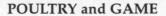

## Chicken on Sunday

1 can cream of celery
  soup
1 can cream of chicken
  soup
1 can cream of mushroom
  soup

3/4 cup milk
1 small box Minute rice
1 chicken, cut up (do not
  flour or salt)
1 envelope dry onion soup
  mix

Mix cans of soup and milk. Add rice to soup and mix well. Pour soup and rice mixture into greased 13 x 9 x 3-inch pan. Place chicken on top of rice mixture. Cover chicken with dry onion soup mix and cover pan with foil. Bake in a 325° oven for 2 hours and 15 minutes.

*Kooking with the Krewe*

## Chicken, Mushroom and Artichoke Bake

4-6 boneless chicken breast
  halves
Salt
Black pepper
Paprika
1/2 cup butter
1/2 - 1 pound mushrooms, sliced

2 tablespoons flour
1 (10-ounce) can condensed
  chicken broth
1/2 cup sherry
1 (14-ounce) can artichoke hearts,
  drained

Season chicken with salt, pepper, and paprika. In a large skillet, melt butter and sauté chicken until lightly browned. Remove to a baking dish. In the same skillet, sauté mushrooms, add flour and mix well. Stir in broth and sherry. Season with salt and pepper. Simmer for 5-10 minutes and pour over chicken breasts. Bake in 375° oven for one hour. Top with artichoke hearts and cook for 20-30 minutes. Makes 4 servings.

*Celebrations on the Bayou*

## *Country Chicken Pie*

4 chicken breast halves,
   cooked and deboned
1 small onion, chopped
2 ribs celery, chopped
1 carrot, chopped
1 small potato, chopped
6 tablespoons butter or
   margarine

6 tablespoons flour
2½ cups milk
2 chicken bouillon cubes
1 teaspoon Worcestershire
   sauce
1 teaspoon salt
Pepper
Biscuits

Boil chicken in enough water to cover until done—about one hour. When cool, remove meat from the bone and chop in bite-size pieces. Chop vegetables into small pieces and boil in a small amount of water about 10 minutes. They should be tender, but not completely done. Drain.

Make sauce by melting butter and adding flour until it is mixed. Gradually add milk, stirring constantly so the sauce will not lump. Add bouillon cubes, Worcestershire, salt and pepper. Cook over low heat until mixture thickens. Mix chicken, vegetables and sauce and pour into a greased 2-quart casserole. Top with biscuits rolled about ½ inch thick. (Any biscuit recipe will do, but a mix made according to directions will do as well.) Bake at 400° for about 30-40 minutes until the casserole is bubbly and the biscuits are brown.

This may be frozen but do not add the biscuits. If frozen, the cooking time will be longer, so the biscuits should be put on top the last 30 minutes of baking. Serves 4-6.

*By Special Request*

## Boneless Chicken Thighs with Curry Sauce

*For curry lovers, this is a splendid dish.*

4 boneless chicken thighs
  (6 ounces each,
  trimmed of excess
  fat and rolled to
  shape of thigh)
3 tablespoons unsalted butter
1 large onion, chopped

2 tablespoons flour
1 cup beef broth
1 tablespoon curry powder
3 tablespoons heavy cream
Chopped cilantro for
  garnish

Preheat oven to 350°. Cook chicken thighs in an uncovered roasting pan approximately 40 minutes. While thighs are cooking, melt butter in a saucepan. Add onion and sauté 10 minutes (do not brown). Add flour and stir constantly for 1 - 2 minutes. Add broth and curry powder and simmer about 15 minutes. Add cream and stir about one minute. If sauce is too thick, add a little more broth. Pour sauce over thighs that have been placed on individual dinner plates, and sprinkle cilantro over the top.

*Golliwogg Cake*

## Chicken Sauce Piquant

1 pound skinned boneless
  chicken breast
3 cups chopped onions
1 cup diced celery
1½ cups chopped bell
  peppers
1 teaspoon chili powder

1 can tomato paste
2 cups water
1 teaspoon black pepper
Dash red pepper
4 ounces light turkey smoked
  sausage, thinly sliced

Cut chicken breasts into strips. Pan fry in non-stick vegetable spray until done. Remove chicken and set aside. Add chopped onions, celery, and peppers and cook until tender. Add chili powder, tomato paste, water, seasonings, and sausage. Add chicken and cook on low heat for 2 hours. Yield: 8 servings.

Cal 187; Chol 187mg; Sat Fat 1gm; Fat 8gm; Sod 213mg; Dietary Fiber 3gm; Exchanges: 2 meat, 2 vegetable.

*Gone with the Fat*

## Chicken Sauce Piquante

4-6 pounds chicken, cut
    in pieces
1 cup oil
2 cups chopped onions
1 cup celery, chopped
1 cup chopped bell pepper
1 (16-ounce) can whole
    tomatoes
1 (16-ounce) can tomato juice
5 cups water
1 (4-ounce) can mushrooms
1 teaspoon sugar
4 cloves garlic, chopped fine
Salt, black and cayenne pepper
1/2 cup green onions and parsley,
    chopped

Season chicken and fry in oil in heavy, covered iron pot. Stirring occasionally, cook for about 1/2 hour or until chicken becomes tender. Take chicken out of pot and set aside. Add onions, celery, and bell pepper to oil and cook slowly until onions are wilted. Add whole tomatoes, tomato juice, and water. Cook over medium heat until oil floats above tomatoes, or about 25 minutes.

Add chicken, mushrooms, sugar, and chopped garlic. Season to taste with salt, black pepper and cayenne, leaning heavily on the cayenne to give the sting (which is piquante). Cook for 20 minutes. Add parsley and green onions. Serve over steamed rice. Serves 8.

*Secrets of The Original Don's Seafood & Steakhouse*

## Crock Pot Chicken Olé

1 medium onion, chopped
2 tablespoons oleo
1/2 cup diced green chilies
1 teaspoon salt
2 (10³/4-ounce) can cream
    of chicken soup
1 (13-ounce) can evaporated milk
3 cups cooked, cubed chicken
8 corn tortillas, cut into eights
1/2 pound sharp Cheddar cheese,

Sauté onion in oleo until clear. Add chilies, salt, soup, and milk. Stir until smooth. Add chicken and bring to a boil. Remove from heat. Layer ingredients in a 6-quart crock pot as follows: chicken mixture, tortillas, grated cheese, repeating layers and ending with cheese. Cover and refrigerate overnight. To serve: Heat in crock pot 3-4 hours on low.

*Cooking with Mr. "G" and Friends*

# Chicken Fricassée
## (Chicken Stew)

1 (3½-pound) hen,
   cut up
Salt and pepper to taste
3 tablespoons cooking oil
5 tablespoons flour
1 cup onion, chopped

½ cup celery, chopped
3 cups water (approximately)
½ cup green onions, chopped
¼ cup parsley, chopped
½ teaspoon dried thyme

Salt and pepper chicken. Brown slowly in oil over medium heat. Remove pieces of chicken when browned. Scrape bottom of pot to remove browned meat juices. Set aside. Stir in flour until smooth. Stir constantly for about 15 minutes or until mixture is a rich brown color. Add onion and celery. Cover and simmer for about 10 minutes on low heat. Gradually add water and the remaining ingredients and browned chicken. Cover and simmer until chicken is tender. Add water if necessary. Skim off excess fat. Serves 6-8.

*Allons Manger*

## Sticky Chicken

6 chicken leg and
  thigh quarters
1/4 pound butter or margarine
1 teaspoon salt
1 teaspoon cayenne pepper
1 cup onion, finely chopped

3 tablespoons garlic, minced
1 tablespoon parsley flakes
3 tablespoons all-purpose flour
1/4 cup white wine
3 cups chicken stock

Wash leg and thigh quarters well. Place on a cutting board and remove the bone. (The butcher will do this for you, if you desire, for a small fee.) Melt 3 tablespoons butter in a skillet on high heat. Place deboned chicken in the skillet, skin-side-down. Set heat to medium-high and fry the chicken until the bottom side is beginning to brown along the edges (about 10 minutes). Sprinkle with salt and pepper and turn. Cook 10-14 minutes or until chicken is done. It will stick—don't worry, just scrap the chicken out and set aside on a plate. Do Not Drain on Paper! To the skillet add remaining butter, and add onion, garlic, and parsley, and sauté 5-7 minutes. Add flour and stir in well. Continue to stir until flour is beginning to stick to the bottom of the pan. Return heat to highest setting and sauté for 30 seconds. Add the wine and remove from heat immediately and stir until pan is clean of stuck residue. (You are de-glazing the skillet.) Return to high heat. Add chicken stock, stirring until all is blended. Adjust liquid for texture. Cover the skillet and simmer on low for 15 minutes. While the pot is simmering, remove the skin from the cooked chicken and discard. Cut the chicken into 1-inch pieces; return the chicken to the skillet and stir well. Continue to simmer for 3 minutes. Remove from heat and set aside, covered, for 10 minutes. Serve with rice or potatoes.

*'Dat Little Louisiana Plantation Cookbook*

## Alma's Chicken

| | |
|---|---|
| Salt | Flour |
| Pepper | 1½ sticks butter |
| Accent | 1 (7-ounce) can mushrooms |
| 6 chicken breasts | 7 ounces dry vermouth |

Sprinkle salt, pepper, and Accent on chicken and roll in flour for frying. Melt butter in skillet and fry chicken until golden brown. Place chicken, bony side up, in roasting pan along with butter in which chicken was fried. Place mushrooms and vermouth (measure in mushroom can) in saucepan and bring to a rolling boil. Pour over chicken; cover and cook in 300° oven for 1 hour or until tender. Baste occasionally. If liquid is insufficient, add additional vermouth. Serve with pepper jelly.

*A Bouquet of Recipes*

## Abbie's Fried Chicken

| | |
|---|---|
| 1½ - 2 cups flour | 2 fryers, cut into pieces |
| Bill's Cajun Seasoning | 2 quarts cooking oil |

Combine flour with seasoning mix. Coat and shake each piece of chicken with the seasoned flour. Using a heavy deep pot, heat oil. When oil is hot, place floured chicken pieces in pot, being careful not to crowd the pieces. Fry until pieces rise to the top and are floating in the oil. Remove chicken from pot and drain on paper towels. Yield: 8 servings.

**Note**: After using oil, strain and reserve for later use.

BILL'S CAJUN SEASONING:

| | |
|---|---|
| 3 teaspoons ground red pepper | 2 teaspoons oregano |
| 1 teaspoon thyme | 2 teaspoons white pepper |
| 2 teaspoons chili powder | 4 teaspoons ground paprika |
| | 2 teaspoons salt |

Sift all ingredients together and store in tightly covered jar.

*Delicious Heritage*

# Southern Pecan Chicken

*Can substitute fish for the chicken for an equally good variation.*

| | |
|---|---|
| 6-8 boneless chicken breasts | 1/2 cup finely chopped pecans |
| Salt and pepper | 1 cup plain bread crumbs |
| 2 eggs | 1/4 cup butter or margarine |
| 2 teaspoons Creole mustard | 1/4 cup vegetable oil |

Lay chicken breasts out on wax paper. Season with salt and pepper. In a small bowl, beat eggs with mustard. In another bowl, combine pecans and bread crumbs. Dip chicken in egg mixture, then coat with bread crumb mixture.

Preheat oven to 350°. In a large skillet over medium-high heat, melt 2 tablespoons butter and 2 tablespoons oil. Sauté half the chicken until golden brown on each side. Place in an ovenproof dish. Wipe out skillet, pouring off any drippings (so second batch will have a clean, fresh look after browning). Sauté the rest of the chicken in the remaining 2 tablespoons of butter and oil. Place in oven and bake for 15 minutes.

**SAUCE:**

| | |
|---|---|
| 1/4 cup butter | 1 teaspoon lemon juice |
| 1/2 cup coarsely chopped pecans | |

Melt butter in a small saucepan over low heat. Stir in pecans and lemon juice. Serve over chicken. Serves 6-8.

*Kay Ewing's Cooking School Cookbook*

# Chicken and Black Bean Enchiladas

*Easy, and will make quite an impression.*

1 pound skinless, bone-
   less chicken breasts
3 slices center cut bacon
2 cloves garlic, minced
1½ cups salsa
1 (15-ounce) can black
   beans, undrained
1 red bell pepper, seeded and
   chopped

1 teaspoon ground cumin
Salt and pepper to taste
1 bunch green onions,
   chopped
12 flour tortillas
6 ounces reduced fat
   Monterey Jack cheese,
   shredded

Cut chicken into cubes; set aside. In skillet, cook bacon until crisp. Remove bacon to paper towel to soak any excess grease and discard any grease in skillet. In same skillet, coat with non-stick cooking spray, and sauté chicken and garlic until chicken is almost done. Stir in ½ cup salsa, beans, red pepper, cumin, and salt and pepper to taste. Simmer until thickened, about 7 minutes, stirring occasionally. Stir in green onions and reserved bacon. Divide chicken-bean mixture among 12 tortillas, placing down center of each tortilla. Top with one tablespoon shredded cheese. Roll up and place seam-side-down in a 13 x 9 x 2-inch baking dish coated with nonstick cooking spray. Spoon remaining one cup salsa evenly over enchiladas. Top with remaining cheese. Bake at 350° for 15 minutes or until thoroughly heated and cheese is melted. Yield: 6 servings.

Cal 467; Chol 52mg; Fat 9.8g; Cal from Fat 18.8%.

*A Trim & Terrific Louisiana Kitchen*

In 1700 B.C., when Ramses II sat on Egypt's throne, a sophisticated Indian civilization flourished in northeastern Louisiana. They built vast earthworks that may have taken generations to complete, including a bird-shaped ceremonial mound one-third the size of the great pyramids. Named Poverty Point after a struggling plantation that once stood on the grounds, this is one of the nation's major archaeological sites.

## Chicken Tetrazzini

1 large onion, chopped
1 large bell pepper,
   chopped
1 stick margarine
2 cans cream of mushroom
   soup
1 large jar sliced mushrooms
1 large jar pimentos

1 large chicken
1 large bag egg noodles
Garlic to taste
Salt to taste
Red pepper to taste
1 large bag grated mozzarella
   cheese

Sauté the onions and bell pepper in margarine. Add the soup, mushrooms and pimentos; simmer. Boil the chicken until very tender and remove from bones; cut into pieces. Boil egg noodles in broth; drain noodles. Add the chicken and soup mixture to noodles and season to taste. Add broth to desired consistency. Pour in a large greased casserole dish. Cover with grated cheese. Bake at 350° until the cheese is evenly melted.

*CDA Angelic Treats*

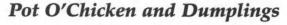

# Pot O'Chicken and Dumplings

**CHICKEN:**

| | |
|---|---|
| 1 large hen | 1 teaspoon salt |
| 3 quarts water | 2 chicken bouillon cubes |
| 1½ teaspoons pepper | 2 tablespoons margarine |

Cut hen into quarters. Place in 6-quart pot. Cover with water. Add pepper, salt and bouillon cubes. Cook over medium-high heat until meat will separate from bone. Remove chicken from broth. Let cool. Remove bones from chicken. There should be 8-9 cups broth in which to cook dumplings. (Additional seasoning may be added to broth at this time. Broth should be highly seasoned to make dumplings flavorful.) Return boned chicken to broth and add margarine.

**DUMPLINGS:**

| | |
|---|---|
| 3 cups flour | 2 eggs |
| 6 tablespoons shortening | ⅔ cup water |
| 1 teaspoon salt | |

To make dumplings, combine flour, shortening, and salt. Blend by cutting shortening into flour with pastry blender. Beat eggs and water together. Gradually add to flour mixture. Stir to make soft dough. Divide dough into 2 equal parts for ease of handling. Roll out dough on generously floured board. Dough should be rolled into very, very thin sheets. Let sheets of dough dry out for 10-15 minutes. Brush excess flour from dough. Cut into 1½-inch squares.

Bring broth to rolling boil. Begin dropping squares of dough, a few at a time, into broth. Stir gently as dumplings are added to broth to prevent dough from sticking together. When desired amount of dough is in broth, reduce heat and simmer on medium-low until dumplings are firm. Serves 10.

*Dinner on the Ground*

## *Chicken Pot Pie*

½ cup liquid butter
  substitute*
3 tablespoons flour
3 cups defatted chicken
  broth
1 cup skim milk
¼ cup celery, sliced

¼ cup onion, chopped
3 cups diced chicken
  breasts
Salt and pepper
1 (16-ounce) package frozen
  mixed vegetables
1 (9-inch) pie crust, uncooked

Combine butter substitute and flour in saucepan over low heat. Gradually add chicken broth and milk, stirring constantly until smooth and thickened. Sauté celery and onion in vegetable spray. Stir in chicken, salt, pepper, mixed vegetables (cook by package instructions), onion, and celery. Mix well. Pour into a 13 x 9 x 2-inch baking dish. Roll pastry to ⅛-inch thickness on lightly floured board and cut into 11-inch wide strips. Arrange in lattice design over chicken mixture. Bake at 350° for 30 minutes or until pastry is golden brown. Yield: 9 servings.

**Note:** *One package Butter Buds mixed with ½ cup water equals ½ cup liquid butter substitute.

Cal 211; Chol 36mg; Sat Fat 1gm; Fat 3gm; Sod 515mg; Pro 18gm; Cho 28gm; Exchanges: 2 meat, 1 bread, ½ vegetable.

*Southern But Lite*

## *Chicken Broccoli Cups*

1 (10-ounce) can (or more)
  refrigerated biscuits
6 boneless chicken breasts,
  cooked, chopped
1 (10-ounce) package frozen
  chopped broccoli, cooked,
  drained

1 (10-ounce) can cream of
  mushroom soup
3/4 cup shredded Cheddar
  cheese

Press the biscuits over bottoms and sides of lightly greased muffin cups. Combine the chicken, broccoli, and soup in a bowl, and mix well. Spoon into the biscuit-lined muffin cups. Top with the cheese. Bake at 400° for 10 minutes. Yield: 5 servings.

*Louisiana Temptations*


## *Tony's Deep-Fried Turkey*

*The most requested recipe by far!*

**1 (approximately 14-pound) turkey**

Mix the following ingredients in a blender 2 days before cooking. Pour into a jar and refrigerate. You can keep this marinade in the refrigerator for months. Use at Thanksgiving then again at Christmas.

1 tablespoon Worcestershire
  sauce
2 tablespoons Creole mustard
3 (2-ounce) bottles garlic juice
3 (2-ounce) bottles onion juice

1 (3-ounce) bottle hot pepper
  sauce
1/4 cup Tony's Creole Seasoning
8 ounces water

Inject turkey with a syringe using the blended mixture. Rub turkey with additional mustard and season generously with Tony's Creole Seasoning. When ready to cook, heat 5 gallons of peanut oil to 350°; submerge turkey and let fry for 4 minutes per pound of turkey. Yields 15 servings.

*Tony Chachere's Second Helping*

## *Fried Turkey*

| | |
|---|---|
| 2 (10-12-pound) turkeys | ⅓ cup chopped bell pepper |
| 1 large onion, minced | or jalapeño |
| 8-10 cloves garlic, peeled, | 2-3 tablespoons salt |
| left whole | 2 tablespoons cayenne pepper |

Clean turkeys thoroughly, leaving the skin flap at the neck intact. In a small mixing bowl, combine the minced onion, whole garlic, chopped peppers, 1½ tablespoons salt and 1 tablespoon of cayenne pepper. With a sharp boning knife, make slits in the breasts and upper thighs of the turkeys and stuff the seasoning mix into the slits with you fingers. Pack well. Season the outside of the turkeys with the remaining salt and cayenne pepper. Place them in large plastic bags and refrigerate overnight.

Before you begin frying, you do have to do a little preparation. First of all, do not try to fry them indoors. It can be dangerous, as oil will splatter and may cause a fire; and, because of the smoke, your smoke detectors may be set off. You will need a butane burner and a large deep pot with a cover. Place cardboard and several layers of newspapers under the burner to protect your patio, deck or yard from grease splatters. Also, have on hand two large paper bags and two long-handled forks, like the kind you use for barbecuing.

Pour enough cooking oil (may use peanut oil, but lard is the best) to fill the pot ¾ full. Oil must be at 350° before adding the turkey. Holding the turkey by the neck skin flap, gently submerge the turkey into the hot oil. Be careful, as the hot grease may overflow and splatter. Cover pot. Every 10 minutes, using the long-handled forks, turn the turkey around in the pot. It will take 45 minutes to one hour to cook one turkey. When the legs start to spread open, the turkey is done. Remove the turkey and put it inside the large paper bag and close tightly. Let it stand for 20 minutes before removing and carving.

*Cajun Men Cook*

## *Seasoning the Turkey*

*Don't worry about bland tasting turkey anymore. Once you prepare a turkey this way, you will never go back to your former method. Cooking the turkey in a baking bag ensures moistness. Because of variation in the size of turkeys, exact proportions are not given.*

Salt, black pepper and
  cayenne pepper
Garlic, chopped
Bell pepper, chopped
Pecan halves

Pimento-stuffed green olives
Butter, cut into pats
Celery, parsley, green onions
Baking bag

Rinse thawed bird and pat dry. Puncture all meaty parts with the point of knife to form deep and narrow pockets. Be sure to make a lot of pockets over the breasts and thighs. Mix salt, black pepper, and cayenne pepper together. Add chopped garlic and chopped bell pepper to salt mixture. Using a small amount of this seasoning, push it down into pockets. Place 1 or 2 pecan halves and 2 pimento-stuffed olives into each of the pockets. Finish by adding a small pat of butter into each pocket. Sprinkle entire outside of turkey with salt, black pepper, and cayenne pepper.

I normally don't stuff my turkey with dressing. I season the cavity with salt and pepper and add 1/3 bunch fresh parsley, 1/3 bunch green onions, and 3 pieces of celery to the cavity. Cook in baking bag. Follow instructions on the bag. Bake until tender. Carve.

*Extra! Extra! Read All About It!*

# *Rabbit Creole*

1 (3-pound) rabbit (cut up)
Salt, black pepper, red
   pepper, to taste
$1/2$ cup flour
$1/2$ cup + 2 tablespoons
   butter
1 onion, chopped
1 bell pepper, chopped
2 ribs celery, chopped

1 can Ro-Tel tomatoes, mashed
$1/2$ cup tomato sauce
$3/4$ cup water
2 teaspoons Worcestershire
$1/2$ teaspoon chili powder
1 small container fresh
   mushrooms, chopped
2 tablespoons chopped green
   onions

Season rabbit with salt and pepper and dredge in flour. Heat $1/2$ cup butter in a large black pot and brown rabbit. Remove rabbit and add onion, bell pepper, and celery. Add tomatoes, tomato sauce, water, Worcestershire sauce, and chili powder. Simmer 5 minutes. Add rabbit. Cover and simmer over low heat until rabbit becomes tender. Sauté mushrooms and green onions in 2 tablespoons butter. Pour over rabbit. Serve over rice.

*Roger's Cajun Cookbook*

# *Smothered Quail*

$1/2$ cup cubed bacon
Salt and pepper
8 quail
6 tablespoons flour
1 medium onion, chopped

$2^1/2$ cups canned chicken
   broth
Pinch thyme
$1/2$ bay leaf
1 tablespoon parsley, chopped

Sauté bacon until brown and remove from skillet. Put lightly peppered and salted quail in drippings, and when browned, remove; add flour and onion, and stir a minute. Add remaining ingredients and return bacon and quail to gravy; cover and simmer 20-30 minutes, turning occasionally until done. Add more chicken broth if needed. Serve with white rice.

*Cajun Cooking*

# Roast Wild Duck Ordinaire

*This might imply that elaborate methods of preparation and marinades are not necessary, however, proper seasoning and roasting are important for all game cooking. Bacon grease is the usual choice for this dish, but health practices encourage us to avoid saturated fats such as bacon. But for taste, bacon gives the best flavor.*

| | |
|---|---|
| 2 ducks, skinned, with backs and necks removed | 1-2 cups of water, to cover |
| ½ cup Crisco | ⅔ of duck breast |
| 3 cups onions, chopped | ½ pound tasso, (sausage) |
| 3 tablespoons minced garlic | defatted and julienned |
| 4 tablespoons Worcestershire | |

Slit breast in 3 places on each side of breast. First wash in a brine-vinegar solution for a few minutes to remove blood and offensive residues. Rinse and then dry and season with a complete seasoning (like Tony Chachere's) with fresh black pepper and garlic powder added. Seasoning should be thorough and rubbed into the meat. Breasts are to be browned throughly for 30-40 minutes. Bones sticking out and affecting the browning should be removed and breasts should be split where necessary for thorough browning.

Place duck breasts down in pot and cover with onions, garlic, Worcestershire, and water. A smoke flavor can be added with tasso. Cook on low fire for 2½ hours or until meat separates from the bones.

A gravy can be made after cooking by de-glazing the pan and adding flour to thicken.

*Cajun Cooking: A Labor of Love*

Louisiana has four million acres of waterfowl-rich marshlands which support unrivaled populations of migratory birds. You can hunt eight months of the year in Louisiana; deer, quail, dove, teal, rail, gallinule, turkey, snipe, woodcock . . . is it any wonder Teddy Roosevelt, Joseph Pulitzer and others came to Louisiana to hunt?

# Wild Ducks à la George

*Ooooh! Heaven!*

4 ducks, dressed
Tony's Creole Seasoning
4 onions, chopped
4 ribs celery, chopped
1 bell pepper, chopped
4 tablespoons oil
1 cup Burgundy wine

2 (10$\frac{1}{2}$-ounce) cans chicken
   broth
$\frac{1}{2}$ cup chopped green onions
$\frac{1}{2}$ cup chopped parsley
1 (8-ounce) can mushrooms
$\frac{1}{2}$ tablespoon all-purpose flour

Season ducks inside and out generously with Tony's Creole Seasoning. In a small bowl, mix the vegetables. Add equally to inside of each duck.

Pour oil in a large black iron pot. Brown ducks. Add wine, chicken broth, and enough water to cover ducks. Bring to a boil. Reduce heat; simmer until tender (about 3-4 hours). Remove ducks from pot. Add green onions, parsley, mushrooms, and mushroom juice thickened with a little flour. Cook 5 minutes. Add water if more gravy is needed. Yields 8 servings.

*Tony Chachere's Second Helping*

## *Grilled Duck Breasts*

8 tablespoons butter
1 tablespoon Worcestershire
sauce
1 garlic clove, finely
minced
3/4 cup thinly sliced fresh
mushrooms

6 duck breasts, removed
from bone and skinned
Salt, freshly ground black
pepper, and cayenne pepper
6 strips of bacon

Melt the butter in a saucepan and add the Worcestershire sauce, garlic, and mushrooms; cook until mushrooms become slightly soft. Remove from heat. Light a fire in the barbecue pit and allow the coals to get glowing red hot. While you're waiting, rub the duck breasts well with salt, black pepper, and cayenne. Carefully wrap each breast with a strip of bacon, securing it with toothpicks. Let them stand at room temperature. (You might want to take this time to fix a green salad with a creamy spicy dressing and some wild rice cooked with a handful of chopped roasted pecans.)

When the coals are ready, grill the breasts quickly, 3-4 minutes on each side if you like them juicy and with a little red in the meat; longer if you prefer your meat well done. Baste with the butter sauce. To serve, place the breasts on toasted slices of bread, and pour the remaining butter and mushroom sauce over each breast. You've never tasted better! Serves 2.

*Who's Your Mama, Are You Catholic,*
*and Can You Make a Roux?*

# Fried Frog Legs

| | |
|---|---|
| 1/2 cup grated onion | 1/2 teaspoon black pepper |
| 3 cloves garlic, minced | 12 frog legs |
| 1/2 teaspoon ground cloves | 1 cup flour |
| 1/4 cup mustard | 1 cup cornmeal |
| 1 tablespoon vinegar | 1 1/2 cups oil |
| 1 teaspoon salt | Lemon wedges |

Combine onion, garlic, cloves, mustard, vinegar, salt and pepper. Wash frog legs, pat dry and place in above mixture for one hour. Combine flour and cornmeal and season to taste with salt and black pepper. Remove frog legs from marinade and roll in flour-cornmeal mixture. Deep-fry frog legs in oil heated to 375°. Fry about 4 minutes on each side. Drain on paper towels and serve hot with lemon wedges around them.

*Roger's Cajun Cookbook*

# Lil' Prairie Hunting Club Deer Roast

| | |
|---|---|
| 1 deer ham roast, deboned | 3 bell peppers, chopped fine |
| 15-20 strips bacon | Seasoning to taste |
| 8 cloves garlic, chopped fine | 1 bottle hot barbecue sauce |
| 3 large onions, chopped fine | |

Slice large slits in roast and fill each slit with a strip of bacon; fill slits with garlic, onions and bell peppers. Sprinkle seasoning over roast. Roll roast and tie with cotton twine. Brown on barbecue fire on high heat. Remove roast and wrap in heavy duty tin foil so it is waterproof; before closing foil, pour barbecue sauce over roast. Cook on low fire on side of barbecue pit (do not place directly over hot coals). Cook 3 1/2 hours; do not puncture foil. Remove, slice and enjoy.

*Cajun Men Cook*

### Alligator Sauce Piquant

| | |
|---|---|
| 1 pound  alligator | 1 can tomatoes with green |
| 1/2 cup flour | chili peppers |
| 3/4 cup cooking oil | 1 can tomato sauce |
| 1 large onion, chopped | 3 cans water |
| 1 garlic pod, chopped | Salt and pepper |
| 1 small bell pepper, chopped | 1/2 cup onion tops |

Cut alligator into 1-inch cubes and season.  Set aside.  Cook flour in oil until medium brown.  Add onions; cook until onions wilt. Add garlic, bell pepper, tomatoes, tomato sauce, and 3 cans of water; cook over low flame 30 minutes.  Add meat, salt and pepper to taste, and onion tops.  Continue cooking until meat is tender.

*C'est Bon, Encore*

### Alligator Stew

| | |
|---|---|
| 2 pounds alligator meat, | 1/2 cup chopped celery |
| cut into small pieces | 1/2 cup chopped bell pepper |
| about 1/2-inch thick | 2 tablespoon minced parsley |
| 1/2 cup oil | 1 (10-ounce) can tomatoes |
| 1/2 cup chopped green onions | with chilies |
| 1/2 cup chopped onion | Salt and pepper, to taste |

Brown meat in oil; add remaining ingredients.  Cover pot; cook over medium heat for 30-40 minutes.  Serve over cooked rice. Yield: 6-8 servings.

*Cajun Cuisine*

# Meats

General Andrew Jackson tips his hat in welcome to the many visitors to Jackson Square. The historic St. Louis Cathedral is in the background. New Orleans.

# Mrs. Maestri's Meatballs and Marinara Sauce

*These meatballs are guaranteed to be the most tender, the most divine you have ever eaten.*

## MEATBALLS:

4 or 5 green onions, tops and bottoms
2 or 3 ribs celery
1 large onion
Handful of fresh parsley
1/2 teaspoon dried thyme
1 1/2 pounds ground chuck
1/4 teaspoon Beau Monde (if available)

Salt, pepper, red pepper, and anise seed to taste
1/2 large loaf stale French bread
2 eggs
1 large tablespoon grated Italian (Romano) cheese
Olive oil for cooking

Grind green onions, celery, onion, parsley, and thyme twice. This is the secret to the lightness of these meatballs. Mix with chuck and add Beau Monde, salt, peppers, and anise. Break stale French bread into small chunks, put in colander, and sprinkle with water. Press out as much water as possible and add to meat mixture with eggs and cheese. Squeeze through fingers until well mixed. Chill for 35-45 minutes.

Shape into golf ball-sized balls and brown quickly in olive oil in heavy skillet. Olive oil should be up about 2 - 2 1/2 inches on side of skillet. Roll meatballs around to brown evenly. I usually have about 4 going at one time. Remove from oil as they brown and drain on paper towels. When all are done, add to marinara sauce; cook 30 minutes more. Serve with sauce over spaghetti.

## MARINARA SAUCE:

1 large onion, chopped
1 green pepper, diced
2 tablespoons olive oil
1 28-ounce can Progresso crushed tomatoes with purée
2 cans boiling water
1 (12-ounce) can Progresso tomato paste
Salt, pepper, Red pepper, anise

1/2 teaspoon Beau Monde
1 can Ro-Tel tomatoes and green chilies
1 teaspoon dried oregano
3 cloves garlic, crushed
2 ribs celery, chopped
Handful parsley, chopped
1/2 cup sauterne

CONTINUED

Sauté onion and pepper in oil in large, heavy pot until tender. Do not let onions brown. Add all remaining ingredients except wine, and cover. Cook slowly for about 1 - 1½ hours, adding water as needed. I sometimes add another can of tomatoes. Just taste as you go along and doctor it up as you see fit. Add the wine last 15 or 20 minutes. Yield: 18-20 golf ball-sized meatballs, 2 quarts of sauce.

*Too Good to be True*

# Meat Balls and Spaghetti

*A very old Italian recipe.*

1½ pounds ground chuck
1 cup Italian grated cheese
8 small crackers (soaked in water and squeezed)
3 large eggs
2 teaspoons salt
1 teaspoon pepper
2 dashes Tabasco
1 large bunch green onions

½ cup olive oil
2 (8-ounce) cans tomato purée
2 pints water
2 large cloves garlic, minced
1 cup parsley, chopped fine
1 teaspoon salt
½ teaspoon red pepper
1 teaspoon oregano

Combine first 7 ingredients. Make into small meat balls—about 1½ inches in diameter. Brown meat balls and onions in olive oil. Remove meat; add tomato purée and water. Add garlic, parsley, and seasonings to taste. Cook one hour or until reduced to about one half. Add meat balls. Simmer one hour. Serve over cooked, drained and buttered spaghetti. Pass additional cheese.

*A Cook's Tour of Shreveport*

 A Fais Do-Do is a Cajun party with music, dancing, and plenty of food. Lagniappe is a little something extra.

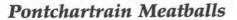

# Pontchartrain Meatballs

**MEATBALLS:**

2 pounds ground pork
2 (15-ounce) cans water
   chestnuts, coarsely chopped
2 cloves garlic, crushed
4 eggs
2 teaspoons salt

1 cup bread crumbs,
   unseasoned
2 tablespoons soy sauce
1 teaspoon MSG
Cornstarch
Peanut oil for frying

In large bowl, mix pork, water chestnuts, garlic, eggs, salt, crumbs, soy sauce, and MSG. Keeping your hands always moist with water, form into small balls. Lay out, as formed, onto large sheet. After all are formed, coat 10-12 meatballs with sifted cornstarch, dusting or shaking off excess, and fry immediately in hot oil. Do not coat all meatballs with cornstarch before beginning the frying process. Coat only as many as you can comfortably fry at one time (otherwise they will absorb too much cornstarch). Set aside.

**SAUCE:**

4 tablespoons peanut oil
2 cups chicken stock (14-
   ounce can equals 2 cups)
1 cup sugar

1 cup vinegar
4 tablespoons cornstarch
1 cup pineapple juice
1 tablespoon soy sauce

In saucepan mix oil, chicken stock, sugar, vinegar, cornstarch mixed with pineapple juice and soy sauce. Heat on low for 3 minutes, stirring constantly. Add meatballs and cook on low about 30 minutes. Serve hot in chafing dish with toothpicks. (Also good as main dish served over rice.) Yield: 150 meatballs.

*LaBonne Cuisine Lagniappe*

# Meat Loaf

1½ pounds ground meat
1 onion, chopped
2 stalks celery, chopped
2 cloves garlic, minced
1 envelope dry onion soup
½ cup evaporated milk
½ cup bread crumbs

1 egg
Salt, white pepper, red pepper
2 tablespoons butter
1 small can tomato sauce
1 teaspoon Worcestershire sauce
2 dashes Tabasco

Combine meat, onion, celery, garlic, and dry onion soup. Mix well and add milk, bread crumbs, egg, and seasonings to taste. Shape into loaf and place in baking dish. Melt butter and add tomato sauce, Worcestershire sauce and Tabasco sauce. Simmer 5 minutes. Pour this over loaf and bake uncovered at 350° for one hour.

*Roger's Cajun Cookbook*

# Mexican Meat Loaf

1 pound ground turkey
1 (15-ounce) can tomato
  sauce, divided
⅓ cup crushed tortilla
  chips
¼ cup chopped onion

2 tablespoons chopped green
  peppers
2 tablespoons chili powder
½ teaspoon cumin
¼ teaspoon garlic powder

Combine ingredients, reserving one cup tomato sauce. Shape into meat loaf, place in a 9 x 5-inch loaf pan. Bake in 350° oven 45-50 minutes. Heat reserved tomato sauce and serve with meat loaf. Yield: 6 servings.

Cal 228; Chol 48mg; Sat Fat 1gm; Fat 12gm; Sod 130mg; Pro 20gm; Cho 10gm.

*Just For Kids*

With 64 rooms, Nottoway Plantation is the largest plantation in the South. Emily Randolph, the wife of Nottoway's builder, confronted Union troops alone and kept them from ransacking her family's home on the Mississippi River between Baton Rouge and New Orleans.

# *Natchitoches Meat Pie*

*Be sure to make the roux. It makes all the difference in this recipe.*

**FILLING:**

| | |
|---|---|
| 2 tablespoons flour | 1/2 pound ground beef |
| 1 tablespoon oil | 1/2 pound ground pork |
| 2 large onions, chopped | 3 tablespoons parsley, chopped |
| 6 green onions, chopped | Salt and pepper to taste |

Make a roux with flour and oil. Add all the other ingredients; salt and pepper to taste and cook thoroughly. Cool in refrigerator before making pies.

**PASTRY:**

| | |
|---|---|
| 4 cups plain flour | 1 1/2 teaspoons salt |
| 1/2 cup Crisco, melted | 2 eggs, beaten |
| 2 teaspoons baking powder | Milk to make stiff dough |

Mix all the preceding ingredients in a large bowl; add enough flour to make the dough stiff. Turn out on floured surface. Roll and cut out circles the size of a saucer. Place chilled meat on half the circle; fold over and dampen edges and crimp with a fork. Fry pies in deep vegetable shortening until golden brown, turning once.

*Recipes from Bayou Pierre Country*

# Cajun Meat Pies

*If you don't have time to make the pastry, pre-made egg roll wrappers work well, but your own home made pastry is much better.*

**PASTRY:**

2¹/₂ cups all-purpose flour
1 teaspoon sugar
1 teaspoon salt

¹/₂ cup shortening
¹/₂ cup milk

In a bowl combine flour, sugar, and salt. Pour into a food processor with the blade attachment. Add shortening in small chunks while processor is on. Mix well until flour and shortening form pea-sized balls, then add milk a little at a time until dough forms together. Pour dough out on floured sheet and roll out to ¹/₁₆-inch thick. Cut out 4-inch circles. Lightly flour both sides and reserve.

**GROUND BEEF FILLING:**

¹/₂ cup chopped bell pepper
¹/₂ cup chopped yellow onion
¹/₂ cup chopped green onion
3 tablespoons bacon fat
1 tablespoon garlic, minced
2 tablespoons parsley flakes

1 teaspoon cayenne
1 teaspoon salt
¹/₂ teaspoon black pepper
¹/₂ pound lean ground beef
2 small eggs, beaten

Add finely chopped pepper and onions to melted fat in skillet. Add everything except beef and eggs and cook for 5 minutes. Add beef and brown. Drain in a colander and let cool before making pies. Place 2 tablespoons filling in center circle of pastry. Moisten ends of circle with egg; fold over to form a half circle and press to seal (a fork works well). Deep fry at 350° until brown. Drain on paper towel. Serve.

**Note:** You can bake in a preheated 350° oven for about 8 minutes; turn over and bake other side 8 minutes or until brown. Makes about 25 (4-inch) pies.

*'Dat Little Cajun Cookbook*

## Taco Pie

1 pound ground beef
1/2 cup chopped onion
1 envelope taco seasoning
    mix
1 envelope chili mix
1 can chopped green chilies

1 1/4 cups milk
3/4 cup Bisquick
3 eggs
2 tomatoes, sliced
1 cup shredded Monterey Jack
    cheese

Sauté ground beef. Add the next 4 ingredients and sauté for a few minutes. Pour into greased baking dish. Blend milk, Bisquick, and eggs together. Pour over ground beef mixture and bake at 400° for 25 minutes. Slice tomatoes on top and sprinkle with cheese. Place in oven for 10 minutes.

*CDA Angelic Treats*

## Biscuit Pie

1 1/2 cans Hungry Jack Biscuits
Parmesan cheese, grated
1 pound mozzarella cheese,
    sliced
1 1/2 pounds ground beef
1 medium onion, chopped
1 medium bell pepper, chopped

1 rib celery, chopped
3 garlic buds, minced
1 package spaghetti sauce mix
1 small can tomato paste
Salt and pepper to taste
1 1/2 - 2 cans water

Use a 13 x 9-inch pan. Press biscuits in the bottom of pan to form a crust. Sprinkle with Parmesan cheese. Place 1/2 of mozzarella cheese on top of Parmesan cheese. Brown ground beef, onion, pepper, celery, and garlic. Add spaghetti sauce mix, tomato paste, seasonings, and water; cook until meat is cooked. Spoon meat mixture on top of cheese in pan. Top with remaining mozzarella cheese slices. Bake at 400° for 15 minutes.

*Sisters' Secrets*

 Rayne is called the "Frog Capital of the World." Each September the town goes "frog-wild" for its Frog Festival.

## *Pistolettes*

2 pounds ground hamburger
  meat and seasoning
2 boxes broccoli-rice
  casserole mix

Velveeta cheese (1 pound or
  as much as desired)
1 can Ro-Tel tomatoes (optional)
2 packages pistolettes

Brown hamburger meat (with onion, optional). Prepare broccoli-rice casserole mix as directed on box. Cut Velveeta into small pieces. Drain hamburger meat. Add cheese and broccoli-rice mixture in large pan until cheese melts. Add Ro-Tel tomatoes if desired and mix well. Take pistolettes and cut off end and hollow out inside. Fill each pistolette with the above mixture and roll in butter and garlic salt. Put in oven and brown at 350° for approximately 15-20 minutes.

*Feast of Goodness*

## *Roger's Cajun Burger*

1 pound extra lean ground
  round steak
1 pound ground turkey
1 pound crawfish tails (boiled,
  peeled, and coarsely chopped)
1/2 onion, chopped

1 teaspoon Worcestershire sauce
1/2 teaspoon Louisiana hot
  sauce
1/4 teaspoon garlic powder
1/4 teaspoon white pepper

Mix ingredients and form into patties.

**BASTING SAUCE:**
1 cup Bar-B-Que sauce
1 stick butter substitute
1 teaspoon Worcestershire
  sauce

1/4 teaspoon garlic powder
1/4 teaspoon white pepper

Mix ingredients and simmer for 2-3 minutes.

Place burgers over hot coals. Add wet hickory chips to coals for added smoked flavor. Baste burgers 2-3 times.

**Note:** Use crawfish tails left over after a crawfish boil.

*Roger's Lite Cajun Cookbook*

## Chili

*This can all be done way ahead of time—it gets better after setting for a while.*

3 pounds coarse ground
  chuck
10 garlic cloves, finely
  chopped
1 quart plus 1 cup water
5 tablespoons chili powder
3 teaspoons salt
1 teaspoon cumin

1 teaspoon oregano
1/2 teaspoon red pepper
1 tablespoon sugar
4 tablespoons paprika
2 cans red kidney beans
  (optional)
3 tablespoons flour
6 tablespoons cornmeal

Brown ground chuck. Add garlic and 1 quart of water; cover and simmer for 1 1/2 hours. Add all spices and simmer for 30 minutes more, covered. (If beans are used, add them at this time.) Mix flour, cornmeal, and one cup water, and add to preceding mixture after bringing it to a boil; cook for about 10 more minutes. Serving size: 6-8.

*Family Favorites*

## Blue Ribbon Chili

2 pounds chili ground
  meat (brown just
  to get red out)
1 large onion, chopped
1 large bell pepper,
  chopped
3 ribs celery, chopped
1 can Ro-Tel tomatoes, diced
3 heaping tablespoon chili
  powder

1 heaping tablespoons paprika
2 teaspoons Accent
1 can tomato sauce
1 can water or more
1 teaspoon cayenne pepper
1 teaspoon salt
3 cans cream-style red
  kidney beans

Cook all but beans together with meat for about 45 minutes. Add the kidney beans and cook another 15 minutes.

*A Shower of Roses*

## Stromboli

1 pound ground meat
1 can tomato sauce
2 cans croissant rolls

1 package Cheddar cheese,
  shredded
1 package mozzarella cheese,
  shredded

Brown ground meat and season to taste. Drain grease, then add tomato sauce. Cook for about 20 minutes or until brown.

Grease 9 x 13-inch pan and lay one can of croissants flat on the bottom of the pan. Layer ground meat, Cheddar cheese, and mozzarella cheese (in that order) on top of croissants. Lay the remaining can of croissants flat on top of the cheese and pinch edges together. Bake in oven 10-15 minutes or until croissants are golden brown. (Check croissant can for oven temperature.)

*St. Philomena School 125th Anniversary*

## Sausage Roll

1 loaf frozen bread
  dough
1/4 cup chopped onion
1/4 cup chopped green
  pepper

1/2 cup fresh sliced
  mushrooms
1 pound ground turkey
  sausage
8 ounces shredded lite
  Cheddar or Colby cheese

Thaw bread dough at room temperature 1 1/2 - 2 hours. Sauté onion, green pepper, and mushrooms in cooking spray until tender; set aside. Brown turkey sausage and drain; set aside. Roll out bread dough to 1/4-inch thickness. Mix sausage with vegetable mixture. Spread this mixture over dough. Sprinkle shredded cheese over meat mixture. Roll up into a jellyroll. Spray with cooking spray and bake at 350° for 20-30 minutes. Let stand 10 minutes before slicing. Yield: 8 servings.

Cal 244; Chol 32mg; Sat Fat 3gm; Fat 8gm; Sod 618; Pro 16gm; Cho 26gm; Exchanges: 2 meat, 1 bread, 1 fat.

*Just For Kids*

## *Chalupa Casserole*

1 pound ground chuck
1 small onion, chopped
1 (23-ounce) can Ranch-
style beans
1 (15-ounce) can tomatoes

1 teaspoon or more hot sauce
1 tablespoon chili powder
$1/2$ teaspoon pepper
Tortilla chips
1 cup shredded cheese

Crumble ground beef into plastic colander over mixing bowl. Mix in the chopped onion. Microwave on high for 5 minutes, stirring after $2^1/2$ minutes. Discard drippings. Blend Ranch-style beans, can of tomatoes, hot sauce, chili powder, and pepper in processor. Add to meat and onion; mix well. Line 12 x 8 x 2-inch baking dish with tortilla chips. Pour mixture over chips. Cover and microwave on roast for 12-14 minutes or until hot. Sprinkle with cheese. Let stand, covered, 5 minutes or until cheese melts. This can be put together ahead of time (except for the cheese), and refrigerated or frozen and then microwaved.

*Feast of Goodness*

## *Broccoli or Spinach Ground Meat Casserole*

2 (10-ounce) packages frozen
broccoli, cooked and drained
1 (4-ounce) can mushroom pieces
1 pound ground meat (browned
and drained of fat)
1 ($10^3/4$-ounce) can cream of
celery soup

1 (8-ounce) carton sour cream
$1/4$ cup minced onion
Garlic salt and pepper to taste
8 ounces mozzarella cheese,
grated

Combine everything but cheese. Place in casserole and top with cheese. Heat in preheated 350° oven until cheese melts and casserole is bubbly (30-45 minutes).

**Note:** 2 (10-ounce) packages of frozen spinach may be substituted.

*Cooking New Orleans Style!*

## Nina's Best Brisket

1 (12-14-pound) brisket,
  trimmed
1 large bottle Worcestershire
  sauce

1 large bottle hot sauce

Place brisket in a large deep pan. Pour Worcestershire and hot sauce over brisket. Cover with foil. Bake at 400° for 2 hours. then lower to 350° for 1½ - 2 hours more.

*A Shower of Roses*

## Best Brisket Ever

*I have never tasted meat like this, and the gravy is good enough to drink. Try it! You won't be disappointed. This is a "must do" recipe.*

1 (4 to 5-pound) brisket
  (point end), trimmed
Tony Chachere's Creole
  Seasoning
Cracked black pepper

Garlic powder
1 (10¾-ounce) can cream of
  mushroom soup
1 (10¾-ounce) can French onion
  soup

Heavily season the brisket on both sides. Use lots of pepper and garlic powder. Do not use salt because there is sufficient salt in Tony's or the seasoning salt you will use. Spoon out the mushroom soup into a heavy, oven-proof cooking utensil with tightly fitting lid. Place seasoned brisket, fat-side-up, on flat rack so it won't be directly on the bottom of whatever you are using. Place rack with the brisket on top of soup. Spoon a can of French onion soup over and around the brisket. Cook covered in preheated, 350° oven for one hour. Lower temperature to 200° and continue to cook covered for 3 more hours. Do not remove cover during cooking. Cool. Slice cross grain with electric knife. Absolutely to die for! The gravy is so good you will want to comb it through your hair. For party buffet, serves 20-25; for family, serves 8.

**Note:** May add 1 can consomme for additional gravy.

*Too Good to be True*

## *Pot Roast*

4 green onion tops,
   chopped fine
1 onion, chopped fine
1 stalk celery, chopped fine
5 cloves garlic, chopped fine
Salt and pepper to taste

1 tablespoon Worcestershire
   sauce
1 (6 to 8-pound) beef or pork
   roast
6 Irish potatoes

GRAVY MIX:
1 large onion, chopped
2 stalks celery, chopped

Green onion tops, chopped

Mix onion tops, onion, celery, garlic, salt, pepper, and Worcestershire sauce. Make deep slits in roast and stuff mixture into slits until all mixture has been used. Let set in refrigerator overnight. Put roast in roasting pan. Brown at 350°. Turn meat occasionally, adding a little water from time to time as needed. When roast is a deep dark brown all around, add water to fill half of your pan. Cover and let cook for about 2 hours or until meat is cooked. Add potatoes and vegetables for gravy, and let cook with roast until done. When serving, cut meat in thin slices and put potatoes around the roast. Makes a pretty dish.

*Nun Better*

# Blackened Rib Eye

*Because the cooking process is very fast in this recipe, thickness is the only way to achieve the desired stage of cooking. Use the suggested chart below to choose the correct thickness of your steak. Be sure to have great ventilation before cooking. I suggest you do this outside if possible, since butter will smoke and pop during the cooking process.*

| | |
|---|---|
| Up to $^1/_4$-inch=Well done | Up to $^5/_8$-inch=Medium rare done |
| Up to $^3/_8$-inch=Medium well done | Up to $^3/_4$-inch=Rare done |
| Up to $^1/_2$-inch=Medium done | Up to 1-inch=Very rare done |

| | |
|---|---|
| **2 rib eye steaks, cut to desired thickness** | **1$^1/_2$ teaspoons paprika** |
| | **1$^1/_2$ teaspoons salt** |
| **1 tablespoon cayenne pepper** | **1$^1/_2$ teaspoons black pepper** |
| **1 tablespoon whole oregano** | **$^1/_4$ cup butter** |
| **1$^1/_2$ teaspoons crushed rosemary** | |

Clean steaks and pat dry. Mix cayenne pepper, oregano, rosemary, paprika, salt and black pepper in a bowl until completely blended. Next sprinkle mixture over both sides of the steak until completely coated. Heat skillet to hot and add 2 tablespoons butter to the pan. Butter will smoke and pop and turn slightly brown. Lift the skillet off the fire and move the butter around until almost melted. Next, place back on fire and as soon as the butter begins to smoke again, place both steaks in the butter for 60 seconds each side. Remove steaks from pan and add remaining butter, scraping the bottom as you stir in the butter. As soon as the butter is melted, pour over each steak and serve.

***'Dat Little New Orleans Creole Cookbook***

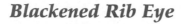

In 1850, two-thirds of America's millionaires were planters on the Great River Road between Natchez and New Orleans. St. Francisville's grandest homes and antebellum gardens stand tribute to this great wealth. Rosedown has 85% of its original furnishings; parts of the mini-series "North and South" were filmed at Greenwood; The Myrtles is the most haunted house in America; and Oakley House was where John James Audubon began work on his famous *Birds of America*.

## Grillades

4 pounds beef/veal rounds,
  1/2-inch thick
1/2 cup bacon drippings
1/2 cup flour
1 cup chopped onions
2 cups chopped green onions
3/4 cup chopped celery
1 1/2 cups chopped green
  peppers
2 cloves garlic, minced
2 cups chopped tomatoes

1/2 teaspoon tarragon (optional)
2/3 teaspoon thyme
1 cup water
1 cup red wine
3 teaspoons salt
1/2 teaspoon black pepper
2 bay leaves
1/2 teaspoon Tabasco
2 tablespoons Worcestershire
  sauce
3 tablespoons chopped parsley

Remove fat from meat. Cut meat into serving-size pieces. Pound to 1/4-inch thick. In a Dutch oven brown meat well in 4 tablespoons bacon grease. As meat browns, remove to warm plate. To Dutch oven add 4 tablespoons bacon grease and flour. Stir and cook to make a dark brown roux. Add onions, green onions, celery, green peppers, garlic, and sauté until limp. Add tomatoes, tarragon, thyme, and cook for 3 minutes. Add water and wine. Stir well for several minutes; return meat; add salt, pepper, bay leaves, Tabasco, and Worcestershire. Lower heat, stir, and continue cooking. If veal rounds are used, simmer covered approximately one hour. If beef rounds are used, simmer covered approximately 2 hours. Remove bay leaves. Stir in parsley, cool; let the grillades sit several hours or overnight in refrigerator.

More liquid may be added. Grillades should be very tender. Heat and serve over grits or rice.

*The Plantation Cookbook*

# Grilled Pork Loin with Honey Sauce

3/4 cup margarine
1 cup honey
1 cup Worcestershire sauce
1/2 cup Italian dressing
1/4 cup lemon juice
3 tablespoons mustard
2 tablespoons brown sugar

2 teaspoons garlic salt
1 1/2 teaspoons celery salt
1 1/2 teaspoons onion powder
1 teaspoon pepper
1 teaspoon liquid smoke
3-4 pound split pork loin

Melt margarine in saucepan. Add remaining ingredients, except loin, to make sauce. Bring to boil. Reduce heat and simmer 2 minutes.

Place loin on grill over medium-high heat. Sear both sides. Baste thoroughly with sauce. Turn and baste every 15 minutes until cooked (approximately 2 1/2 hours. Thicker cuts will require longer cooking time.) Serves 8.

*Dinner on the Ground*

# Grilled Pork Tenderloin

*When a man cooks, who measures!*

1 (8-ounce) jar Caesar salad dressing
Cavender's Greek seasoning
Garlic salt

Freshly ground black pepper
Hot pepper sauce
1 1/2 pounds pork tenderloin

For marinade, pour Caesar salad dressing, 10 "shakes" of Greek seasoning, 8 "shakes" of garlic salt, and 15 "seconds" of freshly ground black pepper into a bowl and stir. Add hot pepper sauce to taste. Pour the marinade over pork tenderloin and place in refrigerator 4-6 hours. Place on grill, cover, and cook until slightly blackened on all sides, about 30 minutes. Each time you rotate tenderloin, dip it in the marinade. This should be served well-done. Remove from grill and let tenderloin cool for 10-15 minutes. Slice in 1/4 to 1/2-inch slices. Makes 4 servings. As cocktail fare, allow 2 ounces meat per person.

*Celebrations on the Bayou*

## Pork Roast

¹/₄ cup finely chopped onion
4 cloves garlic, finely chopped
1 teaspoon salt
¹/₂ teaspoon pepper

1 (4-pound) pork roast
¹/₄ cup oil
2 cups water
Salt and pepper to taste

Combine chopped onion and garlic in a small dish. Season with salt and pepper. Cut slit in the middle of roast and stuff all the onion mixture inside. Season outside of roast with salt and pepper. Heat the oil in a heavy roasting pot. Place the roast in the pot. Brown all sides, adding small amounts of water occasionally. After roast is browned on all sides, add the rest of the water and cover. Cook on low heat about 3 hours. This also makes a wonderful gravy. Serve over rice. Serves 6-8.

**Note:** May cook beef roast in this same manner.

*Classic Cajun*

## Aunt Noonie's Ham Pie

*This one helped make my aunt Noonie very popular.*

1 cup chopped onion
¹/₂ cup chopped celery
¹/₂ cup chopped bell pepper
1 small can mushrooms,
  drained
4 tablespoons butter
2 teaspoons vegetable oil

4 tablespoons flour
2 cups milk
1 cup cubed ham
¹/₂ teaspoon salt
¹/₄ teaspoon black pepper
¹/₂ teaspoon Tabasco sauce
2 baked (9-inch) pie crusts

Sauté vegetables and mushrooms in butter and oil, over medium heat, until vegetables are soft. Blend flour into milk with a wire whisk. Add flour-milk, ham, salt, black pepper, and Tabasco. Stirring constantly, continue to cook until mixture becomes very, very thick (approximately 12 minutes). Pour into baked pastry shells and serve hot. (Pastry shells can be baked in advance; they do not have to be hot.) Serves 4-6 hungry hogs!

*The Hungry Hog*

## Tourtiere
### (Pork Pie)

2 pounds ground lean pork
1/2 cup chopped onion
1 cup chopped celery
1 garlic clove, crushed
1/4 cup chopped parsley
1 teaspoon salt
1/4 teaspoon leaf marjoram,
   crushed

1/4 teaspoon ground cloves
1/4 teaspoon ground mace
1/2 teaspoon ground pepper
2 tablespoons flour
2 beef bouillon cubes
1 cup hot water
Pastry for a 2-crust pie, unbaked
   (can use frozen pie shells)

Sauté pork, onion, celery, and garlic in a large skillet until pork is brown and vegetables are tender. Stir in parsley, salt, marjoram, cloves, mace, and pepper; cover and simmer over low heat for 30 minutes. Drain excess fat from skillet; blend flour into meat mixture. Add bouillon cubes dissolved in hot water.

Return to heat and bring mixture to a boil; simmer for one minute, stirring constantly. Remove from heat and set aside to cool. Pile meat mixture in pie shell; top with other shell, seal and flute edges. (Brush with egg, if desired.) Bake at 400° for 45 minutes or until golden brown. Can be eaten warm or cold. Makes 1 (9-inch) pie. Serves 6.

*The Top 100 Cajun Recipes*

## Pork Dumplings

1/4 cup shortening
1 teaspoon salt
1/4 teaspoon soda
Pepper to taste

3 cups plain flour
1-2 cups broth, cooled and
   seasoned
Pork*

Work shortening, salt, soda, pepper, and flour together. Add broth until dough is sticky. Pour out on a large piece of wax paper which has been generously floured. Roll out, cut in strips and drop into hot broth. Boil in broth about 20 minutes. Add meat* (pork neckbones or any kind of fresh pork that has been cooked and deboned).

*Fiftieth Anniversary Cookbook*

## *J & H Old Bethany Barbecue Sauce*

1 medium onion, chopped
1 teaspoon salt
1 teaspoon paprika
1 teaspoon red pepper
  (optional)
1 teaspoon chili powder
1/4 teaspoon black pepper

4 tablespoons brown sugar
1/4 teaspoon ground cloves
1 (8-ounce) can tomato sauce
4 garlic buttons, chopped
4 tablespoons horseradish
1/2 cup apple cider vinegar

Mix all ingredients in a saucepan and cook 10-15 minutes. Pour through strainer and keep refrigerated. This sauce can be used on beef, pork, sausage, or chicken. This is a table sauce; do not use during cooking.

*Feast of Goodness*

Tabasco® Pepper Sauce was first produced by Edmund McIlhenny from capsicum pepper plants growing on Avery Island in the post Civil War era. Today the same recipe is followed closely at the Tabasco Pepper Sauce Factory, where tours are available.

# Cakes

The Pentagon Barracks along the Mississippi River in Baton Rouge was constructed
in 1823-24 as housing for a US Army garrison. It later was the original site of LSU,
and is now a history museum and offices of the Louisiana Lieutenant Governor.

## *Creamy Coconut Torte*

*It's really worth the wait.*

| | |
|---|---|
| 1 package yellow cake mix | 1 teaspoon vanilla |
| 1 (8-ounce) cream cheese, softened | 1 teaspoon salt |
| | 1 pound powdered sugar |
| 1 cup margarine, softened | 1 cup flake coconut |

Cook cake as directed on cake mix package. You will have 2 layers. When layers are cooled, cut layers in halves with fluted bread knife to make 4 layers. Make creamy filling by mixing softened cream cheese, margarine, vanilla, salt, and powdered sugar. When this is mixed until creamy, fold in flake coconut. Put one cake layer on cake plate and cover generously with creamy filling. Repeat until all layers are stacked, spreading last of creamy filling on top of torte. Place in airtight container for 2 days before serving.

**Recipes from Bayou Pierre Country**

# *Quickie Italian Cream Cake*

*Outstanding!  This is too good and too easy to be true.*

1 (18¼-ounce) package reduced
 fat white cake mix
1 cup low-fat buttermilk
2 large egg whites
1 large egg
¼ cup canola oil

3 tablespoons light brown
 sugar
¼ cup flaked coconut
2 tablespoons chopped pecans
Cream Cheese Frosting

Preheat the oven to 350°.  Coat a 13 x 9 x 2-inch pan with non-stick cooking spray and dust with flour.  In a large mixing bowl, combine the cake mix, buttermilk, egg whites, egg, and oil, beating until well mixed.  In a small mixing bowl, combine the brown sugar, coconut, and pecans together; set aside.  Spread half the batter in the bottom of the pan, sprinkle with the brown sugar mixture, and carefully top with the remaining batter, spreading it out.  Bake for 30 minutes, or until a toothpick inserted in the center comes out clean.  Let cool and spread with the Cream Cheese Frosting.  Makes 28 servings.

**CREAM CHEESE FROSTING:**

1 (8-ounce) package fat-free
 cream cheese, softened
2 tablespoons light stick
 margarine

1 (16-ounce) box confectioners'
 sugar
1 teaspoon vanilla extract

In a mixing bowl, beat the cream cheese and margarine together.  Blend in the sugar, mixing well.  Add the vanilla, mixing well again.

Cal 185: Fat 4.4g; Cal from Fat 21.5%; Sat Fat 1g; Prot 2.8g; Carbo 34g; Sod 190g; Chol 9mg.

*Trim & Terrific One-Dish Favorites*

 Louisiana is the only state in the union that is based on the Napoleonic Code.

## *Cajun Cake*

**CAKE:**

1 (15½-ounce) can crushed pineapple
½ cup softened butter or margarine
1½ cups sugar
2 eggs
2 cups all-purpose flour
2 teaspoons baking powder
½ teaspoon baking soda
¼ teaspoon salt

Drain pineapple, reserving ½ cup juice. Set aside. Cream ½ cup softened butter, gradually add 1½ cups sugar, beating well at medium speed of an electric mixer. Add eggs, one at a time, beating well after each addition. Combine flour, baking powder, soda, and salt; add to creamed mixture alternately with reserved juice, beginning and ending with flour mixture. Mix just until blended after each addition. Stir in crushed pineapple. Pour batter into a greased and floured 10-inch bundt pan. Bake at 350° for 50 minutes or until wooden pick inserted in center comes out clean. Cool in pan 10 minutes; remove from pan and place on serving plate.

**TOPPING:**

¼ cup butter or margarine
½ cup sugar
⅓ cup evaporated milk
½ cup flaked coconut (toasted if desired)
½ cup chopped pecans
½ teaspoon vanilla extract
Toasted flaked coconut (optional garnish)
Pineapple slices (optional garnish)
Fresh pineapple leaves (optional garnish)

Combine ¼ cup butter and next 4 ingredients in small saucepan. Bring to a boil; reduce heat, simmer for 3 minutes. Stir in vanilla. Spoon on top of warm cake. Cool. Sprinkle with toasted coconut and garnish with pineapple slices and fresh leaves.

*Tell Me More*

## Ugly Cake

1 box yellow cake mix      1 stick butter
1 box powdered sugar      1 (8-ounce) package cream cheese

Mix cake mix as directed. Pour into an oblong pan. Combine sugar, melted butter, and cream cheese. Pour this mixture over cake mix and stir with knife to cut into batter just a few swirls.

*Czech-Out Cajun Cooking*

## So-Good Cake

1 (2-layer) package yellow      1 (1-pound) package confectioners'
    cake mix      sugar
1 egg      1 (8-ounce) package cream
1/2 cup melted butter      cheese, softened
1 cup chopped pecans      2 eggs

Combine the cake mix, 1 egg, and butter in a medium bowl, mixing well. Stir in the pecans. Press evenly over the bottom and up the sides of a greased 9 x 13-inch cake pan. Beat the confectioners' sugar, cream cheese, and 2 eggs at medium speed in a mixer bowl until smooth. Pour into the prepared pan. Bake at 350° for 30-35 minutes or until the top is light brown; the center will remain creamy. Cool completely. Cut into squares. Yield: 15 servings.

*Louisiana Temptations*

## Apple Cake

4-5 cups diced cooking
   apples
2 eggs, beaten
2 cups sugar
2 teaspoons cinnamon

1/2 cup oil
1 cup coarsely chopped nuts
2 cups flour
2 teaspoons soda
3/4 teaspoon salt

Place diced apples in a large bowl. Over these break the eggs and add sugar, cinnamon, oil, and nuts. Mix thoroughly with a fork. Sift the remaining dry ingredients together and stir into the apple mixture. Press into a 9 x 13-inch buttered and floured pan. Bake 55 minutes in a preheated 350° oven. Delicious served plain or with a lemon sauce.

*Cooking New Orleans Style!*

## Fresh Apple Cake

3 cups plain flour
1/2 teaspoon salt
1 1/2 teaspoons baking soda
2 teaspoons nutmeg
2 tablespoons cinnamon
2 cups sugar

2 eggs
1 1/2 cups Wesson oil
2 teaspoons vanilla
3 cups peeled and chopped
   apples
1 cup chopped pecans

Sift flour, salt, soda, and spices in bowl. Mix in sugar. Make a hole and put eggs and oil in; mix. Add vanilla, apples and nuts. Blend well. Bake in greased, floured bundt or tube pan at 300° for 1 hour and 15 minutes. Serve with Hot Buttered Rum Sauce.

**HOT BUTTERED RUM SAUCE:**

1 cup sugar
1/2 cup butter or margarine

1 cup light cream
1 teaspoon rum extract

Combine sugar, butter, and cream in saucepan. Mix well. Heat over low heat, stirring occsionally until hot. Stir in rum flavoring. Serve over Apple Cake.

*L' Heritage Du Bayou Lafourche*

## Apple Kuchen

1 (18.5-ounce) box yellow
   cake mix
1/2 cup butter
1 (21-ounce) can apple pie
   filling

1/2 cup sugar
1 teaspoon cinnamon

Cut the butter into the cake mix. Spread this into a greased 9 x 13-inch pan, pressing it with a clenched fist so that it goes up the sides of the pan by one inch. This will serve as a crust. Bake at 350° for 10 minutes. Remove this from the oven and spread the apple pie filling all over the crust. Mix the sugar and cinnamon and sprinkle this all over the apples. Bake an additional 20 minutes at 350°.

*Czech-Out Cajun Cooking*

## Carrot Cake
### (Light Recipe)

**CAKE:**

2 eggs
2 cups sugar
1 1/2 cups applesauce
2 cups all-purpose flour

2 teaspoons baking soda
2 teaspoons cinnamon
1 teaspoon salt
3 cups shredded carrots

Beat eggs, sugar, and applesauce. Mix well. Mix and add dry ingredients to mixture. Add shredded carrots. Mix well and pour into 13 x 9-inch cake pan. Bake at 350° for 40 minutes. Cool on cake rack. Ice with cream cheese icing.

**ICING:**

3 1/2 cups confectioners'
   sugar
4 ounces cream cheese

2 teaspoons vanilla
2 tablespoons skim milk

Cream powdered sugar and cream cheese. Add vanilla and skim milk. Mix well. Spread on cool cake. Yield: 12 servings.

Cal 195; Chol 48mg; Sat Fat 1gm; Fat 3gm; Sod 231mg; Dietary Fiber 1gm; Exchanges: Not acceptable for diabetics.

*Gone with the Fat*

## Fig Cake

| | |
|---|---|
| 2 cups flour | 2 cups mashed figs |
| 2 cups sugar | 2 teaspoons cinnamon |
| 2/3 cup cooking oil | 1/2 teaspoon salt |
| 4 eggs, beaten | 2 teaspoons soda |
| 1 teaspoon vanilla | 1 cup chopped pecans |

Mix together and place in greased 11 x 16-inch pan. Bake at 350° for about 25-30 minutes.

*Family Favorites*

## Orange Slice Cake

| | |
|---|---|
| 1 cup butter or margarine | 1 pound chopped dates |
| 2 cups sugar | 1 pound orange candy slices, |
| 4 eggs |    chopped |
| 1 teaspoon soda | 2 cups chopped nuts |
| 1/2 cup buttermilk | 1 can coconut |
| 3 1/2 cups flour | |

Cream butter or margarine and sugar until smooth. Add eggs, one at a time. Beat well after each addition. Dissolve soda in buttermilk and add to creamed mixture. Put flour in a large bowl and add dates, orange slices, and nuts. Stir to coat each piece. Add flour mixture and coconut to creamed mixture and pour into a greased and floured 13 x 9 x 3-inch cake pan. Bake at 250° for 1 1/2 hours.

**TOPPING:**

| | |
|---|---|
| 2 cups powdered sugar | 1 cup orange juice |

Combine sugar and juice and pour over cake and let stand in pan overnight.

*In The Pink*

# Strawberry Cream Cake

*Light and refreshing.*

1 angel food cake, baked
   according to directions
1 (8-ounce) package cream
   cheese
1 (14-ounce) condensed milk
1/3 cup lemon juice

1 teaspoon almond extract
2 cups sliced strawberries
1 (8-ounce) carton Cool Whip
   or whipped cream
Additional strawberries

Bake cake and cool completely. Cut a 1-inch slice from the top of cake and set aside. Cut one inch from center hole and outer edge and remove center of cake, pulling with fingers. Leave 1 inch at bottom.

Beat cream cheese. Add sweetened condensed milk, lemon juice, and almond extract. Fold in cake pieces and strawberries. Spoon into the center of cake. Top with the reserved top slice. Chill 8 hours or overnight. May frost with Cool Whip and additional strawberries.

**Note:** Can use fat-free cream cheese and fat-free sweetened condensed milk for a very low-fat dessert. It is just as delicious. May use store-bought angel food cake.

*Shared Treasures*

## Mother's Fruitcake

3 cups plain flour
1/4 teaspoon soda
1 teaspoon salt
1 teaspoon baking powder
1/2 teaspoon cinnamon
1/2 teaspoon nutmeg
1/2 teaspoon cloves or allspice
2 cups sugar
1 cup Crisco
4 large eggs

1 1/2 cups applesauce (or pear or pumpkin)
1 1/2 cups preserves (fig, pear or peach)
2 cups blanched, steamed raisins (1 cup each light/dark)
1/2 cup cherries, cut in fourths
1 1/2 cups shredded coconut (optional)
2 cups chopped pecans

Sift together first 7 ingredients and set aside. Cream sugar and Crisco. Add remaining ingredients, mixing after each addition. Add flour mixture. Cream well. Put in greased and floured tube pan. Decorate top with cherries and pecan halves. Bake at 300° for 2½ - 3 hours.

*Feast of Goodness*

# Pineapple-Orange Sunshine Cake

1 package yellow cake mix
1/2 cup salad oil
4 eggs
1 (11-ounce) can mandarin
orange sections (undrained)

Combine cake mix, oil, eggs, and oranges; mix at medium speed in electric mixer until almost smooth. Spoon into 2 greased and floured 8-inch cake pans. Bake at 325° for 25 minutes or until done. Cool cake in pans 10 minutes; remove from pans and cool completely on racks. When very cool, split both layers. Spread frosting between layers and on top and sides of cake. Store in refrigerator.

**PINEAPPLE CHEESECAKE FROSTING:**

1 (20-ounce) can crushed
   pineapple, undrained
1 tablespoon sugar
1 (10½-ounce) package
   cheesecake filling mix
1 (8-ounce) carton sour
   cream
1 (9-ounce) container Cool
   Whip

Combine pineapple, sugar, cheesecake filling mix, and sour cream. Stir until mixture thickens. Fold in Cool Whip, mixing thoroughly.

*Family Favorites*

# Lemon Cake Squares

1 package lemon cake mix
3 eggs
1 cup finely chopped pecans
1 stick butter or margarine
1 (8-ounce) package cream
   cheese, softened
1 (16-ounce) box powdered
   sugar

Mix the cake mix, 1 egg, pecans, and butter together. Beat by hand until well blended. Spread this mixture in the bottom of a greased 9 x 13-inch pan. Use your hands to spread this mixture evenly over the bottom of pan.

Next, mix the cream cheese, powdered sugar, and remaining 2 eggs together. Beat with mixer until smooth. Pour over cake batter in pan. Bake in 350° oven until top is golden brown, about 45 minutes to 1 hour. Cool completely. Cut in small squares.

*Heart of the Home*

## *Lemon Apricot Cake*

3 eggs
1/3 cup canola oil
1 can apricot nectar

1 package yellow cake mix
(pudding in mix)

Heat oven to 350°. Combine all ingredients in large bowl and beat at medium speed for 2 minutes. Bake in greased and floured 10-inch tube pan for 40-45 minutes. Cool right side up for 20-25 minutes before removing from pan. Spread icing while still warm.

ICING:
1/4 cup butter or
   margarine
2 1/2 cups sifted confectioners'
   sugar

1/4 cup lemon juice
1/8 teaspoon grated lemon
   rind (optional)

Blend until smooth and spread over cooled cake.

*L' Heritage Du Bayou Lafourche*

## *Blackberry Wine Cake*

1 box white cake mix
1/2 cup cooking oil
   butter flavored)

1 cup blackberry wine
1 small box blackberry Jell-O
4 eggs

Combine cake mix, oil, wine, and Jell-O. Add eggs, one at a time. Mix well. Bake 45 minutes at 350°.

*In The Pink*

 A po-boy is a long sandwich on French bread usually stuffed with oysters, shrimp or roast beef. A "dressed" po-boy comes with mayonnasie, lettuce and tomato. A muffuletta is a round Italian sandwich as big as your head, made with a variety of meats and olive salad.

# Syrup Cake
### (Gateau de Sirop)

<sup>1</sup>/<sub>3</sub> cup solid vegetable
   shortening
<sup>1</sup>/<sub>3</sub> cup sugar
<sup>1</sup>/<sub>3</sub> cup cane syrup
<sup>1</sup>/<sub>3</sub> cup boiling water
1 egg, beaten

<sup>1</sup>/<sub>2</sub> teaspoon baking powder
<sup>3</sup>/<sub>4</sub> teaspoon ground cinnamon
1 teaspoon salt
1<sup>1</sup>/<sub>2</sub> cups flour
<sup>3</sup>/<sub>4</sub> teaspoon grated nutmeg
<sup>1</sup>/<sub>2</sub> teaspoon baking soda

Preheat the oven to 350°. In a mixing bowl, blend the shortening and sugar, mixing well. Add the syrup and boiling water and mix. Add the beaten egg and mix well. Then add the baking powder, cinnamon, salt, flour, nutmeg, and baking soda, and beat until smooth. Bake in a 9-inch greased cake pan for 35 minutes or until the cake sets. Cool for a few minutes before cutting into wedges to serve. Makes 6-8 servings.

*Cajun Cooking for Beginners*

## Fudgy Peanut Butter Cake

2 cups flour
2 cups sugar
1 teaspoon baking soda
1 cup water
1 cup butter

¼ cup cocoa
½ cup buttermilk
2 eggs
1 teaspoon vanilla

Combine flour, sugar, and soda; mix well and set aside. Combine water, butter, and cocoa in a heavy saucepan on low heat. Bring to a boil, stirring constantly. Gradually stir into flour mixture. Stir in buttermilk, eggs, and vanilla. Pour into a greased and floured 13 x 9 x 2-inch baking pan; bake at 350° for 30 minutes or until a wooden pick inserted in center comes out clean. Let cake cool.

**ICING:**
1 cup peanut butter
1 tablespoon vegetable oil
¼ cup + 1 tablespoon
   butter

3 tablespoons cocoa
1 teaspoon vanilla
3-5 tablespoons buttermilk
2½ cups sifted powdered sugar

Combine peanut butter and oil; mix well. Spread on cooled cake. Combine butter and cocoa in a small saucepan; cook over low heat, stirring constantly, until butter melts and mixture is smooth. Remove from heat; add remaining ingredients. Beat until spreading consistency; spread over peanut butter mixture.

*Cooking with Morehouse Parish Sheriff Ladies' Auxiliary*

# Death By Chocolate

| | |
|---|---|
| 1 box Duncan Hines Swiss chocolate cake mix | 2 cups amaretto |
| | 2 large cartons Cool Whip |
| 4 boxes chocolate mousse mix | 8 Skor bars |

Bake cake in 9 x 13-inch pan. Cool and prick with fork. Make mousse according to package directions. Pour amaretto over cake and let sit overnight. In large bowl, layer 1/2 cake, crumbled; 1/2 mousse; 1 carton Cool Whip; 4 Skor bars, crumbled. Then repeat the layers again. Half of this recipe is enough for a family. Freeze other half of cake for the next time you make this dessert.

*A Shower of Roses*

# Godiva Chocolate Cake

*This cake layered with nuts and chocolate icing is a customer favorite at Bon Appétit!*

| | |
|---|---|
| 2 cups flour | 4 squares Godiva chocolate |
| 1/4 teaspoon salt | melted (or 4 ounces semi- |
| 2 teaspoons baking powder | chocolate chips) |
| 1 stick oleo | 1 1/2 cups milk |
| 2 1/2 cups sugar | 2 teaspoons vanilla |
| 3 eggs, separated | 1 cup chopped pecans |

Sift and measure flour. Sift dry ingredients together. Cream butter. Add sugar, gradually. Add egg yolks one at a time. Then add melted chocolate. Add dry ingredients and milk, alternately, beating well after each addition. Add vanilla and continue beating. Beat egg whites until stiff. Fold in egg whites and pecans. Bake at 350° for 30-35 minutes in 2 greased and floured 9-inch cake pans. Let cool. Remove from pans and frost.

*Fessin' Up with Bon Appétit*

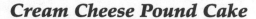

## Cream Cheese Pound Cake

1 Duncan Hines butter cake
  mix
1/2 cup warm water
1/2 cup sugar

1/2 cup oil
4 eggs
1 (8-ounce) package cream cheese
2 tablespoons oleo or butter

Mix cake mix with water and sugar. Add oil and 4 eggs. Add softened cream cheese and oleo (or butter). Mix well. Bake in angel food cake pan or 2 loaf pans at 350° for about 35-40 minutes or until done.

*A Bouquet of Recipes*

## Blueberry Pound Cake

1/4 cup sugar
1 (8-ounce) package light
  cream cheese
1 box yellow reduced-fat
  cake mix
1 cup water

1/2 cup Butter Buds
3/4 cup egg substitute
1 teaspoon butter flavoring
2 cups blueberries
Butter flavor cooking spray

Cream sugar and cream cheese. Mix cake mix, water, Butter Buds, egg substitute, and flavoring. Mix cake mixture and cream cheese mixture. Fold in blueberries. Bake in a tube pan which has been sprayed with butter-flavor cooking spray. Bake at 350° for one hour. Cool slightly before removing from pan. Makes 12-16 servings.

*Cooking with Morehouse Parish Sheriff Ladies' Auxiliary*

---

The Atchafalaya Basin, cutting a 15-mile-wide path across South Louisiana, is the largest and last great river-basin swamp. It comprises an area of 860,000 acres of swamps, lakes and water prairies.

---

## Deluxe Pound Cake

2 sticks oleo
1/2 cup Crisco shortening
3 cups sugar
5 eggs
1 teaspoon rum extract

1 teaspoon coconut extract
3 cups flour
1/2 teaspoon salt
1/2 teaspoon baking powder
1 cup milk

Cream oleo, shortening, and sugar. Add eggs, one at a time. Then add extracts. Sift together dry ingredients and add alternately with milk. Beat well; pour into greased and floured tube pan or large bundt pan. Bake at 325° for 1 1/2 hours.

*Feast of Goodness*

## Vanilla Wafer Cake

1 cup butter
2 cups sugar
6 eggs
1/2 cup milk
1/2 teaspoon lemon extract

2 cups sweetened coconut
2 cups chopped pecans
12 ounces finely crushed
   vanilla wafers

In large bowl of electric mixer, cream together the butter and sugar. Beat in eggs one at a time. Add milk and lemon extract, and mix well. Stir in coconut, pecans, and vanilla wafers. Pour into greased and floured 9 x 13-inch pan. Bake at 350° for 50 minutes or until done. Cut in squares. Sprinkle with powdered sugar.

*LaBonne Cuisine Lagniappe*

# Lily's Blueberry Cheesecake

**PIE CRUST:**

2 cups graham cracker
  crumbs

2 tablespoons sugar
¼ pound butter, melted

Mix well before lining and packing in a 9-inch pie pan. Preheat oven to 350°. Bake for 6 minutes.

**FILLING:**

1 pound cream cheese
¼ pint sour cream
2 tablespoons sugar

1 can blueberries, drained
Sugar for sprinkling

Blend the cream cheese, sour cream, and sugar until smooth. Pour into pie crust and top with blueberries; sprinkle top of berries with sugar and bake 5 minutes at 350°; chill and serve. Serves 8.

*Secrets of The Original Don's Seafood & Steakhouse*

# Coconut Cream Cheesecake

2½ cups grated fresh
  coconut*

1 cup whipped cream,
  scalded

Purée coconut, if using fresh, with hot cream in a blender until finely shredded, about 4 minutes. If using frozen coconut (*can use one {6-ounce} package select shredded quick-frozen; no sugar added), only mix with hot cream. Cool while preparing crust.

**CRUST:**

⅔ cup all-purpose flour
4 teaspoons sugar

5 tablespoons plus 1 teaspoon
  well-chilled butter, cut
  into ½-inch pieces

Preheat oven to 325°. Butter the bottom of a 10-inch springform pan. Blend flour, sugar, and butter until mixture begins to gather together. Press evenly into bottom of prepared pan. Bake until golden brown, about 25 minutes. Set on a rack while preparing filling. Retain oven at 325°.

CONTINUED

**COCONUT FILLING:**

20 ounces cream cheese, room temperature
1½ cups sugar
4 eggs, room temperature
2 egg yolks, room temperature
2½ tablespoons coconut liqueur
1 teaspoon fresh lemon juice
½ teaspoon vanilla
½ teaspoon almond extract
1 cup sour cream
¼ cup cream of coconut*
½ teaspoon coconut liqueur
Coconut flakes, lightly toasted

Using an electric mixer on low speed, beat cream cheese with sugar until blended. Mix in cooled coconut mixture. Blend in eggs and egg yolks, one at a time. Mix in 2½ tablespoons coconut liqueur, lemon juice, vanilla, and almond extract. Pour into prepared crust. Return to oven and bake until sides of cake are dry and center no longer moves when shaken, about one hour. Let cake cool on rack until depression forms in center, about 35 minutes. Mix sour cream, cream of coconut, and remaining ½ teaspoon coconut liqueur. Spread on top of cake. Bake 10 minutes to set topping. Cool completely on rack. Refrigerate until cake is well chilled, about 4 hours. Cover tightly and refrigerate one day to mellow flavors. Can be prepared 3 days ahead. Spread coconut flakes in a 1-inch band around rim.

**Note:** *Cream of Coconut is available at liquor stores and specialty foods section of some supermarkets.

*CDA Angelic Treats*

# Hot Water Gingerbread

*This is a very old recipe! I remember my mother having it ready for me on cold winter days for an after school snack. I did the same for my children.*

| | |
|---|---|
| 1/2 cup sugar | 1/2 teaspoon ginger |
| 1/2 cup vegetable shortening | 1/4 teaspoon allspice |
| 2 eggs | 1 teaspoon cinnamon |
| 1 cup molasses | 2 teaspoons baking soda |
| 2 cups sifted all-purpose flour | 1 cup boiling water |

Cream the sugar and shortening. Beat in the eggs one at a time. Add the molasses. Stir in the flour and spices. Mix the baking soda in boiling water and add to the mixture. Stir gently. Pour into 2 (9-inch) round greased and floured cake pans. Bake at 350° for 20-25 minutes.

Cut into pie-shaped wedges and serve with hot Vanilla Sauce. The gingerbread may be frozen in the pan and reheated when ready to serve.

### VANILLA SAUCE:

This is enough sauce for one pan of gingerbread; double recipe for two pans.

| | |
|---|---|
| 1/2 cup sugar | 2 tablespoons butter or |
| 2 tablespoons flour |   margarine |
| 1/8 teaspoon salt | 1 teaspoon vanilla |
| 1 cup boiling water | |

In a small saucepan, mix sugar, flour, and salt. Slowly add the boiling water, stirring constantly. Bring the mixture to a boil and cook until clear and thick. Remove from heat and add butter and vanilla. Serve hot over gingerbread.

*By Special Request*

# Cookies
# and Candies

*New Orleans cemeteries are tourist attractions since so many of the tombs have architectural significance, often enhanced by iron work done in expressive decorative patterns.*

# Clipper Ship Chippers

*I dare you to find a better chocolate chip cookie!*

| | |
|---|---|
| 1 cup butter, softened | 2 eggs |
| 3/4 cup sugar | 2 1/2 cups all-purpose flour |
| 3/4 cup packed light brown sugar | 1 teaspoon baking soda |
| | 1/2 teaspoon salt |
| 1 tablespoon vanilla extract | 4 cups milk chocolate chips |
| 1 tablespoon coffee-flavored liqueur | 1 cup walnut halves |
| | 1/2 cup pecan halves |
| 1 tablespoon hazelnut-flavored liqueur | 1/2 cup macadamia nuts |

In a large bowl, cream butter, sugars, vanilla, and liqueurs until light and fluffy. Add eggs and beat well. In a separate bowl, combine flour, baking soda, and salt. Gradually beat into creamed mixture. Stir in chocolate chips and nuts. Mix thoroughly. Place in storage container and refrigerate overnight. Drop by teaspoonful onto ungreased cookie sheet. Bake at 325° for 10-13 minutes or until golden brown. Cool slightly and serve immediately. Yields 3-4 dozen cookies.

*Tony Chachere's Second Helping*

# Chocolate Chip Crisp Cookies

| | |
|---|---|
| 1 1/4 cups sifted flour | 1 cup sugar |
| 1/2 teaspoon baking soda | 1 egg |
| 1/4 teaspoon salt | 1 teaspoon vanilla extract |
| 1/2 cup margarine, softened | 2 cups crisp rice cereal |
| | 1 cup chocolate chips |

Sift the flour, baking soda, and salt together. Cream the margarine and sugar in a mixer bowl until light and fluffy. Add the egg and vanilla and beat well. Add the flour mixture and beat well. Stir in the cereal and chocolate chips. Drop by teaspoonfuls onto a greased cookie sheet. Bake at 350° for 8-10 minutes or until golden brown. Remove to a wire rack to cool. Yield: 48 servings.

*Louisiana Temptations*

# Chocolate Chess Bars

*You will get requests for this bar cookie.*

1 (18.25-ounce) package lite devil's food cake mix
1 egg
1/2 cup light margarine, melted
1 tablespoon water

1 (8-ounce) package light cream cheese
1 (16-ounce) box powdered sugar
3 egg whites
1 teaspoon vanilla

In large mixing bowl, combine cake mix, 1 egg, melted margarine, and water. Beat by hand until well blended. Pat batter into bottom of a 13 x 9 x 2-inch baking pan coated with nonstick cooking spray. In mixing bowl, beat cream cheese, powdered sugar, and 3 egg whites until mixture is smooth and creamy. Add vanilla. Pour over batter in pan. Bake at 350° for 45 minutes or until top is golden brown. Cool and cut into squares. Yield: 48 squares.

Cal 103; Chol 7mg; Fat 2.6g; Cal from Fat 22.8%.

*A Trim & Terrific Louisiana Kitchen*


# Authentic Southern Soft Teacakes

*These are soft; just like Granny used to make.*

1 cup shortening
1 3/4 cups sugar
2 eggs
1/2 cup milk

1/2 teaspoon vanilla extract
1/4 teaspoon almond extract
3 cups self rising flour

In a mixing bowl, cream together shortening and sugar; beat in eggs; add milk and extracts; stir in flour. Drop by tablespoons about 2½ inches apart onto greased cookie sheets. Bake 15-20 minutes at 350°. Makes about 3 dozen. These are soft; just like Granny used to make.

*Family Traditions*

## *Darlene's Angel Cloud Cookies*

1 cup butter (room
  temperature)
1/2 cup sugar
2 cups sifted flour

1/2 cup coconut flakes
1 teaspoon vanilla
Confectioners' sugar

Cream butter and sugar. Gradually add flour, coconut, and vanilla and blend well. Roll gently by hand into small balls (about 1 teaspoon each) and place on ungreased cookie sheets. Flatten ball slightly with a fork dipped in cold water. Bake in a preheated 350° oven for 15-20 minutes. Dust cookies with confectioners' sugar and cool. Makes 4 dozen.

*Cooking New Orleans Style!*

## *Coconut Cookies*

*When you taste this cookie, you will know the difference real butter makes! There is really no substitute!*

2 sticks butter
1/2 cup sugar
2 cups flour
1 teaspoon vanilla

1 (3-ounce) can Baker's
  Angel Flake Coconut
Confectioners' sugar

Cream butter and sugar thoroughly. Add flour, vanilla, and coconut. Roll by hand into small balls. Put on a cookie sheet about an inch apart. Flatten these balls with a fork which has been dipped in cold water. Bake at 350° for 20-25 minutes. Cool the cookies and dust with powdered sugar. These are very simple to make but very, very good and pretty on your cookie tray.

*Cooking & Gardening with Dianne*

## *Chocolate Meringues*

2 egg whites
1/8 teaspoon salt
1/8 teaspoon cream of
  tartar
1 teaspoon vanilla

3/4 cup sugar
1 (6-ounce) package (1 cup)
  semi-sweet chocolate
  pieces
1/4 cup chopped pecans

Beat egg whites, salt, cream of tartar, and vanilla until soft peaks form.  Add sugar gradually, beating until peaks are stiff.  Fold in chocolate pieces and nuts.  Cover cookie sheet with plain paper. Drop mixture on by rounded teaspoons.  Bake in slow oven (300°) about 25 minutes.  Cool slightly before removing from paper. Makes about 2 dozen cookies.

*A Cook's Tour of Shreveport*

## *Marshmallow Brownies*

CAKE:
2 stick butter
4 eggs
2 cups sugar
2 teaspoons vanilla

4 tablespoons cocoa
1 1/2 cups flour
1 cup pecans
Marshmallow cream (small)

Mix butter, eggs, sugar, and vanilla; cream well. Add cocoa, flour (sifted together), and 1 cup pecans (more if desired).  Mix well. Pour into a 13 x 9-inch well greased pan and bake at 350° for 25-30 minutes.  Remove from oven and immediately spread marshmallow cream on top.  Set aside and prepare topping.

TOPPING:
1/2 cup butter
3 tablespoons cocoa
1 teaspoon vanilla

2 cups powdered sugar
4 tablespoons evaporated milk

Combine all ingredients and mix well.  Spread over marshmallow cream.  Swirl.  Set in refrigerator until cool; remove and cut as desired.

*Shared Treasures*

## *Chewy Caramel Brownies*

*These indulgent brownies will be the talk of the town. These brownies harden as they cool and become easier to cut, so try to wait—I never can!*

9 ounces caramels,
  unwrapped
1 (14-ounce) can low-fat
  sweetened condensed
  milk
1 (18¼-ounce) box reduced
  fat devil's food cake mix

½ cup (1 stick) light
  margarine, melted
½ cup semi-sweet chocolate
  chips

Preheat the oven to 350°. Coat a 13 x 9 x 2-inch baking pan with nonstick cooking spray and dust with flour. In the top of a double boiler or in the microwave, melt the caramels with ⅓ cup of the milk. Keep warm and set aside. In a large mixing bowl, combine the cake mix, margarine, and remaining milk. Beat at high speed with a mixer until very well combined.

Spread half of the dough into the bottom of the baking pan. Bake for 6 minutes, then sprinkle the chocolate chips over the partially baked dough. Spread the caramel mixture over the chocolate chips. Crumble the remaining dough on top. Return to the oven and continue baking for 15 minutes, or until the sides pull away from the pan. Do not overcook. Cool in the pan on a rack and cut into squares. Makes 48 brownies.

Cal 116; Fat 2.9g; Cal from Fat 22.5%; Sat Fat 1.4g; Sod 127mg; Chol 2mg.

*Trim & Terrific American Favorites*

# Praline Brownies

2 sticks oleo
1 (1-pound) package brown
  sugar
2 eggs
1¼ cups flour
2 teaspoons baking powder
Dash salt
2 cups chopped pecans
2 teaspoons vanilla

Melt margarine and sugar over low heat (or in microwave). Cool mixture and add eggs. Add flour, baking powder, and salt. Stir in pecans and vanilla. Pour into greased 13 x 9 x 2-inch pan. Bake at 350° for 25-30 minutes. Dust with powdered sugar.

*Fiftieth Anniversary Cookbook*

# Amaretto Brownies

1 (20-ounce) box light brownie mix

Prepare brownie mix according to directions. Bake in a 9 x 13-inch pan.

ICING:

3 tablespoons tub margarine
4 ounces light cream cheese,
  room temperature
3 cups confectioners' sugar
1 teaspoon almond extract
1-2 tablespoons milk

Cream margarine and cream cheese together, adding confectioners' sugar and almond extract. Add just enough milk to make smooth and spreadable. Spread over cooled brownies.

TOPPING:

1 (1-ounce) square semi-sweet
  chocolate
2 teaspoons tub margarine
6 tablespoons cocoa powder
1 tablespoon sugar
1 tablespoon cornstarch
¼ cup corn syrup
1 tablespoon skim milk
1 tablespoon amaretto

Melt chocolate square and margarine. Mix cocoa powder, sugar, and cornstarch. Stir corn syrup and milk into cocoa mixture gradually. Add to melted chocolate and continue cooking, stirring until well mixed and smooth. Remove from heat. Mix in amaretto. Cool slightly. Spread over icing. Refrigerate until firm. Cut into small squares. Yield: 32 squares, 1 per serving.

Per Serving: Cal 148; Fat 3.6g; %Fat Cal 22; Sat Fat 1.6g; Chol 9; Sod 99.

*River Road Recipes III*

## Cinnamon Sticks

1¹/₂ sticks butter
1 cup sugar
1 egg, plus 1 egg white

¹/₂ teaspoon cinnamon
1¹/₂ cups flour
1 cup chopped nuts

Cream butter and sugar. Add egg and cinnamon, mix well. Add flour and nuts. Place batter on greased cookie sheet, flatten. Spread top with unbeaten egg white to glaze. Bake at 350° until done (about 20 minutes). Cut in sticks to serve.

*Czech-Out Cajun Cooking*

## Praline Grahams

*Good idea to do 2 packages (2 pans) at one time and double the topping recipe.*

1 package graham crackers
1¹/₂ sticks oleo

¹/₂ cup sugar
1 cup chopped nuts

Separate and arrange crackers close together on Pam-sprayed cookie sheet. Melt oleo in saucepan; stir in sugar and nuts; boil 3 minutes and spread evenly over crackers. Bake 12 minutes at 300°. Remove from pan with spatula and cool on wax paper. Break apart into smaller pieces, if desired.

*Family Traditions*

## Microwave Pralines

1 box butterscotch pie
    filling
¹/₂ cup brown sugar
1 tablespoon butter

1 cup white sugar
¹/₂ cup evaporated milk
¹/₂ teaspoon vanilla
1¹/₂ - 2 cups pecans, chopped

Mix all ingredients except pecans. In microwave dish, cook 3 minutes, stir and cook 2 more minutes, stir and cook 2 more minutes. Then add your pecans and beat until creamy. Drop on wax paper.

*Czech-Out Cajun Cooking*

# Daddy's Pralines

2 cups sugar
1/2 cup white Karo
1/2 cup water
2 cups pecan halves

1/8 teaspoon salt
2 tablespoons butter
1 teaspoon vanilla

Cook sugar, Karo, water, pecans, and salt until soft ball stage. Remove from heat and let cool 15 minutes. Stir and add butter and vanilla. When thick and creamy, drop by spoonfuls on aluminum foil (very quickly).

*Family Favorites*

# Creamy Pecan Pralines

4 cups sugar
1 can condensed milk
1 cup white Karo syrup
1 cup water

4 cups pecan halves
1/4 cup margarine
1 teaspoon vanilla extract

Cook first 4 ingredients over medium heat until mixture reaches firm-ball stage. Remove from heat. Add next 3 ingredients and stir until mixture loses its gloss and is partially cooled. Pour out with spoon onto waxed paper.

*Heart of the Home*

# Mama's Pralines

3 cups sugar
1 cup buttermilk
1 teaspoon baking soda

1/2 stick butter
1 teaspoon vanilla
3 cups pecans

Put all ingredients except pecans into a big boiler and boil until mixture turns brown and forms soft ball in cold water. Add one teaspoon vanilla and beat a little (till slightly creamy). Stir in pecans and drop on waxed paper.

*A Cook's Tour of Shreveport*

# Gold Brick Fudge

*Have the pecans, marshmallow creme and Hershey Kisses measured before you begin.*

5 cups sugar
2 blocks butter

1 large can evaporated milk
1/8 teaspoon salt

Cook the ingredients over medium-high heat, stirring constantly to a soft ball stage, approximately 15-20 minutes. When candy reaches soft ball stage, quickly add following ingredients.

3 cups chopped pecans
1 small jar marshmallow
  creme

160 Hershey Kisses
  (approximately 1½ bags)

Stir rapidly until Kisses are melted and all ingredients are well blended. Pour into a buttered 9 x 13-inch cake pan. The fudge should be 3/4 - 1-inch thick. When cooled and set, cut and store in a covered container. Yield: about 5 pounds.

*CDA Angelic Treats*

# Hurricane Fudge

3 cups sugar
2/3 cup cocoa
1/8 teaspoon salt
1½ cups milk

1/4 cup butter or margarine
1 teaspoon vanilla
1/2 cup chopped pecans

Combine sugar, cocoa, salt, and milk in a large pot. Bring to a boil, stirring constantly over medium heat until it reaches a soft ball stage. Remove from heat. Add butter or margarine and cool mixture to 110° in a pan of water. Add vanilla and chopped pecans. Beat until mixture loses its gloss (about 2 minutes). Pour onto a buttered plate. Slice into squares when cool.

*Tell Me More*

# Fruit Leather

3 pounds peaches, straw-             3 tablespoons honey
   berries, kiwi or apricots

Wash fruit. Cut into small cubes, removing pits, if necessary.
Purée in a blender or food processor. Mix honey with fruit. Heat,
stirring until boiling. Cook 3 minutes. Let cool. Take sheets of
poster paper or cardboard and cover with plastic wrap. Pour
fruit onto this surface in a thin layer. Dry in the sun outdoors
covered with cheesecloth or dry in the oven on the lowest setting. When fruit no longer feels wet, peel off the plastic wrap.
Tear in small pieces. Store in airtight container for several months.
Yield: 10 servings.

Cal 84; Chol 0mg; Sat Fat 0gm; Fat <1gm; Sod 1mg; Pro 1gm; Cho 20gm; Exchanges: 2 fruit

*Just For Kids*

# Rum Balls

1½ cups vanilla wafer              ¼ cup honey
   crumbs                          2 cups ground walnuts
¼ cup rum                          Confectioners' sugar

Use prepared vanilla wafer crumbs or crush vanilla wafers very
fine. (The food processor does this well.) In medium bowl combine all ingredients, except sugar. Mix well. Shape into 1-inch
balls. Roll in confectioners' sugar. Store in tightly covered container until ready to use. Can store in refrigerator. Yields 2½
dozen.

*In The Pink*

## Pecan Kisses

6 egg whites
2 cups sugar
1 teaspoon cream of tartar

1 teaspoon vanilla extract
2 cups chopped pecans

Mix egg whites and sugar without beating and let stand for ½ hour. Add cream of tartar and beat until stiff. Add vanilla and fold in pecans. Drop from tip of teaspoon onto waxed-paper-lined cookie sheet. Bake at 275° for 40-45 minutes. Yield: 100-125 kisses.

*Nun Better*

# Pies and
# Other Desserts

The tallest capitol in the US (34 floors), the Louisiana State Capitol was completed
in 1932 in a mere fourteen months. Governor Huey Long was assassinated there in
1935. His statue and grave face the building he worked hard to have built.

## Lemon Cream Pie

1¼ cups sugar
6 tablespoons cornstarch
2 cups water
3 eggs, separated
⅓ cup lemon juice

1½ teaspoons lemon extract
3 teaspoons vinegar
3 tablespoons butter
1 baked pie shell

Mix sugar and cornstarch in top of double boiler; add water. Add beaten egg yolks and lemon juice and cook until thick; stir often. Remove from heat, add lemon extract, vinegar, and butter. Pour into baked pie shell and allow to cool. Cover with meringue.

**NEVER-FAIL-MERINGUE:**
1 tablespoon cornstarch
2 tablespoons cold water
½ cup boiling water
3 egg whites

6 tablespoons sugar
Pinch of salt
1 teaspoon vanilla

Blend cornstarch and cold water in a saucepan; add boiling water and cook until thick and clear. Let stand until COMPLETELY COLD. Beat egg whites until foamy. Gradually add sugar until stiff, but not dry. Turn to low speed, add salt and vanilla. Stir in the cold cornstarch mixture. Turn again to high speed and beat well. Spread over cool pie, being sure the meringue touches the crust. Bake 10 minutes at 350° or until top is light brown.

*Family Traditions*

## Impossible Buttermilk Pie

1½ cups sugar
1 cup buttermilk (or 1 cup
    milk and 1 tablespoon
    vinegar)

½ cup Bisquick mix
½ cup margarine
1 teaspoon vanilla
3 eggs

Combine all ingredients in blender and beat for 30 seconds. Pour into a greased 9-inch pie plate. Bake at 350° for 30 minutes, or until knife blade inserted in center of pie comes out clean. Cool and serve.

*A Shower of Roses*

## Millionaire Pie

1 cup chopped pecans
1 can sweetened condensed
  milk
1/2 cup lemon juice
1 cup coconut

1 small can crushed pineapple,
  drained
1 (8-ounce) container Cool Whip
1 graham cracker pie shell

Mix all ingredients together and pour into pie shell. Chill and serve.

*Fiftieth Anniversary Cookbook*


## Honey Pecan Pies

*There are as many variations for pecan pie in Louisiana as there are pastry shops. This recipe was given to me many years ago by a wonderful black chef. I often wonder how wealthy she could have become, had she sold this dessert.*

1/4 pound butter
1 cup sugar
3 eggs, beaten
1/2 cup corn syrup
1/2 cup honey
1/2 teaspoon lemon juice

1 teaspoon vanilla
1 cup chopped pecans
Pinch of cinnamon
Pinch of nutmeg
1 (9-inch) uncooked pie shell

Preheat oven to 425°. In a heavy bottom sauté pan, brown butter over medium-high heat. Do not burn. Remove and allow to cool slightly. In a large mixing bowl, combine sugar, eggs, syrup, and honey. Using a wire whisk, blend all ingredients well. Add the brown butter, lemon juice, vanilla, and pecans. Season with cinnamon and nutmeg. Continue to whip until all ingredients are well blended. Pour into pie shell and bake on center rack of oven for 10 minutes. Then reduce temperature to 375° and bake for 35 minutes. Remove and allow to cool.

*The Evolution of Cajun & Creole Cuisine*

## Southern Pecan Pie

1 cup sugar
1/2 cup butter
1 cup light corn syrup
4 eggs, beaten

1 teaspoon vanilla
1/4 teaspoon salt
1 (9-inch) unbaked pie shell
1 1/2 cups pecan halves

Combine sugar, butter and corn syrup, and heat, stirring constantly, until sugar dissolves. Cool. Add beaten eggs, vanilla, and salt. Blend well. Pour in unbaked pie shell and top with pecan halves. Bake at 325° for 50-55 minutes. Test for doneness by inserting knife blade.

*Recipes from Bayou Pierre Country*

## Godiva Chocolate Pie

*Our customers' all-time favorite dessert!*

1/2 cup butter
3 ounces Godiva chocolate
  or 3 ounces milk
  chocolate
4 eggs, well beaten
3 tablespoons white corn syrup
1 1/2 cups sugar

1/4 teaspoon salt
1/4 cup milk
1 teaspoon vanilla extract
1 (10-ounce) pie shell, unbaked
Ice cream (optional)
Whipping cream, whipped
  (optional)

Preheat oven to 350°. Melt butter and chocolate in top of double boiler. Set aside to cool. Beat eggs until light and thick. Add next 5 ingredients. Add chocolate and butter mixture. Mix well. Pour into pie shell. Bake 30-35 minutes or until top is crusty and filling is set. Do not over bake. This pie does not need meringue. Pie can be served warm and topped with ice cream or whipped cream.

*Fessin' Up with Bon Appétit*

---

Cajuns love to go "two-steppin" to the rhythms of "chank-a-chank." Cajun music is a blend of German, Spanish, Scottish, Irish, Anglo-American, African-Caribbean and American Indian influences with a base of western French and French Acadian folk tradition. Broken down more graphically, some call it bluegrass with a French accent, or European folk music. The instruments are the fiddle, accordion, and triangle.

## Chocolate Chip Pie

| | |
|---|---|
| 1 cup sugar | 1 cup milk chocolate chips |
| 1/2 cup flour | 3/4 cup pecans |
| 2 eggs, well beaten | 1 unbaked deep-dish |
| 1 stick melted butter |   pie shell |
| 1 teaspoon vanilla | |

Blend sugar, flour, eggs, butter, and vanilla well. Stir in chocolate chips and pecans. Pour into unbaked pie shell and bake at 350° for 30-35 minutes or until firm.

*St. Philomena School 125th Anniversary*

## Apple Pie

*These apple pies were made by my mother and do not have spices. You have to eat them to know how good they are.*

| | |
|---|---|
| 5 large Winesap apples or | 1 unbaked pie crust |
|   8 small ones such as | 1/2 block margarine (2 sticks) |
|   Jonathan | 3/4 cup sugar |

Peel and core apples. Cut into 1/8-inch rings. Place 2 rows of apples around pie shell. Top with large dots of margarine and cover this row with sugar. Place 2 or 3 more rows of apple rings. Top with remaining margarine and sprinkle remainder of sugar over the top row. Cut strips with remaining dough and criss-cross across the top of the pie. Bake at 400° for 10 minutes and one hour longer at 350°.

*From Mama To Me*

# Spicy Crust Apple Pie

2 pie crusts for 9-inch
  pie pan
2 tablespoons sugar
1/2 teaspoon cinnamon
1/4 teaspoon nutmeg
3/4 - 1 cup sugar

1-2 tablespoons flour
  (if apples are juicy)
1/8 teaspoon salt
6-7 cups peeled, sliced
  tart apples
2 tablespoon butter

Fit one pie crust in pie pan. Combine 2 tablespoons sugar with cinnamon and nutmeg. Brush pastry with milk or water. Sprinkle with 1/2 of sugar-spice mixture. Combine 3/4 - 1 cup sugar with flour and salt; mix lightly through apples. Heap up in pastry-lined pan. Dot with butter. Cover with top crust; cut slits for steam to escape. Brush with milk or water. Sprinkle evenly with remaining sugar-spice mixture.

Bake at 425° 50-60 minutes or until pastry is lightly browned and apples are thoroughly cooked. Cover edges of pie with foil if edges start getting brown.

*Cajun Cooking*

## Sugarless Apple Pie

1 (6-ounce) can frozen
  apple juice concentrate
1/2 can water
2 tablespoons cornstarch

1/2 teaspoon apple pie spice
4 apples
2 pie crust (see below)

Mix all ingredients except apples. Cook until thick. Slice apples into raw crust. Pour mixture over apples. Cover with top crust. Bake at 350° for 45 minutes. Apples may be sprinkled with one package of Sweet & Low, if desired. Yield: 8 slices.

**MAMA BAY'S PIE CRUST:**
3 cups all-purpose flour
1/2 teaspoon salt
2 sticks margarine

1/2 cup ice-cold water
1 tablespoon vinegar

Mix flour and salt. Cut in cold margarine with fork until well blended. Add water and vinegar; work into a ball. Chill one hour before rolling out and placing into pie pans. Bake at 350° until brown. Yields 2 pie crusts.

Cal 256; Chol 0mg; Sat Fat 2gm; Fat 4gm; Sod 261mg; Pro 4gm; Cho 51gm; Exchanges 2 bread, 1½ fruit, 2 fat.

*Southern But Lite*

## Alfred's Sweet Potato Pie

*This pie is truly incredible.*

1 tablespoon softened butter
3/4 cup light brown sugar
1/4 cup finely chopped pecans
1 cup evaporated milk
3 tablespoons brandy (or
  bourbon)

1 1/2 cups cooked mashed sweet
  potatoes
3 large eggs
1/2 teaspoon salt
1/2 teaspoon nutmeg
1 unbaked (9-inch) pie shell

Preheat oven to 425°. Combine all ingredients in large mixing bowl and mix thoroughly. Place in unbaked pie shell. Bake at 425° for 10 minutes; reduce heat to 350° and bake an additional 45 minutes. Serves 1-6 hungry hogs!

*The Hungry Hog*

## Cherry Fruit Pie

1 can sour red cherries
1 small can crushed
  pineapple
2 cups sugar
1 tablespoon red food coloring
  (optional)

7 tablespoons cornstarch
6 chopped bananas
½ cup chopped pecans
Cool Whip

Drain juice from cherries and pineapple. Add water to make 2 cups. Mix all ingredients together except bananas, pecans, and Cool Whip. Cook until thick, then cool. Add bananas and pecans. Pour into baked pie shells. Top with Cool Whip. Chill.

**Feast of Goodness**

The Jazz Funeral is unique to New Orleans. Recognized by the celebratory dance with decorated umbrellas, the Jazz Funeral is rooted in West African culture. Traditionally, mournful music is played on the way to the cemetery (like "Nearer My God to Thee"), and rousing music on the return (like "When the Saints Go Marching In"). Music to African Americans in New Orleans is as much a part of death as it is of life.

# *Peach Cobbler*

*Houmas House had many visitors back in the mid 1800s and often they would write of their experiences at the plantation. One such visitor wrote about the wonderful peas that were grown in the garden and eaten day after day. He mentioned the mint juleps served before breakfast and the fabulous peach cobbler that ended every meal. Here is a rendition of that dish.*

| | |
|---|---|
| **6 cups sliced fresh peaches** | **Pinch of nutmeg** |
| **1¹/₂ cups sugar** | **Pinch of allspice** |
| **¹/₄ cup water** | **1 cup all-purpose flour** |
| **3 tablespoons flour** | **¹/₂ cup sugar** |
| **¹/₄ cup sugar** | **2 teaspoons baking powder** |
| **Pinch of salt** | **³/₄ cup milk** |
| **Pinch of cinnamon** | **¹/₂ teaspoon salt** |

Preheat oven to 400°. In a heavy bottom saucepan, combine peaches, sugar, and water. Bring to a rolling boil, reduce to simmer and allow fruit to cook until softened. In a measuring cup, blend flour, sugar, salt, cinnamon, nutmeg, and allspice. Pour into the peach mixture, stirring constantly until mixture thickens. Remove from heat and pour the mixture into a 9-inch black iron skillet or cobbler pan and allow to cool slightly. In a mixing bowl, combine flour, sugar, baking powder, and milk. Using a wire whisk, whip until well blended. Season with salt. Pour the batter in an irregular shape over the center of the cobbler and bake for approximately 45 minutes or until golden brown.

**Note:** You may wish to garnish the cobbler with fresh sliced peaches, powdered sugar, and a sprig of mint. Serves 8.

*Plantation Celebrations*

---

 New Orleans is below sea level, so the dead are often buried above ground. Many of the cemeteries with their monuments of homage to deceased loved ones are unique and fascinating.

---

## *Fantastic Trifle*

*This is spectacular, can be made ahead, and serves a crowd.*

1 (16-ounce) angel food cake
²/₃ cup sugar
3 tablespoons cocoa
1 tablespoon cornstarch
²/₃ cup evaporated skimmed milk
¹/₄ cup coffee liqueur

3 (1³/₁₆-ounce) English toffee candy bars, crushed
3 (4-serving) packages instant vanilla pudding
3 cups skim milk
2 bananas, peeled and sliced
1 (12-ounce) container frozen light whipped topping

Cube cake and put in bowl. To make chocolate sauce: combine sugar, cocoa, cornstarch, and ²/₃ cup evaporated milk. Cook over low heat until it thickens. Remove from heat; add coffee liqueur. Cool. Pour chocolate mixture over cake in bowl. Add crushed candy to angel cake mixture. In mixer, beat pudding and 3 cups skim milk until thick. Pour over angel food cake mixture. Refrigerate 15 minutes. In trifle dish, layer cake mixture, banana, and whipped topping. Repeat layers, ending with whipped topping. Yield: 16 servings.

Cal 261; Chol 5mg; Fat 3.8g; Cal from Fat 13.2%.

*A Trim & Terrific Louisiana Kitchen*

# *Banana Split Dessert*

*When you're ready to serve this treat, top it with chopped pecans, cherries, and a drizzle of chocolate syrup!*

| | |
|---|---|
| 2 cups graham cracker crumbs | 3 bananas, sliced |
| 6 tablespoons margarine, melted | 1 (20-ounce) can crushed pineapple, drained |
| 2 (3½-ounce) packages instant vanilla pudding mix | 1 (12-ounce) container whipped topping |
| 2 cups milk | |

In a bowl, combine crumbs and margarine. Press mixture into an oblong baking dish and set aside. In another bowl, prepare pudding mix with milk according to package directions. Spread pudding over crumb mixture. Layer with banana slices, then pineapple, then whipped topping. Chill 3 hours or overnight. Cut into squares to serve. Yields 12 squares.

*Tony Chachere's Second Helping*

# *Apricot Dessert*

**1ST LAYER:**

| | |
|---|---|
| 1 stick oleo | ½ cup chopped nuts |
| 1 cup flour | |

Cream together and pack in 9 x 12-inch greased pan. Bake at 350° for 20 minutes or until brown. Cool.

**2ND LAYER:**

| | |
|---|---|
| 1 (8-ounce) package cream cheese | 1 cup Cool Whip |
| | 1 cup confectioners' sugar |

Mix and spread on first layer.

**3RD LAYER:**

| | |
|---|---|
| 1 can apricot pie filling | Whipped topping (optional) |

Spread dessert with pie filling. Whipped topping may be spread over entire dessert.

*A Bouquet of Recipes*

# *Tiramisù*

*The name Tiramisù means "pick me up," so get ready! This recipe was on the cover of* Cooking Light *Magazine's March 1995 issue. If you've never had Tiramisù, this is the perfect time to try making it. I know it requires using a few bowls, but it is worth the effort. You can find instant espresso coffee at the grocery store to make espresso without any special appliances.*

½ cup espresso coffee
¼ cup plus 1 tablespoon
  sugar
3 tablespoons coffee liqueur
1 (8-ounce) package light
  cream cheese, softened
¾ cup confectioners' sugar

1½ cups light frozen whipped
  topping, thawed and
  divided
3 large egg whites
20 ladyfingers, split
Cocoa, for sprinkling

In a small bowl, combine the espresso coffee, one tablespoon sugar, and the coffee liqueur; set aside. In a mixing bowl, combine the cream cheese with the confectioners' sugar, beating until well blended. Fold in one cup frozen whipped topping. In another mixing bowl, beat the egg whites until soft peaks form, add the remaining ¼ cup sugar, and continue beating until stiff peaks form. Fold into the cream cheese mixture.

In a 9 x 9 x 2-inch dish, place a layer of the split ladyfingers across the bottom of the dish. Drizzle with half of the espresso mixture, half of the cream cheese mixture, and repeat the layers, beginning with split ladyfingers and ending with the cream cheese mixture. Spread with the remaining ½ cup whipped topping in a thin layer on top of the dessert and sprinkle with cocoa. Refrigerate until well chilled. Makes 16 servings.

Cal 147; Fat 5g; Cal from Fat 30.6%; Sat Fat 3.5g; Sod 102mg; Chol 57mg.

*Trim & Terrific American Favorites*

 St. Joseph's Cemetery in Rayne was featured in "Ripley's Believe It or Not!" for its idiosyncratic layout: its vaults face north-to-south, while others conform to the tradition of feet-to-east orientation.

## Blackberry Dumplings

*First get a stick to beat the snakes out of the bushes. Pick all the berries you can for the pot and eat just as many. My mother made Christmas wine with a lot of berries. The dumpling was our reward for picking the berries.*

| | |
|---|---|
| 4 tablespoons butter | 3½ cups flour |
| 1 cup milk | 3 teaspoons baking powder |
| 2 eggs | 4 cups water |
| 3½ cups sugar, divided | 1½ quarts blackberries |
| 2 teaspoons vanilla | |

Melt butter and allow to cool. Mix with milk, eggs, and one cup of the sugar and vanilla. Add dry ingredients. Do not over mix. In a large saucepan, combine water, 2½ cups sugar, and berries. Cook over medium heat until mixture thickens. Drop dough by the spoonful into the berry mixture. Cook until dough rises. Test with fork. When it comes out clean, remove dumpling and continue adding dumplings until all dough is used. Serve warm with blackberry mixture. Makes 3-4 dozen.

*Cajun Cookin' Memories, Photos, History, Recipes*

## Chocolate Sin

| | |
|---|---|
| 1 stick soft margarine | 1 cup powdered sugar |
| 1 cup flour | 1 large size whipped topping |
| ½ cup finely chopped pecans | 3 cups milk |
| 1 (8-ounce) package cream cheese | 2 small packages instant chocolate pudding |

Mix margarine, flour and most of the pecans, and pat into a 9 x 13-inch Pyrex pan. Bake for 15 minutes and cool. Mix cream cheese, sugar and one cup of topping. Spread this carefully over the first layer in the pan. Mix the milk into the pudding and beat for 2 minutes. Spread this over second layer. Spread the remaining topping on top and sprinkle with remaining chopped pecans. Refrigerate. When ready to serve, cut into squares and stand aside!

*Cajun Men Cook*

# Chocolate Éclairs

1 cup water
1 stick butter or margarine
1 cup flour
1/4 teaspoon salt
4 large eggs

1 (small) box vanilla pudding
   (regular or instant)
2 cups cold milk
Chocolate Topping

Boil water in heavy pot; add butter and stir till melted. Add flour and salt all at once, stirring and cooking a minute or so till mixture forms soft ball that does not separate. Remove from heat, cool 10 minutes and add eggs one at a time, beating vigorously after each.

Form 12-15 spoonsful batter into smooth capsule shapes on a greased cookie sheet. Bake in 450° oven 15 minutes, then lower to 325° and bake another 25 minutes. While éclairs are baking, prepare and refrigerate pudding (package directions) and Chocolate Topping.

When éclairs are cool, slice top third off with sharp knife. Fill each éclair with about 2 tablespoons pudding. Replace top. Frost with Chocolate Topping. Refrigerate loosely covered (with sheet of waxed paper).

## CHOCOLATE TOPPING:

2 (1-ounce) squares
   unsweetened baking
   chocolate
3 tablespoons butter

1¼ cups powdered sugar
1 teaspoon vanilla
2-3 tablespoons milk

Melt chocolate in microwave on HIGH for 2 minutes (or over hot water on stovetop). Add butter; stir to melt. Add powdered sugar, vanilla and milk for thin consistency. Beat with spoon till glossy.

**Note:** Easier than you imagined, I'll bet. Cream Puffs are similar, but round, and sprinkled with powdered sugar. Try chocolate or lemon filling or stiffly whipped cream.

*The Little New Orleans Cookbook*

# *Brownie Pizza*

**BROWNIE LAYER:**

4 squares unsweetened
  chocolate
³/₄ cup margarine
2 cups sugar

4 eggs
1 teaspoon vanilla
1 cup all-purpose flour

Heat oven to 350°. Grease 12-inch pizza pan. Melt chocolate in double boiler. Add margarine and mix well. Stir 2 cups sugar to melted chocolate and margarine. Remove from heat; stir to cool. Mix in eggs and vanilla until well blended. Stir in flour. Spread in prepared pan. Bake 30 minutes.

**TOPPING:**

1 (8-ounce) package cream
  cheese
¹/₄ cup sugar
1 egg

¹/₂ teaspoon vanilla
Assorted sliced fruit
2 squares semisweet chocolate

Mix cream cheese, sugar, egg, and vanilla in same bowl until blended. Pour over baked brownie crust. Bake 10 minutes or until toothpick comes out with fudge crumbs—don't over bake. Arrange fruit over cream cheese layer. Melt chocolate squares and drizzle over fruit.

*St. Philomena School 125th Anniversary*

## Strawberry Crepes

2¹/₂ cups sliced strawberries
3 tablespoons sugar
³/₄ cup skim milk
¹/₂ cup all-purpose flour
1 egg

¹/₄ teaspoon salt
Nonstick spray coating
¹/₄ cup Mock Sour Cream
4 teaspoons brown sugar

Combine strawberries and sugar. Set aside. Mix milk, flour, egg and salt. Beat until smooth. Spray skillet with nonstick spray. Place over medium heat. Pour ¹/₈ mixture into skillet. Brown for one minute and remove crepe. Repeat procedure.

Lay crepe flat. To center, add strawberries and sugar. Fold over and top with Mock Sour Cream, and top this with brown sugar. Use any excess strawberries for garnish.

MOCK SOUR CREAM:
2 tablespoons skim milk
1 tablespoon lemon juice
1 cup low fat cottage cheese

¹/₄ teaspoon salt
¹/₈ teaspoon Worcestershire sauce

Blend above ingredients well.

*Roger's Lite Cajun Cookbook*

## *Lazy Betty*

2 cans pie filling mix
  (your choice)
1 package yellow cake mix

1 cup chopped nuts
1/2 pound margarine
Cool Whip

Pour pie filling mix into ungreased 9 x 13 x 2-inch baking dish. Smooth filling, sprinkle with cake mix, then with the chopped nuts. Melt margarine and drizzle over entire top. Bake at 375° for about 40 minutes. Serve topped with Cool Whip.

*Cooking with Mr. "G" and Friends*

## *Plantation Pecan Crunch*

2 cups butter
2 cups sugar
1/2 teaspoon salt
1/4 cup water
2 tablespoons corn syrup

1 (6-ounce) package semisweet
  chocolate chips
2 cups finely chopped toasted
  pecans

Melt butter in heavy saucepan. Add sugar, and cook, stirring constantly, until dissolved; do not burn. Add salt, water, and syrup. Cook to brittle stage or to register 290° on candy thermometer, stirring constantly. Remove from heat and pour into 2 shallow pans, spreading evenly to a thin layer. While candy cools, melt chocolate chips in top of double boiler over hot water. Spread chocolate on candy layer and sprinkle with pecans. Let stand to cool, then break into pieces like peanut brittle. Makes 25-30 pieces.

*Cane River's Louisiana Living*

 Ponchatoula, the strawberry capitol of the world, has recently become known for it's small-town antique shops.

## Poached Bosc Pears

*This makes a light but elegant finale to any meal.*

2 cups water
1 tablespoon lemon juice
6 medium ripe, firm pears
2 cups dry red wine
1/2 cup sugar

1 small cinnamon stick
1 strip lemon rind,
  2 x 2 1/2 inches long
2 tablespoons cognac

Combine 2 cups water with lemon juice in a large bowl. Peel pears and immerse in mixture. Bring wine, sugar, cinnamon stick and lemon rind to a boil in saucepan. Add drained pears and bring to a boil. Reduce heat and simmer, turning pears every 5 minutes, just until tender, for 10-15 minutes. Remove with a slotted spoon and place upright in serving dish. Increase heat to high and boil liquid until syrupy and reduced by half, about 5-7 minutes. Remove from heat and add cognac. Discard cinnamon stick and lemon peel. Pour sauce over pears. Cover and cool, then refrigerate at least 2 hours. Serve well chilled with a dollop of nonfat vanilla yogurt or light sour cream, if desired. Yield: 6 servings.

Per Serving: Cal 207; Fat 0.7g; %Fat Cal 3; Sat Fat trace; Chol 0mg; Sod 51mg.

*River Road Recipes III*

## Avocado Cream

*A St. Paddy's Day dessert.*

1 ripe medium-size avocado
1 1/2 tablespoons fresh lime
  juice
6 tablespoons granulated sugar

1/2 cup heavy cream
1 1/2 teaspoons vanilla extract
4 cups French vanilla
  ice cream

Peel and slice avocado. In a blender or food processor, purée avocado with lime juice, sugar, cream, and vanilla. Blend well. Then, in a large mixing bowl, blend softened ice cream with the avocado mixture. Spoon into parfait glasses, cover, and freeze until serving time. Garnish with a slice of lime. Serves 4.

*Who's Your Mama, Are You Catholic,*
*and Can You Make a Roux?*

## *Burnt Cream*

| 8 egg yolks | 1 quart heavy cream |
|---|---|
| 1 cup sugar | 1 tablespoon vanilla extract |

Preheat oven to 350°. With a whisk or electric beater, beat the egg yolks and 1/2 cup of sugar together in a mixing bowl for 3 or 4 minutes or until the eggs are thick and pale yellow. Heat the cream in a heavy saucepan until small bubbles begin to form around the edges of the pan. Pour the cream in a slow stream into the egg yolks, beating constantly. Add the vanilla, and strain the mixture through a fine sieve into a baking dish that is a least 2 inches deep.

Place the dish in another shallow pan and pour enough boiling water into the pan so that the water comes halfway up the sides of the custard dish. Bake for 45 minutes or until a knife inserted in the center comes out clean. Remove the custard dish from the pan of water and cool to room temperature. Refrigerate for at least 4 hours.

About 2 hours before serving, preheat the oven broiler to its highest temperature. Sprinkle the top of the custard with the remaining 1/2 cup of sugar; coat the surface as evenly as possible. Slide the dish under the broiler about 3 inches from the heat; cook for 4 or 5 minutes or until the sugar forms a crust over the cream. Watch carefully for any signs of burning. Allow the cream to cool again and refrigerate before serving. Serves 10.

*Who's Your Mama, Are You Catholic,*
*and Can You Make a Roux?*

# Caramel Cup Custard

| | |
|---|---|
| 1 cup sugar | 4 eggs and 8 egg yolks |
| 2 cups half-and-half | 1 cup powdered sugar |
| 3 cups milk | 2 teaspoons vanilla |

**Caramel:** Melt sugar in a heavy pot. Cook sugar until it is a golden color; pour into custard cups.

**Custard:** Bring cream and milk to a boil. Beat eggs, yolks, and powdered sugar until thick; slowly add hot milk to egg mixture. Add vanilla and mix well; pour into cups. Bake at 325° in a water bath for one hour.

*Tell Me More*

# Flan

| | |
|---|---|
| ½ cup sugar | 1 can evaporated milk |
| 4 eggs | 1 teaspoon vanilla |
| 1 can sweetened condensed milk | |

Caramelize sugar in a heavy skillet over low heat, stirring constantly until it melts and turns golden brown. Pour into 1-quart casserole. Spread around to coat bottom and sides of casserole. Let cool. In a medium bowl, beat eggs and stir in rest of the ingredients. Pour into caramelized casserole. Place in a pan with 1 inch hot water. Bake at 350° for one hour or until knife inserted in center comes out clean. Run spatula around edge and turn out on plate. Pour sauce over top.

*La Bonne Cuisine Lagniappe*

The Cafe Du Monde in the French Quarter is where many tourists begin their morning or end their night, partaking of their famous beignets and cafe au lait.

# Cream Cheese Bread Pudding

*Bread pudding is always a popular dessert, but with the cream cheese topping it reaches new heights!*

| | |
|---|---|
| 1 (16-ounce) loaf French bread | 1 teaspoon imitation butter flavoring |
| 2 large eggs, divided | 3 cups skim milk |
| 4 large egg whites, divided | 1 teaspoon ground cinnamon |
| 1 cup sugar, divided | 1 (8-ounce) package fat-free cream cheese, softened |
| 1 teaspoon vanilla extract | |

Preheat the oven to 350°. Cut the French bread into 1-inch squares. Place the bread in a 13 x 9 x 2-inch baking dish. In a large bowl, lightly beat together 1 egg and 3 egg whites. Add ¹/₂ cup of the sugar, the vanilla, and the butter flavoring; mix well. Slowly add the milk to the egg mixture, mixing well. Pour over the bread squares. Sprinkle the mixture with the cinnamon. In a large mixing bowl, beat the cream cheese with the remaining sugar. Add the remaining egg and egg white, blending until smooth. Spread the mixture evenly over the soaked bread. Bake, uncovered, for 45 minutes, or until firm. Let cool slightly. Makes 8 servings.

Cal 340; Fat 3.1g; Cal from Fat 8.3%; Sat Fat 0.9g; Prot 15.5g; Carbo 61.4g; Sod 573g; Chol 58mg.

*Trim & Terrific One-Dish Favorites*

## Bananas Foster Bread Pudding

| | |
|---|---|
| 1 (12-ounce) loaf stale French bread, broken in small pieces (or 9-11 cups any type stale bread) | 2½ cups sugar |
| | 8 tablespoons butter, melted |
| | 4 eggs |
| | 2 tablespoons vanilla |
| 1 cup milk | 3 sliced bananas |
| 4 cups half-and-half | |

Combine all ingredients; mixture should be very moist but not soupy. Pour into buttered 9 x 13-inch baking dish. Place on middle rack of cold oven. Bake in a 350° oven for approximately 1 hour and 15 minutes until top is golden brown. Serve warm with Bananas Foster Sauce.

**BANANAS FOSTER SAUCE:**

| | |
|---|---|
| ½ cup butter | 2 ounces banana liqueur |
| 2 cups dark brown sugar | 2 bananas cut in small |
| 4 ounces dark rum | pieces |

Melt butter and add brown sugar to form a creamy paste. Stir in liquors until smooth sauce is formed. Add bananas and simmer for 2 minutes. Serve warm over warm bread pudding.

*Cooking New Orleans Style!*


## Old Fashion Bread Pudding

| | |
|---|---|
| 6-8 cups stale biscuits, crumbled or 1 (10-ounce) loaf stale French bread | 2 tablespoons vanilla |
| | 1 cup raisins |
| | 1 cup coconut |
| 4 cups milk | 1 cup chopped pecans |
| 2 cups sugar | 1 teaspoon cinnamon |
| 4 tablespoons melted butter | 1 teaspoon nutmeg |
| 3 eggs | |

Combine all ingredients; mixture should be very moist but not soupy. Pour into buttered 9 x 9-inch baking dish. Place into cold oven. Turn oven to 350° and bake for about 1 hour and 15 minutes, until top is golden brown. Serve warm with whiskey sauce or serve cold slices.

*Pigging Out with the Cotton Patch Cooks*

# Amaretto Bread Pudding

*Better than the average bread pudding—don't pass this one by!*

| | |
|---|---|
| 12 pieces sliced bread | 1¹/₂ cups sugar |
| 4 cups milk | 1 teaspoon almond extract |
| ¹/₄ cup butter | ¹/₂ cup sliced almonds |
| 3 eggs | |

Preheat oven to 350°. Tear up bread into medium-size pieces and place in a large greased baking dish. Heat milk and butter in a large saucepan over low heat until butter melts. Pour over bread. Beat eggs; add sugar and almond extract. Pour over bread and gently stir in. Sprinkle with almonds. Bake about 40 minutes until set.

**SAUCE:**

| | |
|---|---|
| ¹/₂ cup butter | 1 egg |
| 1 cup powdered sugar | ¹/₄ cup amaretto |

Melt butter and powdered sugar in a small saucepan over low heat. Remove from heat and quickly whisk in 1 egg. Stir in amaretto and beat until smooth.

To serve, cut bread pudding into squares and top with sauce. Serve warm, even if made ahead. Can be reheated in microwave. Serves 12.

*Kay Ewing's Cooking School Cookbook*

# Pralines & Cream Dream

1 cup light brown sugar
1/4 cup light corn syrup
1/2 cup half-and-half
  cream
2 tablespoons butter

1 cup coarsely chopped
  pecans
1/2 teaspoon vanilla
Vanilla ice cream

In a small saucepan, combine brown sugar, corn syrup and cream. Place over medium heat and cook for 7-8 minutes. Stir in butter, pecans, and vanilla. Remove and cool completely. To serve, spoon alternate layers of ice cream and praline sauce in a wine glass or parfait glass. Serves 6.

*Kay Ewing's Cooking School Cookbook*

# Strawberries Over Snow

1 large angel food cake
1 (8-ounce) package cream
  cheese, softened

1 (8-ounce) carton frozen
  whipped topping, thawed
3/4 cup milk

GLAZE:
1 cup water
1 teaspoon lemon juice
1 cup sugar
2 tablespoons cornstarch

12 drops red food coloring
2 pints strawberries, cut in
  halves

Trim crust from cake. Tear into chunks and place in 13 x 9 x 2-inch baking dish. Combine cream cheese, whipped topping and milk, blending until smooth. Spread mixture over cake chunks. Chill. Prepare Glaze. Combine water, lemon juice, sugar, and cornstarch in saucepan. Bring to a boil, cook until thickened. Remove from heat. Add food coloring, mix well. Fold strawberries into Glaze. Let stand until cool. Pour Glaze over cake. Chill thoroughly. Serves 8-10.

*Cane River's Louisiana Living*

## *My Favorite Chocolate Pecan Sauce*

*Everyone likes a good chocolate sauce. I like having a jar of this choco-
late sauce in the refrigerator in case I need to come up with a dessert in
a hurry.*

3 (1-ounce) squares
   unsweetened chocolate
1³/₄ cups half-and-half
1 cup sugar
¹/₄ teaspoon salt

¹/₄ cup flour
1 teaspoon vanilla extract
1 tablespoon butter
²/₃ cup chopped pecans

Melt chocolate in half-and-half over low heat in small saucepan.
Cook until smooth, stirring occasionally. Combine the sugar, salt,
and flour. To this dry mixture, add enough of the chocolate mixture to make a smooth paste. Stir well and slowly add to the
chocolate mixture. Cook on medium heat until smooth and thickened, about 10 minutes. After it has thickened, remove from heat
and stir in the vanilla, butter and nuts. Store in tightly sealed jar
in refrigerator. Makes 2¹/₄ cups.

*Extra! Extra! Read All About It!*

## *Praline Ice Cream Sauce*

¹/₂ pound (about 22)
   marshmallows
1¹/₃ cups brown sugar
1 cup light cream

Dash of salt
4 tablespoons butter or oleo
1 teaspoon vanilla
¹/₃ cup broken pecans

Combine first 4 ingredients in 2¹/₂-quart saucepan. Heat and stir
until mixture comes to a boil. Cook over medium heat about 10
minutes or to 224°. Remove from heat; add butter. Cool slightly;
add vanilla and nuts. Serve warm. Makes 2 cups.

*Pigging Out with the Cotton Patch Cooks*

---

The Twin Cities of Monroe and West Monroe are home to the first Coca-
Cola bottling plant and the birthplace of Delta Air Lines.

---

# Blueberry Snow

1 (8-ounce) package cream
  cheese
½ cup milk
¼ cup sugar

Cool Whip
Angel food cake
1 can blueberry pie filling

Cream first three ingredients. Fold in Cool Whip. Bread up angel food cake in 9 x 13-inch pan. Spread part of mixture on cakes, then spread blueberries, then mixture again. Refrigerate. Serve cold. Very good!

*Heart of the Home*

Common expressions you might hear in French Louisiana: C'est tout (Say too): That's all. Fais-do-do (Fay doe doe): A dance. Pauve ti bete (Pove tee bet): Poor little thing. Ca c'est bon (sa say bohn): That's good. Ca va (Sa va): That's enough. Lagniappe (Lahn yop): Something extra. Boucherie (Boo sher ee): Pig roast. Joie de vivre (Jhwa da veev): Joy of living. Laissez les bons temps rouler (Lay say lay bohn tohn roo lay): Let the good times roll.

# Catalog of
# Contributing Cookbooks

*The Shadows on the Teche stands grandly on the banks of Bayou Teche. Built in
1830 by the Weeks family (who built a sugar empire), the Shadows was the
center of much of South Louisiana's gracious social life.*

# CATALOG
## *of*
# CONTRIBUTING COOKBOOKS

All recipes in this book have been selected from the cookbooks shown on the following pages. Individuals who wish to obtain a copy of any particular book may do so by sending a check or money order to the address listed by each cookbook. Please note the postage and handling charges that are required. State residents add tax only when requested. Prices and addresses are subject to change, and books may sell out and become unavailable. Retailers are invited to call or write to same address for discount information.

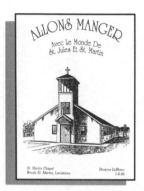

## ALLONS MANGER
### Avec Le Monde De St. Jules et St. Martin

St. Jules Catholic Church
P.O. Box 70
Belle Rose, LA 70341-0070                    504-473-8569

*Allons Manger Avec Le Monde De St. Jules Et St. Martin* was compiled in connection with the annual food festival, Allons Manger. The 600 recipes reflect the area's rich heritage, delicious food, and dear memories that are the natural result of a lifetime of good times spent with family and friends. All proceeds go to the church parish of St. Jules-St. Martin.

$ 10.00  Retail price
$  2.50  Postage and handling
Make check payable to St. Jules Catholic Church

## BIG MAMA'S OLD BLACK POT RECIPES

Stoke Gabriel Enterprises
P.O. Box 12060
Alexandria, LA 71315                    318-487-9577

This one is a classic. Filled with recipes for good old-fashioned, calorie-laden, country-style cooking. Recipes by a Louisiana black family include the simple but delicious—that have been favorites of "country folk" and their "city cousins" the South over. Original art, short stories, and vignettes add flavor to the book. 208 pages.

$ 11.95  Retail price
$   .96  Tax for Louisiana residents
$  2.00  Postage and handling
Make check payable to Stoke Gabriel Enterprises
ISBN 0-929288-00-9

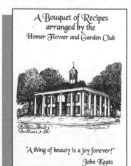

## A BOUQUET OF RECIPES

Homer Flower and Garden Club
c/o Mary Turner
P. O. Box 37
Homer, LA 71040                    318-927-2836

Recipes compiled by members and friends of the Homer Flower and Garden Club includes recipes from appetizers to vegetables followed by some potpourri. The 230-page book contains 600 recipes—some old family favorites as well as up-to-date ones; also great cooking suggestions and measurements.

$ 10.00  Retail price
$  3.00  Postage and handling
Make check payable to Homer Flower and Garden Club

## BY SPECIAL REQUEST

by Leu Wilder
467 Railsback Road
Shreveport, LA 71106          318-797-8689

An intimate book (158 pages) of tasty, but basic recipes (250) that evoke memories of hearth and home. Recipes collected over a lifetime with glimpses of times past and remembrances of growing up in the rural south. Old recipes for a new generation.

$ 12.95  Retail price
$  1.04  Tax for Louisiana residents
$  2.00  Postage and handling
Make check payable to Leu Wilder
ISBN 0-9638840-0-X

## C.D.A. ANGELIC TREATS

Louisiana State Catholic Daughters
Franklin, LA

A wonderful collection of 1,080 recipes and has 450 pages. The recipes were submitted by members from more than 100 of the Catholic Daughters Courts in the state. Selections are identified by the diverse cultures of Louisiana, including many recipes of Cajun, Creole, hill country, and western plains preferences. Seventy-five percent of the profits will go to build a Louisiana Habitat Home. Currently out of print.

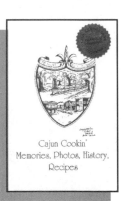

## CAJUN COOKIN'

Franklin Golden Age Club
Franklin, LA

A cookbook of *Cajun Cookin'* compiled by the Franklin Golden Age Club in honor of the 175th anniversary of Franklin, Louisiana. It has memories, photos, and history of the area. 162 pages.

## CAJUN COOKING
## From the Kitchens of South Louisiana

Acadian House Publishing
P. O. Box 52247
Lafayette, LA 70505          337-235-8851

From the pecan orchards to the shrimp docks, from the oyster boats to the crawfish boats, from the sugarcane fields to the rice fields, this is Cajun Cooking, an Acadiana-wide cookbook. Map, history, great recipes. 234 pages.

$ 17.95  Retail price
$  1.35  Tax for Louisiana residents
$  2.50  Postage and handling
Make check payable to Acadian House Publishing
ISBN 0-925417-03-3

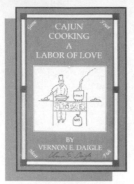

## CAJUN COOKING A LABOR OF LOVE

by Vernon E. Daigle
Baton Rouge, LA

We always prepared special dishes for family visits—crawfish bisques, rice dressings, barbecues, gumbos, jambalayas, sauce piquants, turkey and game specialties, etc. Our book is dedicated to our seven children, their spouses, and all our grandchildren, with the hope that it will encourage them to continue the traditions of family feasts and reunions. Currently out of print.

## CAJUN COOKING FOR BEGINNERS

Acadian House Publishing
P. O. Box 52247
Lafayette, LA 70505                          337-235-8851

We offer this collection of recipes, most of which are simple, to our readers who may not be familiar with Cajun cuisine, or for those who wish to begin learning the basics of Cajun cooking. Cooking should be fun and satisfying. This cookbook is intended to be a means toward these ends.

$  6.95  Retail price
$   .52  Tax for Louisiana residents
$  2.50  Postage and handling
Make check payable to Acadian House Publishing
ISBN 0-925417-23-8

## CAJUN CUISINE: Authentic Cajun Recipes from Louisiana's Bayou Country

Acadian House Publishing
P.O. Box 52247
Lafayette, LA 70505                          337-235-8851

As they have for generations, good Cajun cooks put a lot of tender loving care into preparing meals for their families, and it shows. Though most don't have anything written down ("I can't tell you how I do it; I just do it."), this book contains great recipes that *do* tell you how to do it! 234 pages. Comb bound.

$ 22.50  Retail price
$  1.69  Tax for Louisiana residents
$  2.50  Postage and handling
Make check payable to Acadian House Publishing
ISBN 0-935619-00-3

## CAJUN MEN COOK

Beaver Club of Lafayette
P. O. Box 2744
Lafayette, LA 70502                          337-984-2547

Prize winning 250+ recipes within 254 pages offering food experiences, stories, history, anecdotes, etc., from Louisiana Cajun Country. Hard back, illustrations, everything from appetizers to desserts including a celebrity section. Indexed, glossary, table of contents. Third printing.

$ 16.95  Retail price
$  2.95  Postage and handling
Make check payable to Beaver Club of Lafayette, Inc.
ISBN 0-9642486-0-3

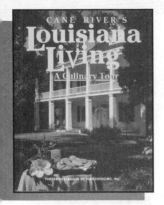

## CANE RIVER'S "LOUISIANA LIVING"
### A Culinary Tour

The Service League of Natchitoches, Inc.
P. O. Box 2206
Natchitoches, LA 71457-2206          318-352-6723 or 800-810-CANE

Quaint Natchitoches, established in 1714, is nestled on the banks of Cane River Lake. A walking tour map and colorful photos accent the many delicious recipes that help make it so unique and flavorful! Profits will be used for educational, civic, historical, and cultural improvement of Natchitoches. Beautiful hard cover, comb bound, 312 pages. Irresistible!

$ 19.95  Retail price
$  4.50  Postage and handling
Make checks payable to *Cane River Cuisine*
ISBN 0-9607674-6-0

## C'EST BON, ENCORE

Vermilion Association for Family & Community Education, Inc.
c/o Mrs. Isaac Broussard
503 N. Lyman
Abbeville, LA 70510                    337-893-4639

*C'est Bon, Encore* meaning It's Good, Again is the second cookbook compiled by the Vermilion FCE members. There are 226 pages of recipes divided into 11 categories. Category titles are both in Cajun French and English. The recipes and Cajun words are typical of this area.

$ 10.00  Retail price
$  2.00  Postage and handling
Make check payable to Vermilion Assn. FCE, Inc.

## CELEBRATIONS ON THE BAYOU

The Junior League of Monroe, Inc.
P. O. Box 7138                    monroejuniorleague.org
Monroe, LA  71211                         800-256-4888

Whether it's a holiday feast or casual summer supper, *Celebrations on the Bayou* captures the rich heritage that makes southern entertaining a legend. The authors of the best selling *The Cotton Country Collection* have created an exceptional cookbook that goes beyond traditional boundaries. Featured are 30 celebrations, parties for all occasions—an elegant collection of menus; a practical cookbook.

$ 19.95  Retail price
$   .80  Tax for Louisiana residents
$  3.50  Postage and handling
Make check payable to Cotton-Bayou Publications
ISBN 0-9602364-1-4

## CLASSIC CAJUN
### Culture and Cooking

by Lucy Henry Zaunbrecher
P. O. Box 99
Dry Prong, LA 71423                    800-257-5829

Revised edition featuring recipes from Mrs. Lucy's television series. "Real" Cajun cooking from a classic authentic Cajun cook plus photos and stories of her Cajun culture. 215 pages of good reading with 200 recipes. Hard cover.

$ 14.95  Retail price
$   .90  Tax for Louisiana residents
$  2.50  Postage and handling
Make check payable to *Classic Cajun*
ISBN 0-9640748-0-X

## THE COOKIN' CAJUN COOKING SCHOOL COOKBOOK

by Lisette Verlander and Susan Murphy
Gibbs Smith, Publisher
116 Riverwalk #1 Poydras Street
New Orleans, LA 70130                          800-523-6425

Traditional and contemporary recipes, tips, techniques, and ingredient information have been carefully sandwiched into one meaty volume by two of New Orleans well known and respected chefs/cooks. 96 pages, 80 recipes, 15 full-color watercolors.

$ 14.95  Retail price
$   .60  Tax for Louisiana residents
$  3.00  Postage and handling
Make check payable to Cookin' Cajun Cooking School
ISBN 0-87905-784-X

## COOKING AND GARDENING WITH DIANNE

by Dianne Cage
119 Glenmar Avenue
Monroe, LA 71201                               318-387-0304

Most cookbooks are just cookbooks. This book is different! It is described as holistic and spiritual. It gives advice on healthy living, gardening and entertaining, plus fabulous recipes.

$ 17.95  Retail price
$  3.00  Postage and handling
Make check payable to Garden District Books
ISBN 0-9654648-0-6

## COOKING NEW ORLEANS STYLE

Episcopal Churchwomen of All Saints, Inc.
100 Rex Drive                                 Fax 504-738-7829
River Ridge, LA 70123                         800-375-1416

*Cooking New Orleans Style* is our newest book of additional wonderful recipes; it has an eye-catching cover and contains interesting information and photographs of New Orleans.

$  6.95  Retail price
$   .28  Tax for Louisiana residents
$  4.00  Postage and handling
Make check payable to *La Bonne Cuisine*
ISBN 0-9696880-2-1

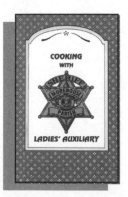

## COOKING WITH MOREHOUSE PARISH SHERIFF LADIES' AUXILIARY

Bastrop, LA

Our cookbook has 262 pages, containing over 700 recipes. Something for everyone; appetizers, beverages, soups, salads, vegetables, main dishes, breads, desserts, and a nice selection of low fat recipes. Currently out of print.

## COOKING WITH MR. "G" AND FRIENDS

by Kevin Grevemberg
117 Grevemberg Road
Anacoco, LA 71403

A handsomely designed cookbook with 300 easy and tasteful recipes. Author, Kevin Grevemberg is a husband, father of 3 daughters, and school teacher has a heartfelt concern for those who live with multiple sclerosis. A portion of the proceeds from this book will be donated to MS research.

$ 10.00  Retail price
$  2.50  Postage and handling
Make check payable to Kevin Grevemberg

## A COOK'S TOUR OF SHREVEPORT

The Junior League of Shreveport
3805 Gilbert
Shreveport, LA 71104                           318-221-6144

*A Cook's Tour* features Shreveport's unique combination of traditional Southern cooking and Cajun spiced dishes. Reprinted in honor of the 60th anniversary of the Shreveport League. It's a journey back into your grandmother's kitchen—classic Southern cookin' alongside old-fashioned sweets recipes to treasure. Comb bound. 336 pages.

$ 14.95  Retail price
$  1.00  Postage and handling
Make check payable to Junior League of Shreveport
ISBN 0-9602246-2-9

## CZECH-OUT CAJUN COOKIN'

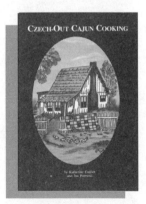

by Katherine Guillot and Ina Potmesil
2631 Village Lane
Bossier City, LA 71112                    318-752-1990 or 352-3979

*Czech-Out Cajun Cooking* is 256 pages of delightful Czech and Cajun recipes written by two Cajuns, one of which married a Czech, thus the Czech recipes. All recipes are simple, easy, country cooking with ingredients commonly found in your pantry. Sprinkled throughout are words of wisdom and Cajun/Czech "kitchen talk glossary" as well as short-cuts.

$ 15.95  Retail price
$  1.29  Tax for Louisiana residents
$  3.05  Postage and handling
Make check payable to *Czech Out Cajun Cookin'*
ISBN 0-9627496-0-5

## 'DAT LITTLE CAJUN COOKBOOK

by Chef Remy Laterrade C. E. C.
P. O. Box 3942
Lafayette, LA 70502-3942

"Big Cookbook" quality recipes in an inexpensive format. Includes popular Cajun recipes like Red Beans and Rice, Okra Gumbo, Oysters Rockefeller, Chicken and Sausage Jambalaya, Crab Bisque, and Cream Cheese Stuffed Mushrooms. Special fried food section "If You Fry It, They Will Come." 144 pages.

$  4.95  Retail price
$   .40  Tax for Louisiana residents
$  2.50  Postage and handling; $1.50 each additional
Make check payable to Relco Enterprises
ISBN 0-9632197-1-5

## 'DAT LITTLE LOUISIANA PLANTATION COOKBOOK

by Chef Remy Laterrade C. E .C.
Lafayette, LA

A popular gift item for a little price. Includes requested Louisiana recipes like Beignets, Crawfish Pie, Pork Jambalaya, New Orleans Pecan Pralines, Hogshead Cheese, and more. Pen and ink illustrations of many of Louisiana's finest plantations by noted illustrator, Joseph Arrigo. 144 pages. Currently out of print.

## 'DAT LITTLE NEW ORLEANS CREOLE COOKBOOK

by Chef Remy Laterrade C. E. C.
P. O. Box 3942
Lafayette, LA 70502-3942

Great Louisiana recipes in a down-to-earth cooking format. New Orleans Style French Bread, Shrimp and Corn Soup, Dirty Rice, Shrimp and Eggplant Remy, Hot Seafood Dip, Oysters Bienville, and more. Complete instructions on how to prepare a successful Dark Roux and other helpful hints. Spiral lay-flat binding. 6 x 3¾ inches. 114 pages.

$   4.95  Retail price
$    .40  Tax for Louisiana residents
$   2.50  Postage and handling; $1.50 each additional
Make check payable to Relco Enterprises
ISBN 0-9632197-2-3

## DELICIOUS HERITAGE

by Nippy Carville
12237 East Millburn Drive
Baton Rouge, LA 70815-6743                                   225-273-3294

Chances are you've read many cookbooks. Your kitchen shelf is probably packed with them. But take it from me, there's nothing like this one, some 450 recipes from more than 150 contributors giving of their talents and themselves, all in the name of good food.

$ 13.95  Retail price
$   1.12  Tax for Louisiana residents
$   2.00  Postage and handling
Make check payable to Delicious Heritage, Inc.
ISBN 0-935545-08-5

## DINNER ON THE GROUND:
### A Southern Tradition

Stoke Gabriel Enterprises
P. O. Box 12060
Alexandria, LA 71315                                         318-487-9577

Whether a kitchen novice or gourmet cook extraordinaire, this cookbook has recipes for everyone. Contains clear concise instructions and short stories that reflect the influence of the church on social activities during the depression era. 244 pages.

$ 11.95  Retail price
$    .96  Postage and handling
$   2.00  Tax for Louisiana residents
ISBN 0-929288-01-7

## THE EVOLUTION OF CAJUN & CREOLE CUISINE

by Chef John Folse
2517 South Philippe Avenue
Gonzales, LA 70737                                        800-256-2433

This hardbound cookbook is the first of its kind to tell the 250-year old history of Cajun and Creole cuisine and culture. More than 250 recipes for stocks, sauces, appetizers, soups, vegetables, poultry, meats, seafood, wild game, desserts and lagniappe ("something extra" in south Louisiana) are featured in the 487-page cookbook.

$ 19.95  Retail price
$  1.60  Tax for Louisiana residents
$  3.50  Postage and handling
Make check payable to Chef John Folse & Co.
ISBN 09625152-0-5

## EXTRA! EXTRA! READ ALL ABOUT IT!

by Corinne H. Cook
P. O. Box 82477
Baton Rouge, LA 70884                          225-293-9770 or 926-4090

After more than 20 years of writing about food, author Corinne Cook gathered her favorite recipes into one volume. *Extra! Extra! Read All About It!* has many "extras" important in a good cookbook. The hard cover, concealed wire binding opens to 237 pages of easy-to-read and easy-to-follow fabulous recipes.

$ 19.95  Retail price
$  1.60  Tax for Louisiana residents
$  3.50  Postage and handling
Make check payable to *Extra! Extra! Read All About It!*
ISBN 0-9646993-0-3

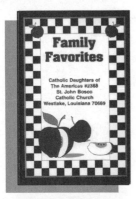

## FAMILY FAVORITES

Catholic Daughters of the Americas #2388
Westlake, LA

Members of our church congregation were asked to submit their own family favorite recipes—thus the name. We compiled our book from great grandmothers on to the very young, and even have recipes from the Mayor of our city and our pastor. Currently out of print.

## FAMILY TRADITIONS
### Recipes & Memories from Possum Valley

by Esta White Freeland
Mer Rouge, LA

*Family Traditions* is a collection of 232 easy-to-follow pages of recipes with 25 extra pages of helpful hints and useful information. Our recipes are kitchen-tested family favorites handed down through several generations. This is an ideal gift for new brides and cookbook collectors. Currently out of print.

## FEAST OF GOODNESS

Jennings Chapel Church
P. O. Box 237
Marthaville, LA 71450                    318-472-6916 or 472-6711

A delightful and attractive collection of "new" and "heritage"
recipes gathered from ladies who love to cook! The looseleaf book
is adaptable for personal recipe additions with space also available for notes. Over 500 recipes in 221 pages with helpful kitchen
and household hints.

$ 10.00  Retail price
$  5.00  Postage and handling
Make check payable to Jennings Chapel Church

## FESSIN' UP WITH BON APPETIT

by Sue Fess
4832 Line Avenue
Shreveport, LA 71106                         318-868-1438

*Fessin' Up* is a tribute to the many customers who have requested
our recipes since we were founded in 1979. These recipes conform
to Bon Appetit's need for quick and simple dishes that can be prepared in a small kitchen, making them perfect for the hurried gourmet in any American home. The cuisine is as distinctly American as
Bon Appetit's red, white and blue decor.

$ 10.95  Retail price
$   .90  Tax for Louisiana residents
$  3.25  Postage and handling
Make check payable to *Fessin' Up*

## FIFTIETH ANNIVERSARY COOKBOOK

Northeast Louisiana Telephone Co., Inc.
P. O. Drawer 185
Collinston, LA 71229                  318-874-7011 or 888-318-1998

In celebration of our fiftieth anniversary, Northeast Louisiana Telephone Co., Inc. compiled over 600 recipes donated by customers,
business associates and friends and created a celebration cookbook.
Some of the recipes are treasured family keepsakes and some are
new.

$ 10.00  Retail price
$   .85  Tax for Louisiana residents
$  1.65  Postage and handling
Make check payable to Northeast Louisiana Telephone Co, Inc.

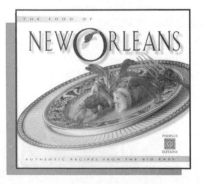

## THE FOOD OF NEW ORLEANS

by John DeMers
Tuttle Publishing Distribution Center
A/P Industrial Park 364 Innovative Drive        Fax 1-800-329-8885
North Clarendon,VT 05759-9436                   1-800-526-2778

Compiled by New Orleans native John DeMers, this new
direction for an award-winning Asian cookbook series bal-
ances respect for tradition with breaking news from the Big
Easy restaurant scene. Carefully tested recipes are showcased
with more than 50 full-color, full-page food photos. Hardcover.

$ 18.95  Retail price
$  4.00  Postage and handling
Make check payable to Hospitality Publications
ISBN 962-593-227-5

## FROM MAMA TO ME: Acadian-Cajun Recipes

Anita G. Guidry
723 W. Canal
Church Point, LA 70525                                   337-684-5853

This book has been published to retain our Cajun heritage and to keep alive the recipes of our area through the years. This is truly Cajun cuisine, past, present and future, which stresses nutrition and taste. From my mother I inherited my love of good food and good cooking.

$ 9.95 Retail price
$ 2.25 Postage and handling
Make check payable to *From Mama to Me*

## GOLLIWOGG CAKE AND OTHER RECIPES

Red River Public Radio
Shreveport, LA

*Golliwogg Cake and Other Recipes* is a 188-page spiral-bound book with recipes divided into seven categories. In addition to great recipes, the cookbook contains tidbits of local and musical trivia. Currently out of print.

## GONE WITH THE FAT

Jen Bays Avis LDN, RD
Kathy F. Ward LDN, RD
200 Professional Drive
West Monroe, LA 71291                                   318-323-7949

*Gone with the Fat* is our newest cookbook, containing a variety of dishes very low in fat. It also contains an "order out" food guide, a substitution list, a 3-day, 20 or 40-gram per day menu plan, and so much more to help you get started losing the fat.

$ 17.95 Retail price
$    .72 Tax for Louisiana residents
$ 3.00 Postage and handling
Make check payable to Avis and Ward
ISBN 0-962683-6-1

## HEART OF THE HOME

East Baton Rouge Extension Homemaker's Council, Inc.
12257 Fairhaven Drive
Baton Rouge, LA 70815                                   225-275-1936

*Heart of the Home* contains treasured recipes by homemakers that are tried and proven. They not only taste good, many are quick and easy. Proceeds are used to fund council-sponsored activities, scholarships, and community projects. 154 pages. Approximately 400 outstanding recipes from local homemakers in the Baton Rouge area.

$ 8.00 Retail price
$ 3.00 Postage and handling
Make check payable to EBRFCE

## THE HUNGRY HOG

by Phil D. Mayers
P. O. Box 53601
Lafayette, LA 70505-3601

*The Hungry Hog®*, a Cajun and Creole cookbook with artwork and quotations about pigs which the author collects (not the real ones of course!). The recipes are precise, simple to follow, and include seafood, beef and poultry, vegetables, salads, breads and desserts. The ingredients are normally found in every kitchen and in keeping with the Cajun and Creole cultures, the book is bilingual (French and English). *The Hungry Hog* cookbook may be purchased at your favorite bookstore.

ISBN 0-9635606-3-8

## IN THE PINK

Beauregard Memorial Hospital Auxiliary
c/o Maurice Burton
P. O. Box 730
DeRidder, LA 70634                                          337-462-7288

In a 1985 meeting, the auxiliary got together and planned this for a fund raiser. The result, a collection of 550 recipes, 182 pages. The cover was designed and drawn by a granddaughter of a "Pinklady," the name of our group. We named the book appropriately.

$ 12.00  Retail price including tax and postage
Make check payable to Beauregard Memorial Hospital Auxiliary

## JUST FOR KIDS

Jen Bays Avis, LDN, RD
Kathy F. Ward, LDN, RD
200 Professional Drive
West Monroe, LA 71291                                       318-323-7949

*Just for Kids* contains recipes your kids will love and love to cook themselves. It includes safety tips when cooking, measuring tips, and nutrition tips for athletes.

$ 12.95  Retail price
$   .52  Tax for Louisiana residents
$  2.50  Postage and handling
Make check payable to Avis and Ward

## KAY EWING'S COOKING SCHOOL COOKBOOK

Kay Ewing's Everyday Gourmet
17921 Inverness Avenue
Baton Rouge, LA 70810                                       225-756-2039

A unique, menu-style cookbook with recipes, instructions and ideas from Kay Ewing's Everyday Gourmet Cooking School. Kay's book offers a sampling of the best of Louisiana and international cuisines from a gifted cook and teacher, featuring over 300 recipes from 75 menu classes including Cajun Creole, French and Italian.

$ 14.95  Retail price
$  1.35  Tax for Louisiana residents
$  2.00  Postage and handling
Make check payable to *Kay Ewing's Cooking School Cookbook*
ISBN 0-9643611-0-8

## KOOKING WITH THE KREWE

Twin Cities' Krewe of Janus
412 Bayou Oaks
Monroe, LA 71203                                    318-343-1776

The Twin Cities' Krewe of Janus cookbook consists of 234 pages with over 600 recipes. It's a collection from Krewe members, their family and friends. Offering a celebrity section, these recipes are a collection of past royalty and local restauranteurs and local personalities.

$ 12.00  Retail price
$  1.02  Tax for Louisiana residents
$  1.75  Postage and handling
Make check payable to Krewe of Janus

## L'HERITAGE DU BAYOU LAFOURCHE

Lafourche Assn. for Family & Community Education
c/o Arvella L. Dupre
614 Catherine Street
Lockport, LA 70374                                  504-532-3503

*L'Heritage Du Bayou Lafourche* proudly presents 650 recipes, many of which are prize winning delights from Lafourche FCE members. The 300 pages also include helpful hints and useful information. The rich heritage of the bayou and exquisite culinary expertise of people from this rich Cajun land is found throughout the book. A section of recipes for special diets add to the large variety of recipes.

$  8.50  Retail price
$  2.00  Postage and handling
Make check payable to Lafourche FCE

## LA BONNE CUISINE LAGNIAPPE

Episcopal Churchwomen of All Saints', Inc.
100 Rex Drive                            Fax 504-738-7829
River Ridge, LA 70123                        800-375-1416

New Orleans is a city where any old excuse becomes a reason to party! This collection will help you begin and end your dinner parties with a flair. These 35 appetizers and 27 desserts will enhance your reputation as a party hostess!

$  3.00  Retail price
$   .12  Tax for Louisiana residents
$  4.00  Postage and handling
Make check payable to La Bonne Cuisine
ISBN 0-960880-1-3

## THE LITTLE GUMBO BOOK

by Gwen McKee
Quail Ridge Press                        www.quailridge.com
P. O. Box 123                            Fax 800-864-1082
Brandon, MS 39043                            800-343-1583

Carefully created recipes by Louisianian, Gwen McKee, plus explanations, definitions, and directions that will enable everyone to enjoy the special experience of gumbo. Step-by-step directions. Recipes, Roux, Rice, Stock, Seasoning—it's all in this charming little book. Hardbound, illustrated.

$  8.95  Retail price
$  3.00  Postage and handling
Make check payable to Quail Ridge Press
ISBN 0-937552-17-8

## THE LITTLE NEW ORLEANS COOKBOOK

by Gwen McKee
Quail Ridge Press
P. O. Box 123
Brandon, MS 39043

www.quailridge.com
Fax 800-864-1082
800-343-1583

Want to capture the cuisine of New Orleans? You can with this nifty little hardcover cookbook that recreates 57 classic Creole recipes that made New Orleans famous—etouffees, jambalayas, drinks, remoulades, pralines, etc. Fascinating secrets, hints, history, origins of recipes, and tales of the Crescent City. Illustrated, photographs.

$ 8.95  Retail price
$ 3.00  Postage and handling
Make check payable to Quail Ridge Press
ISBN 0-937552-42-9

## LOUISIANA TEMPTATIONS

Louisiana Farm Bureau Women
P. O. Box 95004
Baton Rouge, LA 70895-9004

225-922-6200

The temptations of Louisiana are varied and rich, but the most tempting of all the Bayou State has to offer is its cuisine. Be tempted by this collection of recipes from farm wives across our state. 239 recipes, 8 sections, with beautiful color photo divider pages, and nutritional profiles.

$ 16.95  Retail price
$  1.53  Tax for Louisiana residents
$  3.55  Postage and handling
Make check payable to Louisiana Farm Bureau Federation
ISBN 0-9652035-0-6

## NUN BETTER

St. Cecilia School of Sacred Heart Parish
200 West Main
Broussard, LA 70518

800-639-0825 Fax 337-837-1864

*Nun Better* is an original cookbook from the heart of Louisiana's Cajun Country. This classic collection of authentic, time-honored, and tested recipes reflects the unique culinary heritage of the community of Broussard. Providing a broad spectrum of dishes from classic gourmet confections to easy-to-prepare favorites, the meticulously tested recipes insure a variety to satisfy all palates.

$ 18.95  Retail price
$ 3.00  Postage and handling
Make check payable to St. Cecilia School
ISBN 0-9655106-0-3

## PASS THE MEATBALLS, PLEASE!

by Michael Cannatella
P. O. Box 114
Port Allen, LA 70767

225-344-2998

*Pass the Meatballs, Please* is a 160-page, 141-recipe collection of mostly Italian recipes, combined with the Cajun and Creole influences of South Louisiana, and just a hint of the East Coast thrown in for style.

$ 9.95  Retail price
$  .80  Tax for Louisiana residents
$ 2.00  Postage and handling
Make check payable to *Pass the Meatballs, Please!*

## PIGGING OUT
## WITH THE COTTON PATCH COOKS

by Audrey Lee McCollum
1500 Davenport Avenue Apt. 6
Mer Rouge, LA 71261

These wonderful recipes came from people who have lived and worked in and around the cotton patches of Louisiana. Recipes go back to 1816, up through the 1990s. These 496 time-tested recipes are easy, delicious, and money saving.

$ 10.00  Retail price
$  2.75  Postage and handling
Make check payable to Audrey Lee McCollum

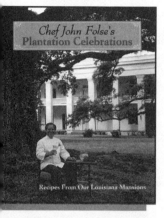

## PLANTATION CELEBRATIONS:
## Recipes from our Louisiana Mansions

by Chef John Folse
2517 South Philippe Avenue
Gonzales, LA 70737                                    800-256-2433

This 335-page hardbound book contains 150 full-color photographs and more than 300 recipes for stocks and sauces, roux, appetizers, soups, vegetables, poultry, meats, seafood, wild game and desserts. This book takes an in-depth look at the 300-year old history of Louisiana's plantations and the cuisine that originated there.

$ 24.95  Retail price
$  2.00  Tax for Louisiana residents
$  3.50  Postage and handling
Make check payable to Chef John Folse & Co.
ISBN 0-9625152-2-1

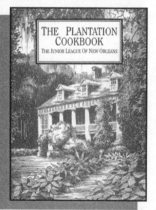

## THE PLANTATION COOKBOOK

Junior League of New Orleans
2727 Prytania Street
New Orleans, LA 70130                                504-891-5845

*The Plantation Cookbook* is in reality two books—half is a history and guide to New Orleans' and Louisiana's plantation homes, and half is a collection of delicious recipes for the elegant type of dining people associate with the area, all handsomely illustrated with 30 line drawings of Louisiana's beautiful plantations.

$ 22.95  Retail price
$  2.07  Tax for Louisiana residents
$  5.75  Postage and handling
Make check payable to B.E. Trice Publishing
ISBN 0-9631952-0-7

## RECIPES FROM BAYOU PIERRE COUNTRY

by Mildred Rachel Norris
Gorum, LA

Recipes of families, children, and grandchildren of the first settlers of Gorum, a small community located off I-49 in the hill country of South Natchitoches Parish on the banks of Bayou Pierre Creek. The first settlers were French Basque, Spanish, and later Anglo Saxon. The Indians were already here, and their influence was deeply felt, and still is today. Currently out of print.

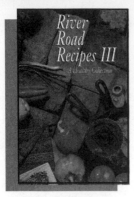

## RIVER ROAD RECIPES III:
## A Healthy Collection
The Junior League of Baton Rouge
P. O. Box 82434                              Fax 225-927-2547
Baton Rouge, LA 70884-2434                 800-204-1726

The newest of the *River Road Recipes* cookbooks will delight people everywhere who want to lower fat and calories, but still want to enjoy great Louisiana food. All recipes have been analyzed by a registered dietitian and are annotated with fat, caloric and nutritional information. Hard cover book with 286 pages and 341 recipes. National Award Winner!

$17.95   Retail price
$1.44    Tax for Louisiana residents
$2.25    Postage and handling
Make check payable to *River Road Recipes*
ISBN 0-9613026-4-X

## ROGER'S CAJUN COOKBOOK
by Vernon Roger
P. O. Box 2841
Baton Rouge, LA 70821

Vernon Roger's culinary expertise was born in his mother's kitchen, and nurtured in cookouts from the banks of Bayou Teche to the shores of Pierre Part Bay. His hosting of a weekly cooking segment on WAFB-TV in Baton Rouge gave birth to this very popular cookbook. Part of the proceeds goes to charity.

$  9.95  Retail price
$   .70  Tax for Louisiana residents
$  1.00  Postage and handling
Make check payable to Roger's Cajun Cookbook
ISBN 09644-16231

## ROGER'S LITE CAJUN COOKBOOK
by Vernon Roger
P. O. Box 2841
Baton Rouge, LA 70821

The concept for this book began when Vernon Roger started trying to "lighten" his traditional Cajun recipes; that is, to reduce the fat and cholesterol content. Cajun dishes such as gumbo, sauce piquante, courtbouillon and étouffee are made lighter. Part of the proceeds goes to charity.

$  9.95  Retail price
$   .70  Tax for Louisiana residents
$  1.00  Postage and handling
Make check payable to Roger's Cajun Cookbook
ISBN 09644-16232

## SECRETS OF THE ORIGINAL DON'S
## SEAFOOD & STEAKHOUSE
The Original Don's Seafood & Steakhouse
301 E. Vermilion Street
Lafayette, LA 70501                       337-235-3551

The first *Don's Secrets Cookbook*, written in 1958, was a staple for anyone wanting to bring the delicious flavors of traditional Cajun cooking into their homes. This revised and updated version includes recipes for gumbos, jambalayas, étouffees and more—95 dishes that represent the Cajun people—hearty and well-seasoned.

$ 11.95  Retail price
$   .90  Tax for Louisiana residents
$  2.00  Postage and handling
Make check payable to The Original Don's Seafood & Steakhouse
ISBN 0-9654883-0-6

## SHARED TREASURES

First Baptist Church, Monroe
201 St. John
Monroe, LA 71201                                    318-325-3126

*Shared Treasures* is the product of 142 years of the First Baptist Church in Monroe. The origins of the 933 recipes (301 pages) reflect the diverse ministries and membership of the church. Recipes are from members of our International Ministry, active members and former staff members, as well as from the files of past members.

$ 15.00  Retail price
$  3.00  Postage and handling
Make check payable to First Baptist Church

## A SHOWER OF ROSES

St. Therese Catholic Church
P. O. Box 609
Abbeville, LA 70511-0609

If you know anything about St. Therese, you will find out how she truly has "let down a shower of roses" in this special cookbook. This book is a collection of 500 recipes from many special people who shared their family favorites, including our pastor's favorite at the end of the book.

$ 12.00  Retail price
$  3.00  Postage and handling
Make check payable to St. Therese Catholic Church

## SISTERS' SECRETS

Beta Sigma Phi
Ville Platte, LA

*Sisters' Secrets* is a collection of over 200 recipes shared by the sorority members of Beta Sigma Phi in Ville Platte to celebrate their twenty-fifth anniversary. The 3-ring hardcover loose-leaf binder has old Cajun traditionals (gumbo, bread pudding, jambalaya) and modern favorites (onion blossom and fettuccini). Currently out of print.

## SOUTHERN BUT LITE

Jen Bays Avis CDN, RD
Kathy F. Ward CDN, RD
200 Professional Drive
West Monroe, LA 71291                                318-323-7949

*Southern But Lite* consists of 279 pages, 263 which contain recipes and vitamin information, nutritional information, and how to read food labels. Below each recipe we label the calories, exchanges, cholesterol, saturated fat and sodium.

$ 17.95  Retail price
$   .72  Tax for Louisiana residents
$  3.00  Postage and handling
Make check payable to Avis and Ward
ISBN 0-9623683-0-2

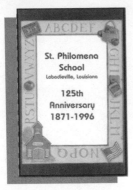

## ST. PHILOMENA SCHOOL 125TH ANNIVERSARY COOKBOOK

St. Philomena Home & School Association
120 Convent Street
Labadieville, LA 70372                                      504-526-8508

*St. Philomena School 125th Anniversary Cookbook* has 97 pages and 335 recipes. In celebrating 125 years of Catholic education, the school and the Labadieville community couldn't think of a better way to celebrate than to share their favorite recipes. The Bayou Country favorites include award-winning dishes from area and state contests.

$ 10.00  Retail price
$  3.00  Postage and handling
Make check payable to St. Philomena School

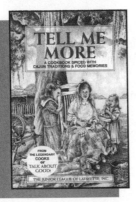

## TELL ME MORE

The Junior League of Lafayette
100 Felecie Street
Lafayette, LA 70506                      337-988-2739 or 800-757-3651

*Tell Me More* is filled with a select collection of recipes and stories chronicling Cajun ways past and present. The recipes contain great dishes using basic pantry items; new recipes from legendary Cajun cooks. Hardcover, 221 pages. Front and back covers as well as divider pages feature prints of nationally recognized Cajun artist, Floyd Sonnier.

$ 16.95  Retail price
$  3.00  Postage and handling
Make check payable to The Junior League of Lafayette
ISBN 0-935032-25-8

## TONY CHACHERE'S SECOND HELPING:
## A Lifetime Collection of the Ole Master's
## Favorite South Louisiana Recipes

519 N. Lombard Street
Opelousas, LA 70570                                      800-551-9066

*Tony Chachere's Second Helping* is truly a unique collection of the cooking and food events of Tony Chachere's life. Book features over 300 recipes, prepared time and again by the well-known chef, who was honored in 1995 as the first inductee into the Louisiana Chefs Hall of Fame. 240 pages, hardcover, inside spiral binding.

$ 22.95  Retail price
$   .92  Tax for Louisiana residents
$  2.00  Postage and handling
Make check payable to Tony Chachere
ISBN 0-9604580-3-4

## TOO GOOD TO BE TRUE

by Chet Beckwith
7065 Boyce Drive
Baton Rouge, LA 70809                                    225-925-9797

The best cookbook to come along in years, now in its fourth printing, offered with money-back guarantee! Delicious no-fail recipes by society columnist, food TV chef that will make guests swoon! An absolute "must have" for the good food enthusiast. Widely acclaimed as "better than the best!"

$ 22.00  Retail price
$  1.76  Tax for Louisiana residents
$  4.00  Postage and handling
Make check payable to C. Beckwith
ISBN 0-935545-17-4

## THE TOP 100 CAJUN RECIPES OF ALL TIME

Acadian House Publishing
P .O. Box 52247
Lafayette, LA 70505                                    337-235-8851

In the process of selecting these "cream of the crop" recipes, we reached one conclusion of which we are fairly certain: Most of the recipes contained in this book have contributed in a real way to South Louisiana's well-deserved reputation for having some of the best food in the United States, if not the entire world.

$   6.95   Retail price
$    .52   Tax for Louisiana residents
$  2.50   Postage and handling
Make check payable to Acadian House Publishing

## TRIM & TERRIFIC AMERICAN FAVORITES:
## Over 250 Fast and Easy Low-Fat Recipes

Holly B. Clegg, Inc.
13431 Woodmount Court
Baton Rouge, LA 70810-5334                             800-88-HOLLY

Enjoy over 250 fast and easy low-fat recipes that are family favorites that can be prepared with little time and even less effort. You'll find great menu ideas along with pasta, vegetarian, and southwestern sections. This is the book you'll use night after night to prepare those familiar favorites with a low-fat twist. Diabetic exchanges and nutritional analysis included.

$ 15.00   Retail price
$  4.00   Postage and handling
Make check payable to Holly B. Clegg
ISBN 0-517-70256-8

## A TRIM & TERRIFIC LOUISIANA KITCHEN:
## An Easy and Lighter Approach to Southern Cuisine

Holly B. Clegg, Inc.
13431 Woodmount Court
Baton Rouge, LA 70810-5334                             800-88-HOLLY

This book contains low-fat fast, easy, everyday recipes that can be prepared in about 30 minutes. There's no sacrifice to taste, nothing that tastes like cardboard! The 375 nutritionally analyzed recipes include all your favorites. Wonderful menu ideas and a fabulous pasta section. Holly appears regularly on the NBC Weekend Today Show. Stay "Trim & Terrific" with these great recipes!!

$ 16.95   Retail price
$  4.00   Postage and handling
Make check payable to Holly B. Clegg
ISBN 0-961-08883-4

## TRIM & TERRIFIC ONE DISH FAVORITES:
## Over 200 Fast and Easy Low-Fat Recipes

Holly B. Clegg, Inc.
13431 Woodmount Court
Baton Rouge, LA 70810-5334                             800-88-HOLLY

Enjoy over 200 delicious fast, and easy low-fat recipes, all in the form of one-dish meals including brunch, pasta, southwestern, meatless, desserts, and menu sections. With limited time, make life easier with these single-pot or low-fat meals that pack a lot of taste, family appeal and nutrition in one dish. Best of all, clean-up's a breeze. Diabetic exchanges, nutritional analysis included.

$ 18.95   Retail price
$  4.00   Postage and handling
Make check payable to Holly B. Clegg
ISBN 0-517-702584

## WHO'S YOUR MAMA, ARE YOU CATHOLIC, AND CAN YOU MAKE A ROUX?

by Marcelle Bienvenu
The Times of Acadiana
P. O. Box 3528
Lafayette, LA 70502                                        337-237-3560

The book is spiral-bound, 111 pages, about 250 recipes. The text contained in the book are stories and anecdotes about recipes, stories about the author's family and their celebrations. The book is divided into the four seasons of the year—Summer, Fall, Winter, Spring.

$ 22.95  Retail price
$  1.72  Tax for Louisiana residents
$  4.50  Postage and handling
Make check payable to The Times of Acadiana
ISBN 0-9631637-1-X

# Index

*The highlight of the Sugar Cane Festival is the official Blessing of the Sugar Cane Fields. New Iberia.*

# INDEX

# INDEX

# INDEX

*A magnificently restored antebellum mansion built in 1835, Rosedown Plantation and Gardens is just off the Great River Road at St. Francisville.*

# Best of the Best State Cookbook Series

**Best of the Best from**
**ALABAMA**
288 pages, $16.95

**Best of the Best from**
**ALASKA**
288 pages, $16.95

**Best of the Best from**
**ARIZONA**
288 pages, $16.95

**Best of the Best from**
**ARKANSAS**
288 pages, $16.95

**Best of the Best from**
**BIG SKY**
288 pages, $16.95

**Best of the Best from**
**CALIFORNIA**
384 pages, $16.95

**Best of the Best from**
**COLORADO**
288 pages, $16.95

**Best of the Best from**
**FLORIDA**
288 pages, $16.95

**Best of the Best from**
**GEORGIA**
336 pages, $16.95

**Best of the Best from the**
**GREAT PLAINS**
288 pages, $16.95

**Best of the Best from**
**IDAHO**
288 pages, $16.95

**Best of the Best from**
**ILLINOIS**
288 pages, $16.95

**Best of the Best from**
**INDIANA**
288 pages, $16.95

**Best of the Best from**
**IOWA**
288 pages, $16.95

**Best of the Best from**
**KENTUCKY**
288 pages, $16.95

**Best of the Best from**
**LOUISIANA**
288 pages, $16.95

**Best of the Best from**
**LOUISIANA II**
288 pages, $16.95

**Best of the Best from**
**MICHIGAN**
288 pages, $16.95

**Best of the Best from the**
**MID-ATLANTIC**
288 pages, $16.95

**Best of the Best from**
**MINNESOTA**
288 pages, $16.95

**Best of the Best from**
**MISSISSIPPI**
288 pages, $16.95

**Best of the Best from**
**MISSOURI**
304 pages, $16.95

**Best of the Best from**
**NEW ENGLAND**
368 pages, $16.95

**Best of the Best from**
**NEW MEXICO**
288 pages, $16.95

**Best of the Best from**
**NEW YORK**
288 pages, $16.95

**Best of the Best from**
**NO. CAROLINA**
288 pages, $16.95

**Best of the Best from**
**OHIO**
352 pages, $16.95

**Best of the Best from**
**OKLAHOMA**
288 pages, $16.95

**Best of the Best from the**
**OREGON**
288 pages, $16.95

**Best of the Best from**
**PENNSYLVANIA**
320 pages, $16.95

**Best of the Best from**
**SO. CAROLINA**
288 pages, $16.95

**Best of the Best from**
**TENNESSEE**
288 pages, $16.95

**Best of the Best from**
**TEXAS**
352 pages, $16.95

**Best of the Best from**
**TEXAS II**
352 pages, $16.95

**Best of the Best from**
**VIRGINIA**
320 pages, $16.95

**Best of the Best from**
**WASHINGTON**
288 pages, $16.95

**Best of the Best from**
**WEST VIRGINIA**
288 pages, $16.95

**Best of the Best from**
**WISCONSIN**
288 pages, $16.95

*Cookbooks listed above have been completed as of December 31, 2003. All cookbooks are ring-bound except California, which is paperbound.*

*Note: Big Sky includes Montana and Wyoming; Great Plains includes North Dakota, South Dakota, Nebraska, and Kansas; Mid-Atlantic includes Maryland, Delaware, New Jersey, and Washington, D.C.; New England includes Rhode Island, Connecticut, Massachusetts, Vermont, New Hampshire, and Maine.*

---

## Special discount offers available! *(See previous page for details.)*

To order by credit card, call toll-free **1-800-343-1583** or visit our website at **www.quailridge.com.**
Use the form below to send check or money order.

*Call 1-800-343-1583 or email* **info@quailridge.com** *to request a free catalog of all of our publications.*

- - - - - - - - - - - - - - - - - - - - - - - - - - - - - - - - - - - - - - - - - - - - - -

# Orderform

Use this form for sending check or money order to:
**QUAIL RIDGE PRESS • P. O. Box 123 • Brandon, MS 39043**

❑ Check enclosed

Charge to: ❑ Visa ❑ MC ❑ AmEx ❑ Disc

Card #_____

Expiration Date _____

Signature _____

Name _____

Address _____

City/State/Zip_____

Phone # _____

Email Address _____

| Qty. | Title of Book (State) or Set | Total |
|------|------------------------------|-------|
|      |                              |       |
|      |                              |       |
|      |                              |       |
|      |                              |       |
|      |                              |       |

Subtotal _____

7% Tax for MS residents _____

Postage ($4.00 any number of books)  **+   4.00**

Total _____